Securing Single-Player Games in Unreal Engine

Techniques to Protect Game Variables, Progress, and Player Trust

Sheikh Sohel Moon

Apress®

Securing Single-Player Games in Unreal Engine: Techniques to Protect Game Variables, Progress, and Player Trust

Sheikh Sohel Moon
Anis Nagor (Master Para)
Khulna, Bangladesh

ISBN-13 (pbk): 979-8-8688-2832-4   ISBN-13 (electronic): 979-8-8688-2833-1
https://doi.org/10.1007/979-8-8688-2833-1

Managing Director, Apress Media LLC: Welmoed Spahr
Acquisitions Editor: Spandana Chatterjee
Editorial Assistant: Rachel Zhang

Cover designed by eStudioCalamar

Distributed to the book trade worldwide by Springer Science+Business Media New York, 1 New York Plaza, New York, NY 10004. Phone 1-800-SPRINGER, fax (201) 348-4505, e-mail orders-ny@springer-sbm.com, or visit www.springeronline.com. Apress Media, LLC is a Delaware LLC and the sole member (owner) is Springer Science + Business Media Finance Inc (SSBM Finance Inc). SSBM Finance Inc is a **Delaware** corporation.

For information on translations, please e-mail booktranslations@springernature.com; for reprint, paperback, or audio rights, please e-mail bookpermissions@springernature.com.

Apress titles may be purchased in bulk for academic, corporate, or promotional use. eBook versions and licenses are also available for most titles. For more information, reference our Print and eBook Bulk Sales web page at http://www.apress.com/bulk-sales.

Any source code or other supplementary material referenced by the author in this book is available to readers on GitHub. For more detailed information, please visit https://www.apress.com/gp/services/source-code.

If disposing of this product, please recycle the paper

This book is dedicated to my wife Maniya and my son Zarrar Mayan.

Maniya, you carried both our child and my dreams through this journey. While writing this book, Mayan, you came into my life and I began learning how to become a father. Every page carries both my professional and personal journey. No matter how far you go, remember that your father was here, building something with his own hands, thinking about you.

Table of Contents

About the Author xv

About the Technical Reviewer xvii

Introduction xix

Chapter 1: Why Security Matters in Single-Player Games 1

The Real Cost of Cheating in Single-Player Games...2

Why the Myth Exists: "It's Single Player, It Doesn't Matter".............................3

The Three Primary Attack Surfaces in Single-Player Games 3

Why Single-Player Security Is Actually Part of Game Design.............................4

Thought Experiment: The Fragile Narrative Arc...4

Historical Context: Why Cheating Shapes Player Expectations 5

Case Study 1: XP Inflation Destroying Progression....................................6

Case Study 2: Save File Corruption in a Survival Game..............................6

Case Study 3: Blueprint Exploits in a Strategy Game 6

Why Cheating Damages More Than Gameplay 7

A Layered Single-Player Defense Mindset...7

Conclusion 8

Chapter 2: Understanding the Cheat Landscape.......................................9

Attacker Motivations in Single-Player Games...10

Attacker Capability Levels...11

Taxonomy of Single-Player Attack Vectors...11

How Cheat Tools Spread and Why Your Game Gets Targeted.........................13

Deep Dive: How Cheat Engine Attacks Unreal Engine Games.........................14

How Basic Scanning Works...14

Code Injection...15

Lua Automation 15

Trainer Platforms: Why WeMod, FLiNG, and Others Are Dangerous 16

Save Editors and Offline Progression Exploitation 16

Case Study: XP Hacks Destroying Progression in Assassin's Creed Odyssey 17

Reflection Abuse: Calling Blueprint Functions Externally 17

Asset and Data Extraction 18

How Attackers Prioritize Targets 18

Why Understanding the Cheat Landscape Matters 19

Conclusion 20

Chapter 3: Designing for Tamper Resistance 21

Why Architecture Matters More Than Any Individual Security Technique 22

Understanding Unreal Engine's Runtime Memory Model 23

Object Headers and Predictable Layout 24

Reflection Metadata (FProperty) 24

Garbage Collection and Deterministic Allocation 25

Memory Fragmentation Does Not Protect You 25

Predictability Is the Enemy of Security 26

Design Principle 1: Minimizing the Attack Surface 27

Design Principle 2: Breaking Up Critical State 27

Design Principle 3: Redundant State and Cross-Validation 28

Design Principle 4: Designing for Unpredictability 28

Text-Only Memory Map Example 29

Developer Mistakes That Cause High Exposure 30

Understanding How Attackers Exploit Layout Patterns 30

Designing Systems That Are Hard to Reverse 31

Component-Based Security Benefits 31

Case Study 1: Why a Simple Float-Based Health System Failed 32

Case Study 2: XP Manipulation in an Indie Action Game 33

Checklist for Designing Tamper-Resistant Architecture 33

Conclusion 34

Chapter 4: Tamper-Proofing Runtime Variables **35**

Why Attackers Target Runtime Memory 36

Understanding the Threat Model for Runtime Variables 37

Why Native Types Are Easy to Manipulate 37

The Secure Wrapper Philosophy 38

Implementing the Secure Float 40

    Extending the Secure Float: Advanced Runtime Defenses 42

Using Secure Floats in Gameplay Systems 55

Case Study: Tamper-Resistant Health System in an Action RPG 56

Red Team Analysis: How Attackers Will Try to Break Your System 56

Conclusion 57

Chapter 5: Anti-debugging and Injection Detection **59**

Why Debuggers Are the Most Dangerous Runtime Tools 60

How DLL Injection Bypasses Traditional Protections 61

What a Debugger Allows an Attacker to Do 62

How Trainers Patch Memory and Hijack Code Paths 62

How These Threats Manifest in Unreal Projects 63

How Debuggers and Injection Tools Attach to Unreal 63

    User-Mode Debug API Attachments 64

    Remote Debugging Pipes and Stealth Attachment 64

    Kernel-Level Assistance for Advanced Debuggers 65

    DLL Injection Entry Points in Unreal Executables 65

    Hooking, Trampolines, and Memory Patching Strategies 66

Direct Debugger Detection Techniques 66

    Detecting Attached Debuggers with IsDebuggerPresent 66

    Detecting External Debuggers with CheckRemoteDebuggerPresent 68

Hardware Breakpoint and Side-Channel Detection 70

    How Hardware Breakpoints Work 70

    Why Hardware Breakpoints Are Difficult to Detect 71

    Timing Analysis for Breakpoint Detection 71

    When Side-Channel Approaches Become Useful 74

Monitoring Suspicious Threads 74

    Why Injectors Spawn Their Own Threads 74

    Differentiating Engine Threads from Unknown Threads 75

    Enumerating Threads Using ToolHelp API 75

Detecting Injected Modules 77

    Why DLL Injectors Are Still Effective 78

    Enumerating Loaded Modules at Runtime 78

    Identifying Suspicious Modules by Name and Pattern 78

    Optional Memory Region Validation 79

Timing-Based Anti-debugging Techniques 81

    Debugger-Induced Frame Delays 81

    Timestamp-Based Breakpoint Detection 81

Memory and Code Integrity Checks 83

Delayed and Passive Countermeasures 84

Dead-Code Guards and Hidden Integrity Points 84

Case Study 1: Debugger-Assisted Stealth Bypass in a Single-Player Stealth Game 85

Case Study 2: Injection-Based Input Hijacking Through a Custom DLL 85

Lessons Learned Across Both Cases 86

Conclusion 87

Chapter 6: Encrypting and Validating Save Data 89

Threat Modeling for Save Data 90

Cryptographic Principles for Game Save Security 91

Introducing the Cryptographic Save Envelope 92

Deriving Cryptographic Keys Securely 94

AES Encryption of Save Data 97

Authenticating Save Data with HMAC 99

Designing a Complete Crypto Envelope 102

Writing Encrypted Save Files 105

Loading and Validating Encrypted Save Files 108

Loader Threat Model 108

Implementing the Secure Loader 108

Handling Save Integrity Failures 112

Case Study 1: The RPG Skill Tree Corruption Incident 113

Case Study 2: The Sandbox Construction Game Rollback Exploit 114

Conclusion 115

Chapter 7: Protecting Save Files Against Tampering 117

Why Save Tampering Requires Behavioral and Structural Defenses 117

Layered Model of Save Security 118

Trap Variables As Early Detection Mechanisms 119

Detecting Implausible Save States 121

Temporal Integrity and Rollback Detection 122

Temporal Consistency Through Metadata Tracking 122

Save Duplication and Device Fingerprinting 124

Detecting Repeated, Identical Save States 126

Session-Level Correlation Checks 127

Cross-Field Semantic Validation 129

Progression Curve Modeling (XP, Gold, Difficulty) 131

Using Regression Curves to Detect Abnormal Progression 131

Reverse-Diff Tamper Reconstruction 133

Save Slot Reputation Scoring 134

Implementing a Basic Reputation Model 135

Designing a Unified Save Tampering Detection Pipeline 136

Soft vs. Hard Countermeasures 139

Soft Countermeasures (Preferred for Single-Player Games) 139

Hard Countermeasures (Use Only When Necessary) 140

Integrating Detection Into Unreal's Save/Load Lifecycle 140

Case Study 1: Platformer Save Duplication Exploit 141

Case Study 2: Open-World RPG Stat Inflation via Save-State Injection 141

Conclusion 142

Chapter 8: Avoiding Blueprint-Based Exploits..**145**

The Blueprint Reflection Surface 146

Exposure Vectors in Blueprint Assets...147

The Five Practical Blueprint Exploit Families 147

Restricting BlueprintCallable Surfaces 148

Blueprint Metadata and Unsafe Annotations..149

Auditing Blueprint Graphs for Exploitability 150

Escalating Critical Logic to C++ 151

Hardening Widget Blueprints and UI Event Graphs 152

Creating a Secure Input Gateway for UI Interaction 152

Hardening Event Dispatchers and Global Triggers 154

Detecting Blueprint Variable Tampering Through State Fingerprinting....155

Securing Blueprint Interfaces and Preventing Unauthorized Implementations 157

Blueprint Construction Script Abuse and Default Value Leakage............159

Preventing Exploits Through Blueprint-Callable Console Commands 161

Securing Blueprint-Exposed Variables and Default Properties 162

Hardening Blueprint Graph Flow Against Direct Trigger Paths...............164

Creating Blueprint Honeypots and Tamper Traps 166

Blueprint Latent Actions and Exploit Timing Windows 167

Protecting Blueprint Data Assets and Data Tables 169

Encrypting Blueprint Parameter Channels Without Cryptography 171

Refactoring Blueprint State Machines for Security..................................173

Case Study 1: Exposed Skill Unlock Paths in an Indie RPG..................175

Case Study 2: UI Button Exploits in a Survival Game 175

Conclusion 176

Chapter 9: Disabling Console and Developer Access **177**

Understanding the Console and CVar Attack Surface 178

    Why CVars Are Dangerous in Shipping Builds 178

    Exec Functions and Hidden Cheat Entry Points...............................179

Disabling the Console in Shipping Builds..180

Build-Level Removal of Console Bindings 182

Input Routing Protection 182

Hardening the CVar System 183

    Making Non-Whitelisted CVars Read-Only 183

    CVar Category Restrictions 188

    Preventing Runtime CVar Overrides 189

Sanitizing Exec Functions 190

    Detecting All Exec Functions at Startup 190

    Restricting Sensitive Exec Commands 194

Configuration File Attacks and Protection 195

    Sanitizing INI Files in Shipping Builds 195

    Config Validation System 197

Build Pipeline Hardening 202

    Removing Developer Modules at Build Time 202

    Removing Debug Commands from PAK Files 206

    Unsafe Build Flags That Must Be Removed 207

    Platform-Specific Rules 208

Case Study 1: Runtime Console Exploitation Unlocks All Debug Commands in a UE Shooter.... 214

Case Study 2: INI Injection Unlocks Hidden God Mode and Developer Cheats 215

Conclusion 216

Chapter 10: Preventing Trainer and Macro Exploits 219

Why Macro Automation Is Fundamentally Different from Debugging 219

Why Single-Player Games Attract Macro-Based Cheating 220

Overview of Modern Trainer Ecosystems 221

    How Input Simulation Bypasses Traditional Anti-cheat Assumptions 222

    Key Threat Categories in Macro Automation 222

How Automation Tools Attack Unreal Games 224

    The Input System Attack Surface 224

    The Gameplay Logic Attack Surface 227

    Menu and UI Automation 227

    Frame-Step Abuse 228

The Timing-Based Attack Surface 228

Detecting Unnatural Input Patterns... 229

Input Timing Analysis.. 230

State-Dependent Input Validation.. 234

Detecting Macro Patterns in Player Behavior 238

Movement Pattern Recognition 238

Action Frequency and Heatmap Analysis 242

Designing Safe and Subtle Countermeasures 245

Delayed Response Strategy... 245

Soft Penalties That Reduce Macro Efficiency 248

Composite Behavior Score.. 251

Implementing a Composite Behavior Evaluator.. 251

Behavior Correlation Across Subsystems 254

Timing vs. Movement Correlation.. 254

Entropy vs. Camera Rotation 255

Action Diversity vs. Gameplay Context 255

Fatigue and Imperfection Modeling... 256

Integrating the Composite Evaluator with Detectors................................... 256

Gameplay-Integrated Deception Systems.. 257

Why Deception Works Better Than Observation Alone 258

Types of Gameplay Deception Traps 259

Pseudo-interactive Targets (Fake Objects)... 259

Timing-Choice Bait (Ambiguous Timing Opportunities)............................... 259

Variability Tests (Micro-Decision Chaos Triggers)...................................... 260

Meaningless Distraction Events 260

Behavioral Branch Traps 261

Design Principles for Successful Deception Systems...................................... 261

Implementing a Simple Deception Trap Component...................................... 262

Using Deception Outputs in the Macro-Detection Pipeline 264

Soft-Penalty Systems and Graduated Response Strategies 265

Why Soft Penalties Are More Effective Than Hard Blocks................................. 266

Categories of Soft Penalties 266

    Reward Degradation Systems 267

    Soft Locks on Progression Gates 267

    Invisible Cooldown Inflation... 268

    Micro-Friction Systems 268

    Quiet Achievement Freezes and Unlock Gating 269

The Suspicion-to-Penalty Curve 269

Integrating Soft Penalties into the Detection Pipeline 270

Using Penalty Levels in Gameplay Systems 273

    Fusing Soft Penalties with Deception and Timing Detection 273

Conclusion 274

Chapter 11: Securing Unreal Build Configurations 275

Why Build Configuration Is a Security Surface 276

Understanding Development, Test, and Shipping from a Security Perspective 277

Hardening Target Rules for Shipping Builds.. 278

Controlling Symbol Files and PDB Handling.. 280

Trimming Dangerous Developer Modules and Plugins 282

Guarding Build Flags That Affect Security.. 284

Automated Configuration Validation in the Build Pipeline......................... 285

Build Pipeline Hardening and Reproducible Security................................ 288

Case Study 1: Shipping a Development Build by Accident......................... 288

Case Study 2: Debug Symbols and Rapid Reverse Engineering 289

Conclusion 290

Chapter 12: Protecting Assets and Game Data...................... 291

Understanding Asset Threats in Single-Player Games.............................. 292

Securing PAK Files Using Unreal Build Settings...................................... 293

Introducing an Asset Integrity Manager 294

Obfuscating Critical Game Data 297

Runtime Verification of Game Data Tables 299

Map Integrity Validation 302

Lightweight Encryption for Custom Data Files 303

Conclusion 305

Chapter 13: Monitoring Tampering in the Wild **307**

Why Post-Launch Monitoring Matters 307

Collecting Signals Without Hurting Performance 309

Event-Driven Security Logging 311

Monitoring Integrity Failures Across Systems 313

Building a Tamper Telemetry Buffer 316

Detecting Patterns Over Time 318

Using Crash Reports As Security Signals 320

Case Study 1: Repeated Save File Rollback Attempts 321

Case Study 2: Map Integrity Failures Exposing Hidden Shortcuts 322

Conclusion 322

Chapter 14: The Line Between Cheating and Modding **323**

What Makes Modding Different from Cheating 323

The Security Boundary: What Must Never Be Moddable 324

Structuring Unreal Projects for Safe Modding 325

Safe Modding Categories 325

What Should Never Be Exposed to Modders 326

Building a Safe Modding API 326

Case Study 1: Safe UI Modding Without Gameplay Access 329

Case Study 2: A Gameplay "Mod" That Turned into Cheating 329

Conclusion 330

Appendixes **331**

Glossary of Terms **339**

Index **351**

About the Author

 **Sheikh Sohel Moon** is a game developer, technical author, and Unreal Engine specialist with a focus on immersive systems, VR/AR interaction, and game security. He is the author of *Game Development Concepts in C++: Elevate Your Skills with Unreal Engine* (Apress, 2025).

Sohel has led multiple cross-platform game and VR development initiatives, integrating C++, Blueprints, and multiplayer systems for simulation, racing, and open-world environments. He is also actively involved in security-driven game design, helping small studios and solo developers protect their games from tampering, memory editing, and save game exploitation. With an emphasis on hands-on coding and implementation-first design, Sohel is dedicated to helping indie creators deliver secure, polished experiences at any scale.

About the Technical Reviewer

Massimo Nardone has more than 30 years of experience in security, web/mobile development, and cloud and IT/OT/IoT architecture. His true passions are security and Android. He has been programming and teaching how to program with Android, Perl, PHP, Java, VB, Python, C/C++, and MySQL for more than 30 years. He holds a master of science degree in computing science from the University of Salerno, Italy. He has worked as chief information security officer (CISO), software engineer, chief security architect, security executive, and OT/IoT/IIoT security leader and architect for many years. He works currently as VP, OT Security, for SSH Communications Security.

Introduction

This book is uniquely designed for intermediate to advanced game developers, offering a comprehensive guide to creating complex, engaging, and performance-driven games using Unreal Engine (UE) and C++. Whether you are an indie developer, a student, or a professional, this book will equip you with the tools and knowledge to take your skills to the next level.

Why This Book?

As indie games grow in depth and complexity, players have more opportunities to manipulate game systems using external tools like Cheat Engine and WeMod (Wand) or by modifying save files. Many developers assume that because their game is single player, security isn't important. But when players bypass game progression, unlock everything instantly, or break carefully tuned mechanics, it compromises the experience you've crafted.

This book bridges the gap between Unreal Engine development and practical game security, offering a step-by-step guide to protecting the most vulnerable parts of your game. With detailed explanations, hands-on code samples, and real-world case studies, you'll learn how to secure runtime variables, encrypt save files, detect tampering, and more.

Who Is This Book For?

This book is intended for

- Indie developers using Unreal Engine for single-player games

- Developers familiar with Blueprints and/or basic Unreal C++

- Anyone interested in preventing tampering, cheating, or save file exploitation in their games

You should already be comfortable with

- Creating and packaging a game in Unreal Engine

- Working with variables and logic in Blueprints

- (Optionally) Writing or reading simple C++ classes and functions in Unreal Engine

If you're brand new to Unreal Engine, we recommend completing beginner-level tutorials or reviewing the official documentation before starting this book.

Structure of the Book

The book is divided into multiple parts and chapters, each focusing on different aspects of single-player game security in Unreal Engine:

Chapter 1: Why Security Matters in Single-Player Games

- Debunks common myths and highlights real-world damage caused by tampering

Chapter 2: Understanding the Cheat Landscape

- Explores popular cheating tools, methods, and the motivation behind them

Chapter 3: Designing for Tamper Resistance

- Outlines architectural principles and defensive design patterns that make systems more resistant to manipulation

Chapter 4: Tamper-Proofing Runtime Variables

- Discusses how to implement secure float wrappers and honeypots that detect or resist real-time memory editing attacks

Chapter 5: Anti-debugging and Injection Detection

- Shows how to detect debuggers and DLL (Dynamic Link Library) injection attempts at runtime using low-level Windows APIs

Chapter 6: Encrypting and Validating Save Data

- Explains how to protect Unreal Engine save files from editing, duplication, and rollback using encryption and integrity checks

Chapter 7: Protecting Save Files Against Tampering

- Describes how to defend against unauthorized save file edits, duplication, and rollback by using encryption, checksums, and save-time validations

Chapter 8: Avoiding Blueprint-Based Exploits

- Shows how BlueprintCallable functions, exposed variables, and open Blueprint logic can be abused to bypass game rules and how to prevent that

Chapter 9: Disabling Console and Developer Access

- Walks through disabling the in-game developer console, cheat console variables (CVars), and default config file abuse in shipped builds

Chapter 10: Preventing Trainer and Macro Exploits

- Explains how to detect unauthorized automation such as macros, input simulators, and auto-farming bots using heuristic and behavioral techniques

Chapter 11: Securing Unreal Build Configurations

- Discusses how to protect your game during the build and packaging process using secure shipping configs, symbol stripping, and program database (PDB) management

Chapter 12: Protecting Assets and Game Data

- Describes how to prevent players from extracting or tampering with assets (.pak files, maps, etc.) using encryption and obfuscation

Chapter 13: Monitoring Tampering in the Wild

- Explains how to detect and learn from tampering attempts post-launch using logging, telemetry, and crash reporting tools

Chapter 14: The Line Between Cheating and Modding

- Explores how to mod safely without compromising security and defines boundaries between creative customization and tampering

Each chapter contains real-world case studies and practical code snippets to help you understand how and why each system is targeted and how to defend it.

Continuous Learning

Security is not a one-time task. As tools and exploits evolve, so must your strategies. Engage with other developers, follow anti-cheat and reverse engineering forums, and keep up with Unreal Engine updates to stay ahead of potential threats.

This book is your guide to fortifying your Unreal Engine games without bloating your project or alienating your players. By the time you reach the final chapter, you'll have the confidence and practical ability to defend your single-player game against cheating, tampering, and unintended manipulation.

CHAPTER 1

Why Security Matters in Single-Player Games

Single-player security is one of the most misunderstood topics in game development. Many developers believe that because their game has no online competition, no leaderboards, and no server-driven progression, players are free to modify or skip content as they choose. The assumption is that cheating harms no one, that offline games are immune to tampering risk, and that security measures are unnecessary. This chapter challenges that belief.

Security matters in single-player games because tampering destroys the pacing, meaning, and structure of your design. When a player bypasses difficulty, unlocks everything instantly, or manipulates narrative progression, they experience a distorted version of your work. They reach moments they should not reach, achieve things they did not earn, and lose the emotions you built through careful timing and progression. The player may feel powerful in the moment, but their long-term experience becomes hollow. Worse, they may blame the game's design rather than their own manipulation. A broken save file, a trivialized challenge, or an unintended skip can become a negative review. Once this happens, other players searching for help encounter guides and cheat tables that spread the same issues to thousands more.

Security in single-player games is therefore not about policing players. It is about protecting the structure of your design so the intended experience can survive contact with the real world.

S. S. Moon, *Securing Single-Player Games in Unreal Engine*, https://doi.org/10.1007/979-8-8688-2833-1_1

The Real Cost of Cheating in Single-Player Games

Cheating in offline games is often framed as a personal choice. However, data from modding communities, cheat forums, and player reviews reveals that tampering leads to widespread misunderstandings about game balance, pacing, and progression systems. Many negative reviews originate from players who unintentionally broke their progression through external tools.

The following consequences appear frequently in untreated single-player security:

- Distorted progression curves where players trivialize experience points (XP) or currency and then blame the game for being too short or too easy

- Broken narrative pacing when players skip required content or unlock late-game mechanics prematurely

- Incorrect perceptions of difficulty when health, stamina, or damage multipliers are modified

- Unrecoverable save files when players use trainers or editors that corrupt core systems

- Community spread of exploits as tampered saves circulate online and normal players unknowingly download compromised files

- Reduced retention because players lose meaningful goals when everything becomes instantly available

- Public misconception of design quality when bypassed systems are misinterpreted as poorly built

Security is therefore directly connected to gameplay meaning. A secure single-player ecosystem is not about enforcement. It is about protecting the emotional and structural integrity of the work.

Why the Myth Exists: "It's Single Player, It Doesn't Matter"

The myth originates from two assumptions:

1. There is no competitive element, so cheating harms no one.

2. Only multiplayer games require anti-cheat systems.

These assumptions ignore the fact that single-player games rely on carefully constructed pacing, resource management curves, challenge barriers, and emotional beats. Tampering breaks these structures. When players circumvent your design, they are not playing your game. They are playing a compromised simulation that resembles your work but does not reflect your intentions.

Several developers from indie studios have expressed regret post-launch when they discovered that their negative reviews were caused by tampered or modified saves. When a system breaks, the player blames the developer, not the cheat tool.

The myth also survives because developers underestimate how easy modern tools have made offline tampering. Debuggers, memory scanners, and save editors are freely available. Many players use trainers simply out of curiosity, not malicious intent. They do not expect the consequences.

The Three Primary Attack Surfaces in Single-Player Games

Before diving into the technical systems throughout this book, it is important to establish the three major categories of tampering. These form the security model that structures the remaining chapters.

- Runtime Memory Tampering

  Editing health, XP, currency, stamina, or timers by modifying RAM as the game runs

- Save File Manipulation

  Editing, replacing, duplicating, or rolling back save files to remove consequences or unlock progression

- Scripting and Engine Exposure Abuse

  Calling Blueprint-exposed functions, running console commands, or manipulating config files and user interface (UI) logic

Each of the next chapters aligns with one of these layers. Understanding these layers prevents conceptual overlap and creates thematic consistency for the rest of the book.

Why Single-Player Security Is Actually Part of Game Design

Security is often treated as a technical discipline, but in single-player ecosystems, it is inherently tied to design. A secure game feels fair, consistent, and meaningful. Without security, the following design pillars collapse:

- Pacing loses meaning when players jump progression steps.

- Challenge loses meaning when enemies or obstacles are bypassed.

- Reward structures lose meaning when items or XP are obtained instantly.

- Choice and consequence lose meaning when players can undo failure through rollback saves.

- Achievement loses meaning when unlocks are trivialized.

Security reinforces design rather than constraining it. It ensures that each system you build remains intact, predictable, and narratively coherent throughout the player's journey.

Thought Experiment: The Fragile Narrative Arc

Imagine a story-driven RPG where the first few hours are designed to introduce the player to limited tools, moderate difficulty, and early narrative conflict. Early-game scarcity is a core part of the tension. Now imagine a player who uses a trainer at the beginning to unlock every ability and obtain unlimited resources.

The following design pillars collapse instantly:

- No tutorial pacing

- No sense of growth

- No meaning to leveling up

- No emotional investment in early difficulty

- No attachment to new unlocks

- No tension in resource management

- No connection to failures or consequences

The game was not designed to be played this way, yet without security measures, this is exactly how many players will encounter it. Some players will enjoy the power. Many others will quit midway and describe the game as boring or unbalanced. Both outcomes damage your design's intent.

Historical Context: Why Cheating Shapes Player Expectations

Cheating in single-player games has always existed, but modern tools have made it dramatically easier. Earlier cheats required

- Hex editors

- Memory address hunting

- Command-line debugging

- Complex reverse engineering

Today, a player can achieve the same results in seconds by

- Clicking "Unlimited Health" in a trainer

- Dragging a save file into an editor

- Calling Blueprint functions through an external script

- Enabling test features left in development builds

- Injecting DLLs with ready-made tools

The ease of tampering has changed players' expectations. They expect to see cheats, shortcuts, and modifications available. If your game does not anticipate this environment, it risks being interpreted as poorly tested or poorly balanced when those tools distort your systems.

Case Study 1: XP Inflation Destroying Progression

A turn-based indie RPG released with a simple float variable for XP. Trainers instantly discovered the XP address. Thousands of players used cheats to gain massive amounts of XP early. They reached end-game abilities within minutes. Reviews described the game as shallow and unbalanced.

The developer later admitted the progression curve was never meant to operate under tampered values. But by that point, players were judging the compromised version of the game, not the real one.

Case Study 2: Save File Corruption in a Survival Game

An early-access survival game used plain JSON for saves. Players used text editors to modify resource amounts. Corrupted saves began circulating on forums. New players unknowingly downloaded broken saves, loaded them, and lost their progression. Many blamed the game for "unreliable saving."

The issue was never the save system itself. It was the lack of integrity checks that allowed invalid saves to be loaded without warning.

Case Study 3: Blueprint Exploits in a Strategy Game

A developer left several BlueprintCallable debugging functions exposed for testing. Trainers discovered them and began calling:

- GiveAllUnits

- UnlockAllTech

- RevealMap

- AddResources

Players unintentionally triggered these functions by clicking buttons in certain cheat tools. Many then left negative reviews stating that the game lacked challenge or had instant-win mechanics.

Once again, the game was blamed for a tampered experience.

Why Cheating Damages More Than Gameplay

Beyond moment-to-moment distortion, tampering creates long-term consequences for developers:

- Misleading analytics when tampered saves produce impossible playtime or economy data

- Incorrect difficulty adjustments based on data from cheaters

- Unrealistic testing conditions when tampered builds affect balancing cycles

- Inconsistent user experience across players and platforms

- Damaged reputation when public sentiment blames the game for side effects of cheats

Security is therefore not about enforcement. It is about preserving the integrity of the data you rely on and the experience you have authored.

A Layered Single-Player Defense Mindset

This book teaches you how to build layered resilience, not absolute protection. No technique stops every possible tampering attempt, but when multiple systems work together, tampering becomes noticeable, detectable, or costly.

The layered model introduced in this book follows three principles:

- Obscure and obfuscate the easy attack paths.

- Validate and verify assumptions at every boundary.

- Detect and record implausible behavior, even if you do not block it.

Security becomes part of the architecture rather than a bolt-on afterthought. This mindset prepares the reader for the remainder of the book.

Conclusion

Single-player security is not about denying players freedom. It is about protecting the intended emotional and structural experience of your game. Without security, progression loses meaning, pacing collapses, narrative order breaks, and player trust erodes. The chapters that follow build a comprehensive defensive model across runtime variables, memory, saves, Blueprints, and internal logic. The objective is not perfect protection. It is integrity. By understanding why security matters, you can begin designing systems that retain their purpose even when players experiment, explore, or attempt to bypass your rules.

In the next chapter, we will explore the tools, motivations, and techniques used by cheaters in real-world scenarios. Understanding these tools is essential, because every defensive method in the remaining chapters is built in response to specific attack patterns. By learning how single-player games are targeted, you will be ready to design tamper-resistant systems from the ground up.

CHAPTER 2

Understanding the Cheat Landscape

Understanding the cheat landscape is an essential step toward building secure single-player experiences. A game's security does not exist in isolation. It enters a diverse environment shaped by real tools, real communities, and real behaviors. This chapter explores the motivations and methods used by players who modify, manipulate, or experiment with game systems. It also examines how these actions interact with the structures you build in Unreal Engine.

The goal of this chapter is not to teach cheating. Instead, it aims to provide a clear insight into the techniques and workflows players commonly use so you can build defenses that tolerate tampering attempts. By understanding how memory scanning, save file manipulation, asset extraction, and scripting exposure work, you gain the perspective needed to create resilient systems in later chapters.

Modern cheating has become widespread and accessible. Tools that were once used only by technical users are now packaged into single-click trainers supported by large communities. Some players cheat out of curiosity, while others do it for convenience or experimentation. Regardless of the motivation, the impact remains consistent: progression curves break, difficulty becomes unpredictable, analytics lose meaning, and narrative pacing loses its structure.

This chapter creates the foundation for the technical strategies that follow. By mapping the tools, motivations, and behaviors that shape the single-player cheating ecosystem, you will be better prepared to understand why specific systems are targeted and how attackers choose their methods.

© Sheikh Sohel Moon 2026
S. S. Moon, *Securing Single-Player Games in Unreal Engine*, https://doi.org/10.1007/979-8-8688-2833-1_2

Attacker Motivations in Single-Player Games

Players modify games for a wide range of reasons. Understanding these motivations helps anticipate which systems are likely to attract tampering and why certain patterns repeat across titles. The motivations below represent the most common scenarios observed in real game releases:

- Curiosity

  Many players simply want to see how the game works. They scan for values, change them, and experiment.

- Convenience

  Players tired of grinding may adjust XP, currency, or item counts to accelerate progression.

- Testing Boundaries

  Some players enjoy discovering unintended mechanics, physics exploits, or event triggers.

- Content Unlocking

  Players who want to skip ahead in a narrative or obtain post-game content early often modify saves.

- Power Fantasy

  Trainers allow players to feel invulnerable or overwhelmingly strong.

- Content Creation

  Streamers often use cheats to showcase content, which normalizes cheating for viewers.

- Frustration

  Players stuck in a difficult section may turn to trainers or save editors.

Although not all cheat users act with harmful intent, their actions can distort progression, corrupt saves, and create misleading analytics data. Recognizing this variety of motivations helps guide defensive design.

Attacker Capability Levels

Not all players who modify games possess the same skill level. The following categories describe typical attacker capabilities, helping you anticipate the complexity of attacks and the level of protection needed to address them. These levels form a practical mental model for designing layered defenses.

- Level 1: Casual Editor Users

  These users open save files in a hex editor or a JSON editor. They typically search for numbers like gold or XP.

- Level 2: Basic Cheat Engine Users

  These attackers scan memory, search for changing values, and freeze or modify them.

- Level 3: Trainer Users

  These rely on packaged cheat tools like WeMod (Wand) or FLiNG, which require no skill. They simply click options like "Unlimited Health."

- Level 4: Scripted Tool Users

  These individuals write Cheat Engine Lua tables, signature scans, or basic automation scripts.

- Level 5: Reverse Engineers

  These attackers use debuggers, disassemblers, custom DLL injectors, or code hooks to modify game logic itself.

Understanding these levels clarifies why even low-skill attacks can reshape your game experience if left unprotected.

Taxonomy of Single-Player Attack Vectors

All cheating techniques used in single-player games ultimately fall into a few recurring categories. Organizing these categories early prevents conceptual overlap later in the book and prepares you for the layered security structures discussed in subsequent chapters. The list below outlines the primary attack surfaces you will encounter:

- Runtime Memory Manipulation

  Directly editing values in RAM such as health, gold, stamina, damage multipliers, cooldowns, or XP

- Save File Tampering

  Editing serialized saves to change inventory, unlocks, stats, or world state

- Scripting Layer Abuse

  Calling BlueprintCallable or exec functions, manipulating widget logic, or triggering events externally

- Code Injection

  Injecting DLLs to override functions, hook engine calls, or patch logic

- Function Hooking and Patching

  Manipulating assembly instructions to bypass checks or enforce cheats

- Input Automation

  Using macros or simulated inputs to farm resources or spam actions

- Asset and Data Extraction

  Inspecting DataTables, uassets, or configs to uncover developer variables, debug flags, or hidden mechanics

- Configuration Manipulation

  Changing .ini values to enable cheats, unlock console commands, or alter internal CVars

Each upcoming chapter addresses one or more of these attack vectors. Understanding this taxonomy early prevents conceptual overlap and prepares you to build layered defenses.

How Cheat Tools Spread and Why Your Game Gets Targeted

Cheating rarely happens in isolation. Cheat tools spread through communities, influencers, and automated platforms that make them easy to access. By understanding how these tools circulate, you can better anticipate when and why your game becomes a target. The patterns below illustrate how cheating ecosystems form and grow around new releases:

- Trainer Request Hubs

  Platforms like WeMod allow users to vote for which games should receive trainers. High-demand games are prioritized.

- Influencer Amplification

  Once a cheat is showcased by a streamer, many players adopt it, often without understanding its consequences.

- Community Collaboration

  Cheat tables spread rapidly through forums, Discord groups, and Reddit communities.

- Update Cycles

  When you release a patch, cheat authors release a new trainer within hours.

- Content Discovery

  Players curious about debugging or modding often begin by editing your game's memory or save files.

These patterns create predictable stages of cheat adoption, which defensive systems must anticipate.

Deep Dive: How Cheat Engine Attacks Unreal Engine Games

Cheat Engine is one of the most common tools used to tamper with single-player games. Understanding how its workflows interact with Unreal Engine helps explain why certain defensive patterns appear later in the book. Each technique below shows a different approach that attackers use when targeting live memory.

How Basic Scanning Works

At its simplest, Cheat Engine allows players to search for values in memory, refine their search, and edit or freeze results. This process is straightforward yet powerful, and many early-stage attacks begin here.

- Search for a number (e.g., 100 for health).

- Take damage and search again for the new value.

- Narrow results until one or a few addresses remain.

- Modify or freeze those addresses.

Even this basic process can break unprotected systems instantly.

Pointer Scanning

Pointer scanning targets the underlying memory references used by Unreal Engine's object model. This method aims to find stable offsets that persist across sessions.

- Scanning for pointers to the health variable

- Finding stable offsets (e.g., +0x34)

- Building a pointer map

- Saving the pointer chain across sessions

Without countermeasures, this technique remains effective across patches.

Array-of-Bytes (AOB) Pattern Scans

AOB scanning allows cheat authors to find functions by matching byte patterns rather than relying on memory addresses. This enables trainers to remain functional even after updates.

- Target code around damage handling or XP functions.
- Identify unique byte sequences.
- Use AOB patterns to locate functions post-update.

This makes AOB scanning a reliable option for persistent cheats.

Code Injection

Code injection replaces or modifies internal logic through custom assembly. This allows attackers to rewrite behavior entirely.

- Overwrite damage logic.
- Skip validation checks.
- Force functions to return fixed values.
- Use NOP (no operation) instructions to bypass comparisons.

These techniques motivate the anti-debugging systems explored in Chapter 5.

Lua Automation

Lua scripting extends Cheat Engine with automation capabilities. This enables sophisticated workflows that adapt to updates or complex memory structures.

- Automate scanning.
- Rebuild pointer paths.
- Update cheat tables after patches.
- Create GUI trainers.

Through Lua, attackers with moderate skill can produce advanced cheats.

Trainer Platforms: Why WeMod, FLiNG, and Others Are Dangerous

Trainer platforms package memory edits into accessible interfaces. The danger lies not in complexity but in how easy they make cheating. These platforms offer a consistent set of cheats that reshape the game experience with no technical effort required.

- Unlimited health
- Unlimited ammo
- Unlimited currency
- No cooldowns
- Unlock all skills
- Freeze timers
- Slow enemy AI
- Teleport

For many players, the trainer becomes their "default experience." They judge your game based on this distorted version. Many negative reviews come from players who accidentally activated cheats or did not realize trainers alter game balance.

Save Editors and Offline Progression Exploitation

Save file tampering is extremely common because it does not require advanced tools. Players use editors to modify serialized data and reshape progression according to their preferences. The methods below represent the broad range of edits seen across games:

- Hex editors
- JSON editors
- Custom-built save editors
- Tools like Gibbed Save Editor (for Borderlands)
- Online save editors available through browser tools

The most frequently edited values include

- Currency increases

- XP increases

- Inventory modification

- Unlocking skills or levels prematurely

- Rolling back progress to retry events

- Removing consequences such as permadeath

These actions connect directly to the concepts in Chapters 6 and 7.

Case Study: XP Hacks Destroying Progression in Assassin's Creed Odyssey

When Odyssey launched, many players used cheat tools to inflate their XP gain. The progression system was designed around slow, steady leveling, but cheat users skipped dozens of hours of content.

As a result:

- Players unlocked the entire skill tree prematurely

- Combat encounters became trivial

- Difficulty felt inconsistent

- Narrative cues no longer matched the player's level

Many players wrote reviews claiming the game was poorly balanced. In reality, their experience had been tampered with unintentionally.

Reflection Abuse: Calling Blueprint Functions Externally

Unreal Engine exposes UFunction metadata at runtime, allowing attackers to find and call BlueprintCallable or exec functions. This allows external tools to trigger internal behaviors without normal game flow.

Commonly targeted functions include

- GiveXP

- UnlockAll

- Teleport

- Debug menus

- Hidden mechanics

- Level transitions

- Test functions

These risks connect directly to the protections in Chapter 8.

Asset and Data Extraction

Even without modifying memory or code, attackers can extract assets and data from packaged files. These values often reveal sensitive design parameters or hidden mechanics. The extracted elements typically include

- DataTables

- Enemy damage tables

- Drop rates

- XP curves

- Unlock conditions

- Crafting data

- Dialogue states

These extraction attacks motivate the systems discussed in Chapter 12.

How Attackers Prioritize Targets

Attackers focus on areas of the system that provide immediate impact or easy reward. Understanding these target preferences helps guide where you apply defensive layers. The most commonly targeted elements include

- Frequently changing values such as health or XP

- Timers and cooldowns

- Inventory arrays

- Player state structs

- Unlock functions

- Widget logic

- Save file fields

- Debug flags

- Console commands

These patterns help identify where memory structures require added protection.

Why Understanding the Cheat Landscape Matters

The chapters that follow describe defensive techniques that operate at runtime, in serialization, in scripting, and in packaging. Each defense gains strength when aligned with attacker workflows. By recognizing the motivations and methods described above, you will better understand

- Why certain values are particularly vulnerable

- How attacker workflows locate sensitive data

- Which systems are likely to be modified

- Where memory-resistant structures are most useful

- How to protect save files from trivial edits

- How to control Blueprint exposure

- Why console and config protection matters

- When asset security becomes essential

These insights help ensure that defensive systems fit the actual threats your game will face.

Conclusion

Cheating in single-player games emerges from predictable workflows, community ecosystems, and widely accessible tools. By understanding these behaviors, you can design systems that preserve core mechanics even when players attempt to bypass them. The next chapter moves closer to the internal structure of your game. Chapter 3 explores architectural design principles that support tamper-resistant systems, including distributed state, assumption validation, and the avoidance of single points of failure.

CHAPTER 3

Designing for Tamper Resistance

Security in single-player games is not achieved through a single technique or a handful of code-level adjustments. It is achieved through deliberate architectural choices. Strong defenses begin long before encryption, anti-debugging checks, or obfuscated variables are added. They begin at the design stage, where you decide how gameplay data flows, how the game stores and updates state, and how much information is exposed at any given moment.

This chapter explores the architectural foundations of tamper resistance. While Chapter 2 focused on understanding attacker tools and motivations, this chapter focuses on the internal structure of your game. The goal is to help you build systems that resist manipulation by design, even before advanced protection layers are introduced in later chapters.

Tamper-resistant architecture does not eliminate cheating entirely. Instead, it forces attackers to work significantly harder, reduces the reliability of automated tools, and increases the cost of producing stable cheats. These outcomes create meaningful security for single-player games because they preserve difficulty curves, progression pacing, and narrative flow.

This chapter introduces conceptual patterns, memory flow considerations, and structural principles that underpin all later defenses. Understanding these concepts ensures that techniques introduced in Chapter 4 and beyond integrate smoothly into your project.

Figure 3-1 illustrates a simplified example of a tamper-resistant gameplay architecture where gameplay state is distributed across multiple components rather than stored in a single structure.

© Sheikh Sohel Moon 2026
S. S. Moon, *Securing Single-Player Games in Unreal Engine*, https://doi.org/10.1007/979-8-8688-2833-1_3

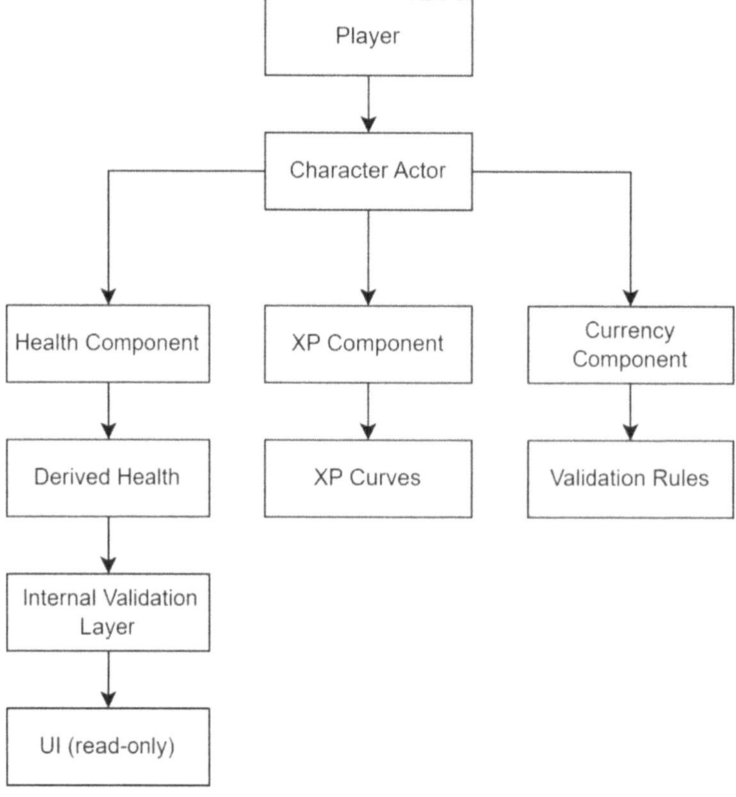

Figure 3-1. *Example of a distributed gameplay architecture that separates critical state across components and validation layers*

Why Architecture Matters More Than Any Individual Security Technique

Many developers jump directly into encryption, honeypots, or anti-debugging. While these tools are helpful, they cannot compensate for an architecture that exposes too much data or allows values to be directly manipulated.

A strong security foundation begins with architectural thinking. Before implementing advanced protection mechanisms, developers should examine how gameplay data flows through the system and how easily attackers might locate and manipulate critical values. The following structural questions help guide that evaluation:

- Where does your game store critical values?

- How is state shared between systems?

- How predictable is the memory layout for attackers?

- Do your functions leak information through exposed interfaces?

- Can your game continue functioning if a variable is tampered with?

- What assumptions does your gameplay rely on that an attacker can break?

Architectural choices shape how easily attackers can understand and manipulate your systems. Several key aspects of system design directly influence how predictable your memory layout and gameplay state become:

- How easily attackers can locate variables

- How reliably they can freeze, scan, or patch values

- How stable pointer paths are

- How consistently property offsets appear in memory

- How much game state becomes exposed to cheat-layer reflection

Bad architecture makes advanced defenses unnecessary because attackers can directly modify values without resistance. Good architecture makes tampering unpredictable, risky, or counterproductive.

Understanding Unreal Engine's Runtime Memory Model

Unreal Engine's flexibility is one of its greatest strengths. However, from a security perspective, it also creates a relatively transparent runtime environment. Attackers rely on several structural characteristics of Unreal Engine's memory model that appear in nearly all projects.

Understanding these characteristics helps developers design systems that reduce exposure while still maintaining performance and maintainability.

Object Headers and Predictable Layout

Every UObject begins with a predictable layout in memory. This layout contains several elements that help the engine manage objects and dispatch functions. Because this structure is consistent across classes, attackers often use it as an entry point when navigating memory.

[UObject Pointer / VTable]

[Internal Flags]

[UObject ID / Outer]

[Class Pointer]

[Property Data Block (contiguous)]

When attackers scan memory, they often search for recognizable patterns surrounding these structures. The following elements commonly become starting points for memory exploration:

- Class pointers

- Property blocks

- VTable signatures

- Consistent offsets around known variables

This allows them to easily navigate object memory.

Reflection Metadata (FProperty)

Unreal Engine uses a powerful reflection system to describe properties at runtime. Each UPROPERTY contains metadata that describes the variable's type, location, and behavior. While this system is extremely valuable for development, it also creates an additional discovery surface for attackers.

- Type (float, int, bool)

- Offset within the object

- Size

- Flags (BlueprintReadWrite, SaveGame, EditAnywhere)

Attackers can enumerate reflection tables and search for gameplay-related variables. These frequently include values such as

- Health

- XP

- Currency

- Damage multipliers

- Unlock flags

- Cooldowns

If a property is visible through reflection and has a predictable offset, attackers may locate it without scanning memory at all.

Garbage Collection and Deterministic Allocation

Unreal Engine's garbage collector and object allocator follow consistent rules. These behaviors help maintain performance and memory stability, but they can also introduce predictable patterns that attackers learn to recognize.

Several patterns often appear during normal gameplay execution:

- Objects often spawn in predictable order.

- Memory regions for common classes group together.

- Re-loading a level often re-creates objects in the same sequence.

- Many objects retain the same offset structures across builds.

This predictability allows attackers to build pointer chains that remain stable across sessions. Even when variable addresses change, pointer paths frequently remain consistent.

Memory Fragmentation Does Not Protect You

Some developers assume that dynamic allocation or memory fragmentation provides a form of protection. In practice, modern cheat tools are designed to handle fragmented memory environments.

Tools typically rely on automated scanning techniques that search the entire address space. These tools can

- Scan every region of memory

- Detect changing values automatically

- Use pattern scans to bypass fragmentation entirely

- Build pointer maps independent of addresses

Because of these capabilities, fragmentation alone does not provide meaningful protection.

Predictability Is the Enemy of Security

Attackers rely heavily on patterns. Whenever a system behaves in a predictable way, the effort required to locate and manipulate values becomes much lower. Architecture that exposes consistent patterns therefore becomes easier to reverse engineer.

Several common design patterns unintentionally make systems easier to analyze. The following examples illustrate architectural choices that can increase exposure.

Common predictable patterns that harm security:

- Storing all stats in a single struct (Health, MaxHealth, Armor, XP)

- Using sequential offsets for abilities or inventory

- Exposing variables through BlueprintReadWrite unintentionally

- Keeping values in plain floats instead of encapsulated types

- Allowing UI widgets to access critical variables directly

- Using obvious variable names (Coins, XP, GodMode)

- Keeping developer debug variables in the final build

- Relying on global singletons for progression values

These patterns make your architecture easy to reverse.

Design Principle 1: Minimizing the Attack Surface

Every system exposes some portion of the game's internal state. A secure architecture limits how much information is visible and reduces the number of entry points that attackers can use to manipulate that state.

Several practical techniques can help reduce the exposed attack surface of gameplay systems.

Practical techniques:

- Avoid exposing sensitive UPROPERTY variables unless required.

- Mark unnecessary members as private.

- Use accessors instead of public variables.

- Keep core values in controlled subsystems, not scattered in Blueprints.

- Restrict the number of functions marked BlueprintCallable.

- Remove or isolate developer toggles and debug values.

Reducing entry points lowers the number of ways attackers can interfere with gameplay systems.

Design Principle 2: Breaking Up Critical State

Attackers prefer simple and linear data structures. When a gameplay system depends on a single float for health or progression, that variable becomes a single point of failure.

Breaking up critical state forces attackers to locate and manipulate multiple values instead of one. The following examples illustrate ways that developers can distribute gameplay state.

Examples:

- Track health using separate components (base health, bonus health, shield layers).

- Store XP progress as a combination of factors instead of a raw number.

- Split currency into session earnings and persistent earnings.

- Tie unlocks to multiple state checks instead of single flags.

Attackers must now

- Find more values

- Patch more functions

- Maintain more pointers

This additional complexity discourages trainer developers and increases opportunities for tampering detection.

Design Principle 3: Redundant State and Cross-Validation

Redundancy provides a powerful conceptual defense. When multiple systems store overlapping information, inconsistencies can be detected automatically. Attackers who modify one value must modify all related values to maintain stability.

Several gameplay systems benefit from this form of cross-validation:

- Health displayed to the UI should be cross-validated against internal health.

- Currency should appear in multiple subsystems with matching rules.

- XP should be validated by progression curves and achievement logic.

- Unlocks should depend on state, not flags.

When redundancy exists, attackers cannot reliably freeze or overwrite a single variable.

Design Principle 4: Designing for Unpredictability

Systems that behave identically in every frame are easier to analyze and automate. Introducing controlled unpredictability can break automated scanning tools and reduce the reliability of persistent trainers.

Several architectural techniques can introduce this form of unpredictability. Introducing controlled unpredictability:

- Randomize internal offsets (within safe bounds).

- Introduce occasional non-linear calculations.

- Use proxy variables that jump in unexpected ways.

- Update multiple values simultaneously.

- Use indirect references instead of direct values.

These techniques complement later layers such as encryption and obfuscation.

Text-Only Memory Map Example

The following map demonstrates how a simple Unreal character might appear
in memory:

0x1000AA00 [UObject Base]

0x1000AA10 [Class Pointer -> AMyCharacter]

0x1000AA18 [Component Array Pointer]

0x1000AA20 [Property Block Start]

0x1000AA24   Health (float)

0x1000AA28   MaxHealth (float)

0x1000AA2C   Armor (float)

0x1000AA30   XP (int32)

0x1000AA34   Level (int32)

0x1000AA38   bIsAlive (bool)

0x1000AA39   Padding

Attackers often prefer tightly grouped properties because they reveal patterns and
relationships between values.

A more secure design spreads gameplay state across multiple structures such as

- Components

- Managers

- Internal data structures

- Derived values instead of raw values

This increases the cognitive effort required to analyze the system.

Developer Mistakes That Cause High Exposure

Certain implementation mistakes unintentionally expose game systems to tampering. These mistakes frequently appear in early prototypes and sometimes remain in production builds.

Common mistakes include

- Exposing too many variables to Blueprints

- Keeping all stats in one struct

- Using linear data structures with predictable offsets

- Allowing UI layer direct access to gameplay values

- Using SaveGame fields without validation

- Leaving debug functions or variables in the final build

- Using public variables where private ones are sufficient

- Building inventory systems with sequential numeric IDs

- Storing both "value" and "max value" together in plain floats

Each of these mistakes increases the visibility of internal state.

Understanding How Attackers Exploit Layout Patterns

Attackers often rely on structural patterns when searching memory. By recognizing these patterns, they can infer the location of variables even without scanning for specific values.

Common patterns used during analysis include

- Memory alignment (4 or 8 bytes)

- Patterns in adjacent values

- Sequential property offsets

- Fixed-size arrays

- String patterns used for variable names

- Virtual function table addresses

This knowledge allows them to detect your variables even without searching for numbers.

Example:

If Health is stored next to MaxHealth, attackers may freeze both values to avoid unintended side effects. If Armor always appears after MaxHealth, attackers can infer its location even without scanning.

Architecture that disrupts these patterns increases the difficulty of reverse engineering.

Designing Systems That Are Hard to Reverse

Certain gameplay structures are naturally more difficult to analyze and manipulate. Systems that rely on multiple interacting components or derived values create additional layers of complexity.

Examples include

- State machines instead of simple Booleans

- Event-driven logic with conditional triggers

- Calculations dependent on multiple internal parameters

- Encapsulation through C++ private members

- Stateless reward calculations

- Derived values that never appear in memory as raw numbers

Selecting these structures early reduces vulnerability later.

Component-Based Security Benefits

Component-based architecture distributes gameplay state across several smaller systems. This approach naturally aligns with Unreal Engine's design and provides several security benefits.

Examples:

- HealthComponent manages health, regeneration, and damage history.

- XPComponent handles leveling, skill progression, and thresholds.

- CurrencyComponent stores multiple currency types with validation.

- AchievementTracker validates consistency between systems.

This distribution

- Reduces clustering

- Increases complexity for pattern scanning

- Adds natural cross-validation

- Obfuscates pointer paths

- Prevents single-variable exploits

Component-based design therefore strengthens both maintainability and resilience.

Case Study 1: Why a Simple Float-Based Health System Failed

A small RPG stored health, max health, defense, and stamina in a single struct. Trainers quickly identified predictable offsets and stable pointer chains.

Attackers found

- Predictable offsets

- Simple calculations

- Clear adjacent patterns

- Stable pointer chains

The system became easy to exploit. After redesigning the architecture, the developers split values into

- Base values

- Modifiers

- Temporary effects

- Derived statistics

Once these structural changes were introduced, existing trainers stopped functioning and were rarely updated.

Case Study 2: XP Manipulation in an Indie Action Game

An indie action game originally stored XP as a single int32 value. The UI displayed this value directly, making it easy to locate.

Attackers quickly

- Located the XP value in seconds

- Froze it

- Built a stable pointer path

- Published a trainer within a week

After redesign

- XP became derived from multiple sources

- UI displayed a processed value

- The game used XP curves instead of raw points

- Milestones validated cross-system consistency

This architectural redesign eliminated most XP cheats.

Checklist for Designing Tamper-Resistant Architecture

The following checklist summarizes the key architectural ideas introduced in this chapter. These principles help reduce exposure and create a stronger foundation for later runtime defenses:

- Avoid single points of failure.

- Use multiple interacting systems.

- Distribute values across components.

- Avoid exposing sensitive values to Blueprints.

- Use private members and accessor functions.

- Break linear data structures.

- Use derived values instead of raw ones.

- Implement cross-validation between systems.

- Remove debug variables before shipping.

- Design unpredictable memory patterns.

- Avoid storing duplicate value and max value together.

- Limit use of global singletons.

This checklist guides your initial design process.

Conclusion

Architecture plays a central role in determining how easily attackers can understand and manipulate your game. Later chapters introduce techniques such as encryption, runtime protection, anti-debugging, and save validation. However, these techniques are most effective when the underlying system design already limits exposure.

The next chapter moves from conceptual architecture into practical implementation. Chapter 4 focuses on protecting runtime variables using secure wrappers, honeypots, obfuscation, and detection techniques that operate directly on your game's memory. These techniques build directly on the architectural principles discussed in this chapter.

CHAPTER 4

Tamper-Proofing Runtime Variables

Runtime memory represents one of the most active battlegrounds in modern single-player game tampering. While save files represent long-term data stored on disk, runtime variables represent the living state of the game while it is executing. These variables track the player's progression, health, currencies, position, and many other critical gameplay systems.

Memory editing tools such as Cheat Engine operate by observing, modifying, and freezing these values while the game is running. When a variable exists in memory in a predictable location and stores its value in an unprotected form, it becomes an immediate target that attackers can locate and manipulate.

This chapter explores how to defend runtime values using a layered approach. We begin with a conceptual analysis of why native types are vulnerable and then introduce a complete system for securing floats and other numerical values. These protections include obfuscation, derived keys, shadow variables, freeze detection, dynamic noise, and redundant validation.

The goal of this chapter is not to create unbreakable protection. Instead, the objective is to increase the effort required by attackers, create ambiguity in memory structures, detect interference, and ensure that tampering leaves observable signals.

By the end of this chapter, you will understand how to design secure variable types, how to implement them in Unreal Engine, and how to combine multiple defensive layers to produce runtime variables that resist manipulation in real time.

S. S. Moon, *Securing Single-Player Games in Unreal Engine*, https://doi.org/10.1007/979-8-8688-2833-1_4

Why Attackers Target Runtime Memory

Attackers frequently focus on runtime memory because it contains the most immediate representation of gameplay state. Values such as health, experience points, damage multipliers, and currencies are constantly updated and often stored in simple numeric formats.

Memory editing tools typically rely on a predictable workflow when locating these values. Understanding this workflow helps explain why native variables are vulnerable.

The typical Cheat Engine workflow follows these steps:

1. Search for a value that the player can influence, such as health or coins.

2. Narrow the search by updating the value in game and repeating scans.

3. Modify the memory location directly.

4. Freeze the address so the value cannot change.

5. Inject new logic once the memory region is mapped.

This process succeeds largely because native numeric types behave in predictable ways within memory.

Several characteristics of runtime variables contribute to this vulnerability:

- Native floats and integers store values directly.

- Their size and memory layout are fixed.

- Their access pattern is predictable.

- Their behavior is observable through scanning.

For example, if the health variable is stored as a single float in memory and that value changes from 75 to 60 after taking damage, Cheat Engine can locate it in seconds. As a result, complexity or unpredictability must be deliberately introduced into the design of protected variables.

Understanding the Threat Model for Runtime Variables

Before implementing defensive mechanisms, it is important to understand the types of attackers that typically interact with runtime memory. In single-player environments, these attackers range from casual users experimenting with memory editors to experienced reverse engineers developing trainers.

The most common attacker categories include

- *Casual Editors*: Players who attempt basic scans and value changes

- *Intermediate Tinkerers*: Players who know how to freeze values and attach debuggers

- *Reverse Engineers*: Players who search for pointer chains, use symbol lookup, or rewrite logic

- *Trainer Developers*: Individuals who create general purpose tools for a wide audience

Each of these attacker groups interacts with runtime memory in slightly different ways.

Common runtime attack behaviors include

- Reading values directly from memory

- Replacing values with extreme numbers

- Freezing values so they never change

- Searching for structures through pattern matching

- Inspecting code paths using memory breakpoints

The defensive systems introduced in this chapter are designed to disrupt these behaviors without requiring kernel-level anti-cheat systems or online verification.

Why Native Types Are Easy to Manipulate

Unreal Engine stores floats, integers, and Booleans in predictable locations within memory. While the engine's garbage collector manages memory ownership, it does not obscure the values themselves.

Additionally, Unreal Engine's reflection system exposes metadata that tools can use to inspect variable names and properties, especially within Blueprint-accessible classes. The Unreal Header Tool also produces deterministic struct layouts that remain stable across builds.

Although these systems improve development efficiency and engine stability, they also create recognizable patterns that attackers can exploit.

Native numeric types become vulnerable because of several structural characteristics:

- Their stored representation is the actual value.

- Gameplay logic accesses them directly.

- Their location in memory often remains stable.

- Their binary signature reveals their intent.

Protecting runtime variables therefore requires breaking this predictability by introducing surrogate representations that hide the real value behind controlled logic.

The Secure Wrapper Philosophy

Rather than storing gameplay values directly, a secure wrapper stores transformed or obfuscated versions of the value. The real value is reconstructed only when required and only within controlled code paths. Any external observation of memory therefore reveals incomplete or misleading information.

Figure 4-1 illustrates the internal flow of a secure float wrapper, showing how gameplay values are transformed and validated before they are used by gameplay systems.

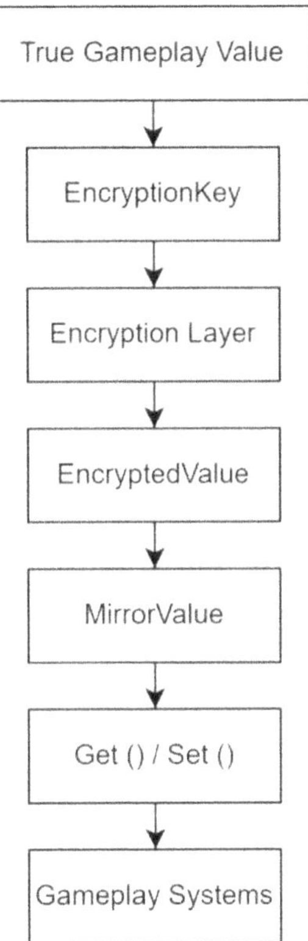

Figure 4-1. *Secure float wrapper architecture showing how gameplay values are stored in encrypted and redundant representations*

A secure wrapper typically provides several defensive capabilities:

- *Obfuscation*: Prevents direct scanning

- *Integrity*: Detects edits, freezes, or inconsistencies

- *Unpredictability*: Prevents attackers from deriving the correct value

- *Redundancy*: Stores the value multiple ways to check for tampering

- *Behavior Tracing*: Monitors changes for signs of manipulation

- *Fail-Safe Behavior*: Enforces consistent correctness under attack

The following sections implement these ideas through a series of progressively stronger secure float designs.

Implementing the Secure Float

The simplest secure float hides its value by adding or removing a key during storage and retrieval. The underlying representation becomes meaningless to memory scanners, although skilled attackers can still identify the pattern. This approach provides a foundation that can be extended.

Below is the full implementation of this base wrapper.

Listing 4-1 protects the variable by using a random encryption key and performing integrity checks through redundant storage. It creates a foundation for further security layers.

- EncryptedValue: Stores the obfuscated float

- EncryptionKey: Random value applied during encryption

- MirrorValue: Redundant obfuscated storage for cross-validation

- Set and Get Functions: Provide controlled read and write access

- IsTampered: Detects if any component has diverged

Listing 4-1. FSecureFloat.h

```cpp
#pragma once

#include "CoreMinimal.h"

struct FSecureFloat
{
private:
    float EncryptedValue;
    float EncryptionKey;
    float MirrorValue;

public:
    FSecureFloat();
    FSecureFloat(float InValue);

    void Set(float InValue);
    float Get() const;

    bool IsTampered() const;
};
```

This structure ensures that modifying the memory for a single storage location is insufficient for successful tampering.

Listing 4-2 handles key generation, encryption, decryption, redundant storage, and tamper detection. Each component in this implementation contributes to hiding the true value and verifying its integrity.

- FSecureFloat() generates a random encryption key and initializes the encrypted value to zero through the Set() function.

- FSecureFloat(float InValue) assigns a new randomized key at construction and stores the provided value in encrypted form.

- Set(float InValue) applies the encryption transformation and writes both the primary obfuscated value and its mirrored companion.

- Get() const reconstructs the original float by reversing the encryption step.

- IsTampered() const compares MirrorValue against a derived expression to detect any external modification to the stored data.

Listing 4-2. FSecureFloat.cpp

```
#include "FSecureFloat.h"
#include "Math/UnrealMathUtility.h"

FSecureFloat::FSecureFloat()
{
    EncryptionKey = FMath::FRandRange(50.f, 500.f);
    Set(0.f);
}

FSecureFloat::FSecureFloat(float InValue)
{
    EncryptionKey = FMath::FRandRange(50.f, 500.f);
    Set(InValue);
}
```

```cpp
void FSecureFloat::Set(float InValue)
{
    EncryptedValue = InValue + EncryptionKey;
    MirrorValue = EncryptedValue + 17.0f;
}

float FSecureFloat::Get() const
{
    return EncryptedValue - EncryptionKey;
}

bool FSecureFloat::IsTampered() const
{
    return FMath::Abs((EncryptedValue + 17.0f) - MirrorValue) > KINDA_
SMALL_NUMBER;
}
```

This implementation forms the basic foundation for the layered security system developed in the remainder of the chapter.

Extending the Secure Float: Advanced Runtime Defenses

While simple encryption discourages casual tampering, experienced attackers may analyze decryption paths or trace value reconstruction through debugging tools. To address these scenarios, additional layers of protection must be introduced.

These layers include

- Shadow variables

- Key rotation

- Freeze detection

- Value history tracking

- Memory noise pools

Each layer increases the complexity of reverse engineering and improves the reliability of tamper detection. Figure 4-2 illustrates the layered runtime protection model used throughout this chapter, where multiple defensive systems work together to conceal, validate, and monitor sensitive gameplay variables.

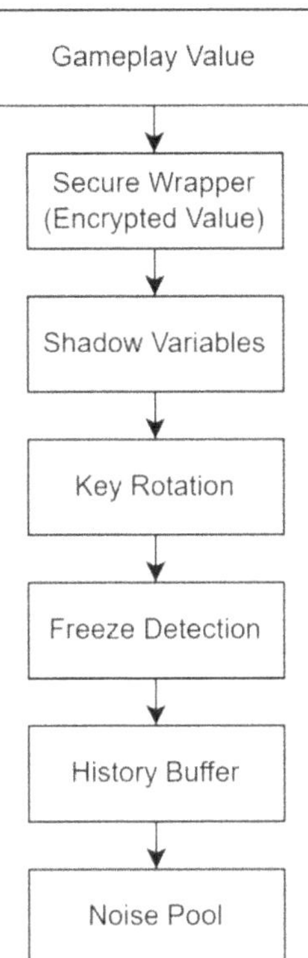

Figure 4-2. *Layered runtime variable protection combining secure wrappers, redundancy, behavioral monitoring, and memory noise to resist manipulation*

Shadow Variables for Cross-Validation

A shadow variable stores the value in a different form, usually with a non-linear transformation. Attackers must modify both the primary and shadow representation in order to bypass detection.

Listing 4-3 improves resilience by generating a secondary key and transforming the value differently. Each field inside the struct contributes to a two-layered protection model that makes external modification significantly harder.

- EncryptedValue stores the primary obfuscated value using the main encryption key.

- MirrorValue stores a companion offset version of the primary encrypted data for integrity checking.

- EncryptionKey is the random main key used to encode and decode the primary value.

- ShadowEncrypted stores a second transformed representation of the true value using a different mathematical rule.

- ShadowKey provides an independent encryption key for the shadow representation.

- IsTampered() compares both storage layers to detect inconsistencies caused by memory edits.

Listing 4-3. FSecureFloat_Shadow.h

```
#pragma once

struct FSecureFloat_Shadow
{
private:
    float EncryptedValue;
    float MirrorValue;
    float EncryptionKey;

    float ShadowEncrypted;
    float ShadowKey;

public:
    FSecureFloat_Shadow(float InValue = 0.f);

    void Set(float InValue);
    float Get() const;

    bool IsTampered() const;
};
```

Listing 4-4 validates the memory integrity by comparing the primary and shadow storage. The implementation encodes the value across two independent transformations and ensures both layers remain synchronized.

- The constructor generates two unrelated encryption keys (EncryptionKey and ShadowKey) to make pattern matching more difficult.

- Set() encodes the true value twice: once through additive encryption and once through a multiplicative transformation for the shadow layer.

- MirrorValue stores a fixed offset of the primary encoding so any edit breaks the derived relationship.

- ShadowEncrypted stores a mathematically different transformed version of the same true value.

- PrimaryMismatch detects tampering by comparing MirrorValue and the derived offset.

- ShadowMismatch checks whether the shadow representation is still mathematically consistent with the primary value.

- IsTampered() returns true if either protection layer is out of alignment.

Listing 4-4. FSecureFloat_Shadow.cpp

```cpp
#include "FSecureFloat_Shadow.h"
#include "Math/UnrealMathUtility.h"

FSecureFloat_Shadow::FSecureFloat_Shadow(float InValue)
{
    EncryptionKey = FMath::FRandRange(10.f, 1000.f);
    ShadowKey = FMath::FRandRange(5.f, 2000.f);
    Set(InValue);
}

void FSecureFloat_Shadow::Set(float InValue)
{
    EncryptedValue = InValue + EncryptionKey;
    MirrorValue = EncryptedValue + 123.45f;

    ShadowEncrypted = (InValue * 3.17f) + ShadowKey;
}
```

```cpp
float FSecureFloat_Shadow::Get() const
{
    return EncryptedValue - EncryptionKey;
}

bool FSecureFloat_Shadow::IsTampered() const
{
    bool PrimaryMismatch = FMath::Abs((EncryptedValue + 123.45f) -
MirrorValue) > 0.001f;
    bool ShadowMismatch = FMath::Abs(((EncryptedValue - EncryptionKey) *
3.17f) + ShadowKey - ShadowEncrypted) > 0.1f;

    return PrimaryMismatch || ShadowMismatch;
}
```

This discourages tampering by increasing the number of dependent values required for manipulation.

Key Rotation

Some attackers freeze keys instead of values. To avoid this, keys must be updated periodically.

Listing 4-5 adds a RotateKey method that periodically changes the encryption key while preserving the correct internal value. This header file introduces the function that will handle key regeneration and force a fresh encryption cycle on the stored data.

- RotateKey() is a public function that triggers a controlled regeneration of the encryption key.

- The new key will be applied without exposing the true underlying value.

- The method integrates naturally with the base FSecureFloat workflow.

- The header extends the original wrapper using inheritance, allowing all existing logic to remain intact.

Listing 4-5. FSecureFloat_KeyRotation.h

```
#pragma once

#include "FSecureFloat.h"

struct FSecureFloat_KeyRotation : public FSecureFloat
{
public:
    void RotateKey();
};
```

Listing 4-6 defines the RotateKey implementation and shows how the secure float briefly reconstructs the true value, assigns a fresh encryption key, and then re-encrypts the value using the new key. This keeps the memory representation unstable over time while ensuring the gameplay logic always sees a consistent number.

- TrueValue captures the decrypted value before any modification.

- EncryptionKey is reassigned using a randomized range to avoid predictability.

- Set(TrueValue) writes the value back through the standard encryption path.

- The external behavior of the variable remains identical from the game's perspective, but its memory signature does not; this complicates pointer tracing and static analysis.

Listing 4-6. FSecureFloat_KeyRotation.cpp

```
#include "FSecureFloat_KeyRotation.h"
#include "Math/UnrealMathUtility.h"

void FSecureFloat_KeyRotation::RotateKey()
{
    float TrueValue = Get();
    EncryptionKey = FMath::FRandRange(50.f, 500.f);
    Set(TrueValue);
}
```

Key rotation disrupts pointer chains and static pattern inspection, raising the difficulty for tampering.

Freeze Detection

When attackers freeze variables, the game logic still updates the value internally, but the memory location refuses to change. This discrepancy can be measured.

Listing 4-7 computes the natural movement of the variable over time. If a value does not change when expected, tampering is suspected. This header introduces the component that tracks temporal behavior and identifies frozen memory states.

- TrackedValue stores the secure float being monitored for suspicious behavior.

- LastValue keeps the previously observed decrypted value to compare against new updates.

- LastUpdateTime records the last moment when a legitimate change occurred.

- Initialize() sets up the component with an initial value and baseline timestamp.

- Update() receives new values from game logic and detects if the value is being blocked from changing.

- IsFrozen() determines whether too much time has passed without a valid update, suggesting external freezing.

Listing 4-7. FreezeDetectorComponent.h

```
#pragma once

#include "CoreMinimal.h"
#include "Components/ActorComponent.h"
#include "FSecureFloat.h"
#include "FreezeDetectorComponent.generated.h"

UCLASS(ClassGroup=(Security))
class UFreezeDetectorComponent : public UActorComponent
```

```cpp
{
    GENERATED_BODY()
private:
    FSecureFloat TrackedValue;
    float LastValue;
    float LastUpdateTime;

public:
    void Initialize(float InitialValue);
    void Update(float NewValue);
    bool IsFrozen(float ThresholdSeconds = 1.0f) const;
};
```

Listing 4-8 implements the freeze detector. This file defines how the tracked value updates over time and identifies any periods where the memory location fails to change even though the game logic expects movement.

- Initialize() encrypts and stores the starting value while establishing baseline history markers.

- Update() compares the current decrypted value with LastValue to detect whether a real change occurred.

- When legitimate movement is detected, the component updates LastValue and refreshes LastUpdateTime.

- If a trainer freezes memory, the stored value will not change even though updates are requested, triggering freeze detection.

- IsFrozen() checks if the elapsed time since the last genuine update exceeds the allowed threshold.

Listing 4-8. FreezeDetectorComponent.cpp

```cpp
#include "FreezeDetectorComponent.h"

void UFreezeDetectorComponent::Initialize(float InitialValue)
{
    TrackedValue.Set(InitialValue);
```

```cpp
    LastValue = InitialValue;
    LastUpdateTime = 0.f;
}

void UFreezeDetectorComponent::Update(float NewValue)
{
    float CurrentValue = TrackedValue.Get();
    float CurrentTime = GetWorld()->GetTimeSeconds();

    if (FMath::Abs(CurrentValue - LastValue) > KINDA_SMALL_NUMBER)
    {
        TrackedValue.Set(NewValue);
        LastValue = NewValue;
        LastUpdateTime = CurrentTime;
    }
}

bool UFreezeDetectorComponent::IsFrozen(float ThresholdSeconds) const
{
    float CurrentTime = GetWorld()->GetTimeSeconds();
    return (CurrentTime - LastUpdateTime) > ThresholdSeconds;
}
```

Freeze detection is one of the most important behavioral signals for recognizing tampering.

Value History Buffers

A history buffer captures past values. Sudden impossible jumps often indicate external modifications. By storing several previous samples, the game can analyze whether changes follow normal gameplay patterns or show signs of forced manipulation.

Listing 4-9 tracks multiple previous values for behavioral analysis. Each part of the struct contributes to building a compact rolling window of recent secure float states.

- History[10] stores the last ten recorded values used for detecting anomalies.

- Index keeps track of the current insertion position and wraps around when reaching the array end.

- The constructor initializes all history values to zero and resets the index.

- AddSample() inserts a new sample into the rolling buffer while advancing the index.

- ComputeMaxJump() examines consecutive samples to detect sudden value spikes that may indicate tampering.

Listing 4-9. FSecureFloatHistory.h

```
#pragma once

struct FSecureFloatHistory
{
private:
    float History[10];
    int32 Index;

public:
    FSecureFloatHistory();
    void AddSample(float InValue);
    float ComputeMaxJump() const;
};
```

Listing 4-10 implements the ring buffer. This file defines how historical values are stored and analyzed to identify abnormal jumps that do not align with legitimate gameplay.

- The constructor zeroes out all entries in History to ensure a clean initial state.

- AddSample() writes a new value to the current index and uses modulo arithmetic to wrap around the buffer.

- ComputeMaxJump() iterates through all stored samples to compute the largest difference between adjacent entries.

- Large deltas between consecutive samples signal abrupt, unnatural changes often caused by external memory edits.

- The ring buffer maintains constant size and never reallocates memory, avoiding predictable memory signatures.

Listing 4-10. FSecureFloatHistory.cpp

```cpp
#include "FSecureFloatHistory.h"
#include "Math/UnrealMathUtility.h"

FSecureFloatHistory::FSecureFloatHistory()
{
    Index = 0;
    for (float& Sample : History)
    {
        Sample = 0.f;
    }
}

void FSecureFloatHistory::AddSample(float InValue)
{
    History[Index] = InValue;
    Index = (Index + 1) % 10;
}

float FSecureFloatHistory::ComputeMaxJump() const
{
    float MaxJump = 0.f;

    for (int i = 0; i < 9; ++i)
    {
        float Delta = FMath::Abs(History[i] - History[i + 1]);
        MaxJump = FMath::Max(MaxJump, Delta);
    }

    return MaxJump;
}
```

History-based analysis provides strong signals when values are externally manipulated.

Memory Noise Pools

The easiest way to mislead attackers is to create multiple fake variables with realistic patterns. The real value hides among decoys, making it significantly harder to identify through scanning. By surrounding your real data with numerous moving noise values, memory scanners receive false leads that weaken the attacker's ability to isolate meaningful data.

Listing 4-11 creates a set of randomized values updated periodically to simulate believable patterns. Each part of this component introduces either the protected value or a group of noise entries meant to disguise it.

- TrueValue: Holds the actual sensitive data in a secure float wrapper

- DecoyValues: Stores an array of meaningless numbers intended to confuse memory scans

- Initialize(): Sets the true value and fills the decoy array with randomized noise

- UpdateValue(): Updates the real secure float while leaving decoys untouched

- UpdateDecoys(): Slightly changes each decoy entry every tick to mimic natural gameplay behavior

Listing 4-11. NoisePoolComponent.h

```cpp
#pragma once

#include "CoreMinimal.h"
#include "Components/ActorComponent.h"
#include "FSecureFloat.h"
#include "NoisePoolComponent.generated.h"

UCLASS(ClassGroup=(Security))
class UNoisePoolComponent : public UActorComponent
{
    GENERATED_BODY()
```

```
private:
    FSecureFloat TrueValue;
    TArray<float> DecoyValues;

public:
    void Initialize(float InitialValue);
    void UpdateValue(float NewValue);
    void UpdateDecoys();
};
```

Listing 4-12 implements the noise pool. This file shows how the decoy values fluctuate over time and how the secure float is updated separately, ensuring the real value remains concealed among rapidly shifting noise.

- Initialize(): Assigns the true encrypted value and fills the decoy array with random noise in a large numeric range

- DecoyValues.SetNum(20): Ensures a consistent number of decoy entries in memory for pattern misdirection

- UpdateValue(): The true value is safely re-encrypted with each update, while decoys remain intentionally unsynchronized

- UpdateDecoys(): Applies small random adjustments to each decoy entry to simulate lifelike memory changes

Listing 4-12. NoisePoolComponent.cpp

```
#include "NoisePoolComponent.h"
#include "Math/UnrealMathUtility.h"

void UNoisePoolComponent::Initialize(float InitialValue)
{
    TrueValue.Set(InitialValue);

    DecoyValues.SetNum(20);
    for (float& Val : DecoyValues)
    {
        Val = FMath::FRandRange(0.f, 10000.f);
    }
}
```

```cpp
void UNoisePoolComponent::UpdateValue(float NewValue)
{
    TrueValue.Set(NewValue);
}

void UNoisePoolComponent::UpdateDecoys()
{
    for (float& Val : DecoyValues)
    {
        Val += FMath::FRandRange(-5.f, 5.f);
    }
}
```

Noise pools create an environment in which the true variable cannot be reliably identified through scanning.

Using Secure Floats in Gameplay Systems

Using the secure float wrapper is straightforward, but integration decisions are important. The following guidelines ensure consistent behavior:

- Use secure floats for critical gameplay systems such as health, damage multipliers, player currencies, XP, and unlock thresholds.

- Avoid using secure floats for high-frequency or purely cosmetic values because overhead accumulates.

- Keep secure floats inside C++ systems rather than exposing them directly to Blueprints.

- Always perform sanity checks when applying large or unbounded modifications.

- Use secure wrappers on server-side values even in local multiplayer projects.

Secure variables introduce intentional unpredictability into your data flow, increasing the difficulty for attackers to understand or modify your systems.

Case Study: Tamper-Resistant Health System in an Action RPG

A developer shipped an action RPG where the player's health was stored as a simple float. Trainers quickly discovered that freezing the address made the player invulnerable. After switching to a secure float with shadow validation and freeze detection, the health system became significantly harder to manipulate.

The final configuration included

- Secure float wrapper with redundant storage

- Shadow key and secondary encoding

- Frame-based freeze detection

- Value history monitoring

- Slight random noise applied to damage intake

Attackers now had to modify multiple synchronized values within acceptable tolerances. Attempts to freeze addresses caused immediate tamper detection.

Red Team Analysis: How Attackers Will Try to Break Your System

A realistic security design must also consider how attackers will respond once defensive systems are introduced. Experienced attackers rarely stop at the first obstacle. Instead, they analyze how the protection works and attempt to bypass it through several investigative techniques.

Common strategies attackers may use include

- Searching memory for repeated patterns that reveal encoded values

- Inspecting runtime changes with conditional breakpoints

- Attempting to locate the `Get()` function responsible for decryption

- Freezing entire structs through stable pointer paths

- Tracing execution through the call stack to identify transformation logic

- Patching decryption routines in compiled code

Your secure float implementation resists many of these strategies, but it is not intended to be invincible. This is both acceptable and expected. The goal of the system is to increase the difficulty of manipulation, produce detectable signals of tampering, and raise the effort required to build reliable cheats.

When combined with debugger detection (Chapter 5), encryption techniques (Chapter 6), and trap mechanisms (Chapter 7), runtime tamper protection becomes part of a broader defensive system rather than a single isolated mechanism.

Conclusion

Runtime variables form the foundation of your game's behavior. If they can be manipulated freely, no amount of save file protection or architectural design will matter. By replacing native types with secure wrappers, adding shadow validation, rotating keys, detecting freezes, tracking history, and generating noise pools, you build a system that resists tampering and identifies unauthorized manipulation.

This chapter prepares the reader for the next major threat: runtime intrusion through debuggers and DLL injection. Chapter 5 builds on the foundations established here by teaching how to detect external tools, block inspection of memory, and maintain control of the execution environment even under attacker observation.

CHAPTER 5

Anti-debugging and Injection Detection

Many attackers no longer rely solely on memory scanning to manipulate single-player games. Instead, they target the execution environment itself. Debuggers, injected DLLs, and live code patchers allow an attacker to influence your game while it is running and reshape internal logic in ways that no save validator or secure float wrapper can prevent.

In Unreal Engine projects, this becomes particularly dangerous because of the predictable class structures, accessible reflection metadata, and globally reachable engine subsystems. These characteristics simplify reverse engineering and make it easier for attackers to identify valuable gameplay systems.

Before building defensive systems that detect these behaviors, it is important to understand how attackers interact with the process at runtime and what capabilities these tools provide once attached.

Figure 5-1 illustrates how external debugging and injection tools interact with the game process and where detection mechanisms operate within the runtime environment.

© Sheikh Sohel Moon 2026
S. S. Moon, *Securing Single-Player Games in Unreal Engine*, https://doi.org/10.1007/979-8-8688-2833-1_5

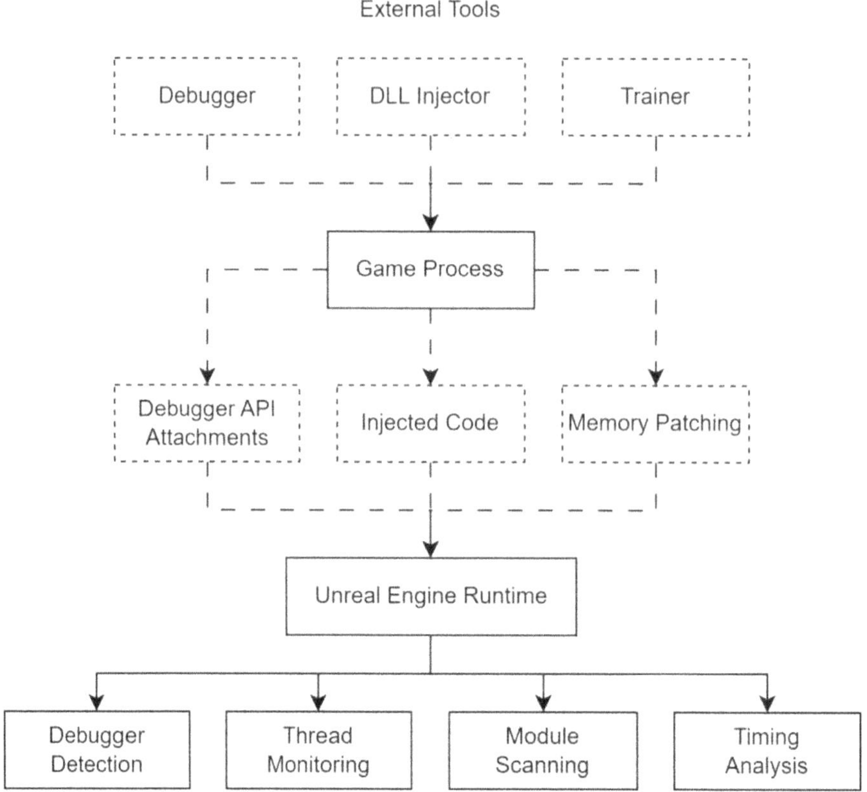

Figure 5-1. *Runtime intrusion pathways showing how external tools attach to the game process and how detection systems within the Unreal Engine runtime monitor these behaviors*

Why Debuggers Are the Most Dangerous Runtime Tools

Debuggers give attackers complete control over the execution of your game. Once attached, a debugger can pause the CPU, capture stack frames, inspect internal variables, and alter state before the next instruction executes. This level of visibility makes it possible to bypass structural security measures because the attacker is not guessing about your logic, they are observing it directly.

Because a debugger exposes nearly every internal aspect of the program, it becomes one of the most powerful tools available to an attacker. With this level of control, attackers can analyze how gameplay systems operate and intervene at precise moments during execution.

The following capabilities illustrate why debuggers are so dangerous in runtime environments:

- A debugger can pause the process at any instruction boundary.

- Memory can be read, modified, or frozen in place.

- Breakpoints can be set on functions, lines, or conditions.

- Execution flow can be redirected at runtime.

- Internal values such as XP, cooldowns, or Booleans can be altered precisely.

- Attackers can trace through C++ logic one instruction at a time.

Because debuggers expose every component of your game's architecture, they represent one of the most critical threats to real-time system integrity.

How DLL Injection Bypasses Traditional Protections

DLL injection allows attackers to load their own code inside your game's process. Once injected, this module executes the same privileges as the game itself, bypassing most architectural safeguards. Unreal Engine's modular subsystems and predictable memory layout give injected DLLs immediate footholds for further exploration.

Once an attacker successfully injects a DLL into the process, they gain several powerful capabilities inside the runtime environment.

These capabilities often include the following:

- Injected modules can intercept or replace engine functions.

- Attackers can install hooks on UWorld, PlayerController, or Tick loops.

- Arbitrary threads can be spawned inside the process.

- Memory regions can be scanned, patched, or overwritten.

- BlueprintCallable functions can be invoked externally.

- Internal subsystems become directly accessible through global pointers.

With an injected DLL, the game effectively becomes an execution environment for attacker-controlled code.

What a Debugger Allows an Attacker to Do

A debugger attached to the process grants an attacker surgical precision when analyzing gameplay logic. Instead of guessing where important variables or functions exist, attackers can inspect the program while it executes and observe exactly how systems behave.

This level of visibility allows attackers to analyze gameplay systems in detail and manipulate execution flow directly.

Common debugger-driven analysis techniques include the following:

- Track where variables change during gameplay.

- Observe every call to damage, XP gain, or unlock conditions.

- Patch instructions to eliminate checks or restrictions.

- Trigger events manually by forcing function calls.

- Set conditional breakpoints to monitor specific game states.

- Discover and isolate persistent gameplay structures.

Once a debugger has been attached, every line of your logic becomes transparent.

How Trainers Patch Memory and Hijack Code Paths

Even when a debugger is not attached, trainers and cheat tools often rely on targeted memory patching to disrupt internal logic. These tools typically locate functions inside your game's executable or DLL regions and replace instructions with simplified or modified alternatives.

Rather than manipulating gameplay variables directly, attackers may instead modify the code that updates those variables.

Typical memory patching strategies include the following:

- Comparison instructions can be replaced with no operations.

- Conditional branches can be forced to always succeed.

- Decrements (such as ammo or cooldown reduction) can be overwritten.

- Function calls can be redirected to injected code.

- Jump trampolines can hijack logic before it returns to the engine.

These techniques allow attackers to modify gameplay behavior without interacting with variables directly. Instead, they alter the logic that manipulates those values.

How These Threats Manifest in Unreal Projects

Unreal Engine's architecture provides predictable anchor points that simplify reverse engineering. Reflection metadata, UObject layout, and uniform virtual function table structures make it easier for attackers to identify important gameplay systems.

Although these design patterns improve development efficiency, they also introduce structural consistency that attackers can analyze.

In practice, these attacks often appear in several common forms:

- Trainers scan for UObject collections using structural patterns.

- Attackers set breakpoints on Blueprint execution nodes.

- Injected DLLs hook into Tick functions to override logic.

- External tools search for BlueprintCallable methods to abuse.

- Memory patchers replace internal function instructions.

- Debuggers trace through C++ logic and find hidden developer paths.

Unreal's consistency is a strength for development but a vulnerability for attackers who exploit predictable structures.

How Debuggers and Injection Tools Attach to Unreal

Before building defensive layers, it is essential to understand how debuggers and injected modules enter the process. Unreal Engine games run on top of the Windows process model and inherit its debugging APIs, remote handles, and module loading interfaces.

Attackers exploit these mechanisms to observe execution, redirect logic, or insert new code during runtime.

Understanding these pathways allows developers to design detection systems that monitor suspicious behavior with minimal performance overhead.

User-Mode Debug API Attachments

Most debugger attachments rely on the standard Windows debugging APIs. These APIs allow external tools to connect to a running process, inspect memory, and control execution flow.

Tools such as x64dbg, OllyDbg, and Cheat Engine's built-in debugger rely on these official interfaces to interact with the game process.

Common Windows debugging APIs include the following:

- DebugActiveProcess attaches an external debugger to your game.

- WaitForDebugEvent forces the game to pause when events occur.

- ContinueDebugEvent resumes execution after debugger handling.

- Debuggers gain access to your call stack, registers, and memory layouts.

- Everything that happens inside the game becomes observable.

Because these APIs are widely used and deeply integrated into Windows, they offer a predictable surface to detect debugger presence.

Remote Debugging Pipes and Stealth Attachment

Some advanced debugging tools avoid the standard debugging APIs and attach through alternative communication channels. These techniques attempt to bypass simple detection methods by avoiding traditional debug flags.

These stealth attachment strategies typically include the following:

- Remote debuggers communicate through pipe-based interfaces.

- Some tools attach via injected threads that act as silent breakpoints.

- Stealth debuggers manipulate system calls to hide their presence.

- Debugger handles may not be exposed through the usual APIs.

Although harder to detect, these tools still leave indirect behavioral traces: thread anomalies, suspicious timing gaps, or the presence of unexpected modules.

Kernel-Level Assistance for Advanced Debuggers

Kernel-assisted debuggers operate below user mode and can conceal their presence by intercepting system calls. Tools such as ScyllaHide or TitanHide modify internal debugging structures to prevent detection.

These tools frequently use the following techniques:

- Kernel drivers can hook NtQueryInformationProcess.

- They mask debug ports and flags inside the Process Environment Block (PEB).

- Hardware breakpoints become invisible to user-mode detectors.

- They bypass typical user-mode debug detection methods.

Although extremely difficult to detect directly, you can still detect the *effects* of kernel-level debugging through timing analysis and execution inconsistencies. These strategies appear later in this chapter.

DLL Injection Entry Points in Unreal Executables

Injected DLLs are a major threat because they execute inside your game's process with full privileges. They can run arbitrary logic, hook engine functions, and modify gameplay dynamics without interacting with memory directly.

- *Standard Injection*: LoadLibraryA/LoadLibraryW

- *Remote Thread Injection*: CreateRemoteThread

- *Manual Mapping*: Loading modules without the Windows loader

- *APC (Asynchronous Procedure Call) Injection*: Queueing a function invocation on a thread

- *Thread Hijacking*: Rewriting stack contexts

Injectors use many of the same techniques malware uses, making it essential to monitor module lists and thread behavior to detect intrusion.

Hooking, Trampolines, and Memory Patching Strategies

Once a DLL is inside the process, attackers often hook functions by overwriting the first few bytes of executable instructions with a jump to their own code.

- Overwriting the prologue of functions with JMP instructions

- Replacing operations with no-ops (NOP)

- Redirecting logic through "trampolines" placed in attacker memory

- Hijacking virtual function tables (VTables)

- Overwriting key engine functions such as UWorld::Tick

These methods tamper with the code itself, making it essential to detect module anomalies and runtime inconsistencies.

Direct Debugger Detection Techniques

The most fundamental defense against runtime manipulation is the ability to detect whether a debugger is currently attached to the process. Windows exposes several APIs that reveal debugger presence. While any single API is easy to bypass, combining multiple checks increases reliability. Unreal Engine allows us to integrate these checks into lightweight subsystems and components that run every frame or at controlled intervals.

Detecting Attached Debuggers with IsDebuggerPresent

IsDebuggerPresent checks a flag inside the Process Environment Block (PEB) indicating whether the current process is being debugged. Although simple to bypass, it is inexpensive, safe, and effective against basic debugging tools.

Listing 5-1 explains the structure of the debugger monitor.

- UDebuggerMonitor defines a component for per-frame inspection.

- TickComponent runs the debugger check every frame.

- IsDebuggerAttached wraps the Windows API call safely.

- Integration inside Unreal's component model keeps it flexible.

Listing 5-1. DebuggerMonitor.h

```cpp
#pragma once

#include "CoreMinimal.h"
#include "Components/ActorComponent.h"
#include "DebuggerMonitor.generated.h"

UCLASS(ClassGroup=(Security))
class UDebuggerMonitor : public UActorComponent
{
    GENERATED_BODY()

public:
    virtual void TickComponent(float DeltaTime, ELevelTick TickType,
FActorComponentTickFunction* ThisTickFunction) override;

private:
    bool IsDebuggerAttached() const;
};
```

Listing 5-2 defines the implementation and shows how the component interacts with the Windows API to check for attached debuggers.

- Calls IsDebuggerPresent() inside a private helper

- Logs alerts whenever a debugger is detected

- Keeps detection isolated to avoid interfering with gameplay

- Demonstrates Unreal's platform header wrapping

Listing 5-2. DebuggerMonitor.cpp

```cpp
#include "DebuggerMonitor.h"
#include "Windows/AllowWindowsPlatformTypes.h"
#include <windows.h>
#include "Windows/HideWindowsPlatformTypes.h"

void UDebuggerMonitor::TickComponent(float DeltaTime, ELevelTick TickType,
FActorComponentTickFunction* ThisTickFunction)
{
```

```cpp
    Super::TickComponent(DeltaTime, TickType, ThisTickFunction);

    if (IsDebuggerAttached())
    {
        UE_LOG(LogTemp, Warning, TEXT("Debugger detected via
        IsDebuggerPresent."));
    }
}

bool UDebuggerMonitor::IsDebuggerAttached() const
{
    return IsDebuggerPresent();
}
```

This introductory detector offers basic protection by exposing when common debuggers attach to the game. Although bypassable, it lays the foundation for more advanced layered detection mechanisms.

Detecting External Debuggers with CheckRemoteDebuggerPresent

CheckRemoteDebuggerPresent identifies whether the current process has been opened by a debugging tool, even if the debugger tries to hide by manipulating the PEB. It evaluates external handles rather than internal flags, which makes it useful against remote or stealth debuggers.

Listing 5-3 outlines a game-instance subsystem dedicated to external debugger monitoring.

- Encapsulates detection in a persistent engine subsystem

- Provides a global monitoring point across all gameplay contexts

- Designed to run on demand or at scheduled intervals

- Offers a more reliable perspective than frame-based monitoring

Listing 5-3. RemoteDebuggerSubsystem.h

```
#pragma once

#include "CoreMinimal.h"
#include "Subsystems/GameInstanceSubsystem.h"
#include "RemoteDebuggerSubsystem.generated.h"

UCLASS()
class URemoteDebuggerSubsystem : public UGameInstanceSubsystem
{
    GENERATED_BODY()

public:
    void CheckDebugger();
};
```

Listing 5-4 provides the subsystem implementation using the Windows API.

- Calls CheckRemoteDebuggerPresent() on the current process

- Detects debuggers that manipulate the PEB to hide their presence

- Logs alerts for further security layers to respond

- Demonstrates correct use of Windows platform header wrapping

Listing 5-4. RemoteDebuggerSubsystem.cpp

```
#include "RemoteDebuggerSubsystem.h"
#include "Windows/AllowWindowsPlatformTypes.h"
#include <windows.h>
#include "Windows/HideWindowsPlatformTypes.h"

void URemoteDebuggerSubsystem::CheckDebugger()
{
    BOOL bDebuggerPresent = FALSE;
    CheckRemoteDebuggerPresent(GetCurrentProcess(), &bDebuggerPresent);
```

```
    if (bDebuggerPresent)
    {
        UE_LOG(LogTemp, Error, TEXT("External debugger detected via
        CheckRemoteDebuggerPresent."));
    }
}
```

This subsystem adds an additional layer of defense by detecting debugging activity that operates outside normal flags. It complements the previous listing and increases the reliability of debugger detection.

Hardware Breakpoint and Side-Channel Detection

Most advanced debuggers use hardware breakpoints rather than software breakpoints. Hardware breakpoints allow the debugger to pause execution without modifying instructions in memory, which makes them harder to detect. However, hardware breakpoints almost always introduce timing irregularities or interruptions in natural execution flow. These timing distortions give us an indirect opportunity to detect debugger involvement. Unlike user-mode flag checks, timing-based detectors are resilient against PEB manipulation and kernel-level hiding because they rely on the *observable behavior* of the debugger rather than its internal state.

Timing analysis works by measuring how long the game takes to execute code that should be near-instantaneous. When a debugger halts execution at a breakpoint, even for milliseconds, this pause becomes detectable as an abnormal timing gap. While false positives are possible, especially on lower-end hardware, these timing discrepancies, when combined with other signals, form a powerful approach to exposing hidden debugging activity.

How Hardware Breakpoints Work

Hardware breakpoints rely on CPU debug registers (DR0–DR7). When an instruction accesses or executes memory linked to one of these registers, the debugger halts the process.

- They do not modify memory, making them invisible to basic checks.

- They trigger before the instruction executes, allowing deep inspection.

- They can be set on read, write, or execute conditions.

- Access to debug registers requires privilege that attackers can obtain through debuggers or kernel drivers.

Although user-mode applications cannot read debug registers directly, the pauses caused by breakpoint hits still produce detectable timing anomalies.

Why Hardware Breakpoints Are Difficult to Detect

Because hardware breakpoints do not alter the game's memory or executable code, traditional integrity checks cannot detect them.

- They leave no visible traces in memory.

- They do not change instructions or opcodes.

- They cannot be scanned with pattern matching.

- Kernel tools can hide them from user-mode queries.

This forces defenders to rely on indirect methods, where side-channel timing analysis becomes the primary defensive technique.

Timing Analysis for Breakpoint Detection

Timing analysis detects hard-to-hide debugger interference by measuring how long it takes for a section of code to execute. If the timing exceeds natural thresholds, it suggests the process was paused.

Listing 5-5 introduces a timing detector component that logs abnormal stall patterns.

- LastTimestamp stores the previous frame's time.

- Threshold defines the maximum acceptable gap.

- DetectPause computes deviations caused by debugger halting.

- Designed as an actor component for per-frame evaluation.

Listing 5-5. BreakpointTimingDetector.h

```cpp
#pragma once

#include "CoreMinimal.h"
#include "Components/ActorComponent.h"
#include "BreakpointTimingDetector.generated.h"

UCLASS(ClassGroup=(Security))
class UBreakpointTimingDetector : public UActorComponent
{
    GENERATED_BODY()

private:
    float LastTimestamp;
    float Threshold;

public:
    UBreakpointTimingDetector();

    virtual void TickComponent(float DeltaTime, ELevelTick TickType,
    FActorComponentTickFunction* ThisTickFunction) override;

private:
    bool DetectPause(float CurrentTime) const;
};
```

Listing 5-6 implements the timing-based logic and exposes how breakpoints cause measurable delays.

- LastTimestamp initialized to zero for early validity.

- DetectPause compares elapsed time against the threshold.

- Logs warnings when unnatural delays suggest debugging.

- Does not rely on Windows APIs—purely behavioral detection.

Listing 5-6. BreakpointTimingDetector.cpp

```cpp
#include "BreakpointTimingDetector.h"

UBreakpointTimingDetector::UBreakpointTimingDetector()
{
    PrimaryComponentTick.bCanEverTick = true;
    LastTimestamp = 0.0f;
    Threshold = 0.25f; // 250ms stall likely indicates breakpoint
}

void UBreakpointTimingDetector::TickComponent(float DeltaTime, ELevelTick
TickType, FActorComponentTickFunction* ThisTickFunction)
{
    Super::TickComponent(DeltaTime, TickType, ThisTickFunction);

    float CurrentTime = GetWorld()->GetTimeSeconds();

    if (LastTimestamp > 0.0f)
    {
        if (DetectPause(CurrentTime))
        {
            UE_LOG(LogTemp, Error, TEXT("Debugger breakpoint detected via
            timing analysis."));
        }
    }

    LastTimestamp = CurrentTime;
}

bool UBreakpointTimingDetector::DetectPause(float CurrentTime) const
{
    float Delta = CurrentTime - LastTimestamp;
    return Delta > Threshold;
}
```

This timing-based detector catches many forms of hidden debugger behavior,
including hardware breakpoints and kernel-assisted pauses that bypass user-mode
detection APIs.

When Side-Channel Approaches Become Useful

Side-channel detectors are most valuable when

- Attackers use kernel drivers to hide debugger flags

- Patching-based detection fails due to lack of memory changes

- Breakpoints exist on internal engine functions

- Step-through debugging produces micro-pauses each frame

- Manual mapping DLL injectors avoid Windows loader involvement

While timing alone cannot confirm debugger presence, combining timing signals with thread anomalies and module scanning (introduced next) builds a reliable multi-layer detection system.

Monitoring Suspicious Threads

Injectors and debuggers frequently create new threads inside the game process. These threads may handle communication, breakpoints, debugger housekeeping, or hooks. Unreal Engine normally manages its own threads using well-defined naming and patterns. Any unexpected thread suggests potential tampering.

Thread scanning becomes an essential defensive layer when dealing with advanced attackers because many injection and hooking tools leave distinct thread signatures.

Why Injectors Spawn Their Own Threads

DLL injectors often rely on custom threads to execute payloads. These threads typically do not align with Unreal's threading model.

- Injector-created threads run attacker logic.

- They can monitor memory addresses for changes.

- They maintain communication with remote UIs.

- They may host hooks or breakpoints internally.

- Unreal does not create arbitrary unnamed worker threads like these.

This makes thread enumeration one of the most effective ways to detect injected modules.

Differentiating Engine Threads from Unknown Threads

Unreal Engine threads usually follow identifiable patterns:

- Named threads (e.g., "RenderThread," "RHIThread," "TaskGraphThread")

- Known stack sizes and priorities

- Expected creation timing (startup or subsystem initialization)

In contrast, attacker threads often exhibit

- Generic names or no names

- Suspicious start addresses outside engine DLLs

- Unusual priorities

- Unexpected creation timing during gameplay

Detecting these differences allows us to flag threads that do not belong.

Enumerating Threads Using ToolHelp API

The following listings implement a thread scanner that enumerates all threads in the current process.

Listing 5-7 introduces a thread-scanning utility that inspects thread IDs and execution addresses.

- Uses Windows ToolHelp API for thread enumeration

- Tracks suspicious thread entries for further inspection

- Exposes a clean Unreal-friendly interface

- Allows integration with higher-level security logic

Listing 5-7. ThreadScanner.h

```
#pragma once

#include "CoreMinimal.h"

struct FThreadScanResult
{
    TArray<uint32> SuspiciousThreads;
};

class FThreadScanner
{
public:
    static FThreadScanResult ScanThreads();
};
```

Listing 5-8 implements the thread-scanning logic and identifies anomalies.

- Uses CreateToolhelp32Snapshot to capture thread information

- Filters threads based on process ID

- Checks for unusual start addresses or characteristics

- Aggregates suspicious thread IDs into a structured result

Listing 5-8. ThreadScanner.cpp

```
#include "ThreadScanner.h"
#include "Windows/AllowWindowsPlatformTypes.h"
#include <windows.h>
#include <tlhelp32.h>
#include "Windows/HideWindowsPlatformTypes.h"

FThreadScanResult FThreadScanner::ScanThreads()
{
    FThreadScanResult Result;

    DWORD CurrentPID = GetCurrentProcessId();

    HANDLE Snapshot = CreateToolhelp32Snapshot(TH32CS_SNAPTHREAD, 0);
```

```
if (Snapshot == INVALID_HANDLE_VALUE)
    return Result;

THREADENTRY32 Entry;
Entry.dwSize = sizeof(THREADENTRY32);

if (Thread32First(Snapshot, &Entry))
{
    do
    {
        if (Entry.th32OwnerProcessID == CurrentPID)
        {
            // Simple heuristic: threads with very low thread IDs or
                unexpected states
            if (Entry.th32ThreadID < 50)
            {
                Result.SuspiciousThreads.Add(Entry.th32ThreadID);
            }
        }
    }
    while (Thread32Next(Snapshot, &Entry));
}

CloseHandle(Snapshot);

return Result;
}
```

Thread enumeration provides valuable clues about injection attempts, especially when paired with module scanning, which will be covered in the next section.

Detecting Injected Modules

Injected DLLs are one of the clearest and most reliable indicators of tampering inside a running Unreal Engine game. Unlike thread anomalies or timing irregularities—which may produce rare false positives—the presence of an unauthorized module is nearly always malicious. DLL injection gives attackers a direct foothold in your process, enabling them to intercept engine calls, rewrite instructions, or manipulate gameplay systems externally. Because Unreal Engine loads modules predictably, scanning the module list at runtime provides an effective method of detecting injected code.

Module enumeration works by capturing a snapshot of all loaded modules in the current process and comparing them against expected patterns. Suspicious modules often contain keywords such as "inject," "hook," "cheat," or "trainer," but even when they do not, their mere presence outside the project's packset is cause for concern. The following listings introduce a module-scanning system integrated into Unreal's runtime logic.

Why DLL Injectors Are Still Effective

Despite modern OS protections, DLL injection remains a powerful attack tool because

- Injected code runs *inside* your process

- Attackers gain direct access to Unreal memory and function calls

- They can hook engine functions such as UWorld::Tick

- Injected DLLs operate with the same privileges as the main game

- Even manual-mapped DLLs behave like standard modules once loaded

This makes module scanning a vital detection layer.

Enumerating Loaded Modules at Runtime

The ToolHelp API provides an accessible method to enumerate modules inside the current process. This method offers excellent compatibility across Windows versions and integrates cleanly into Unreal Engine.

Identifying Suspicious Modules by Name and Pattern

The simplest detection heuristic checks for suspicious substrings include

- Inject

- Cheat

- Mod

- Trainer

- Overlay

In more advanced scenarios, you can validate module paths, compare against approved module sets, or perform hash-based integrity checks.

Optional Memory Region Validation

Some attackers attempt "manual mapping" of DLLs—loading modules without invoking LoadLibrary. Although these modules may not appear in the default module list, they still occupy memory regions that can be inspected through PE parsing. Advanced engines may implement this, but for this chapter, we focus on standard module enumeration.

Listing 5-9 introduces a module-scanning utility that collects suspicious modules.

- FModuleScanResult stores names of flagged modules.

- ScanModules performs ToolHelp-based enumeration.

- Provides Unreal Engine-friendly data for higher detection layers.

- Separates the scan logic from gameplay code cleanly.

Listing 5-9. ModuleScanner.h

```
#pragma once

#include "CoreMinimal.h"

struct FModuleScanResult
{
    TArray<FString> SuspiciousModules;
};

class FModuleScanner
{
public:
    static FModuleScanResult ScanModules();
};
```

Listing 5-10 implements the module scanner using the ToolHelp32 API.

- Captures a snapshot of all loaded modules

- Iterates through each entry and lowercases the module name

- Filters modules for suspicious patterns

- Aggregates results for further security actions

Listing 5-10. ModuleScanner.cpp

```cpp
#include "ModuleScanner.h"
#include "Windows/AllowWindowsPlatformTypes.h"
#include <windows.h>
#include <tlhelp32.h>
#include "Windows/HideWindowsPlatformTypes.h"

FModuleScanResult FModuleScanner::ScanModules()
{
    FModuleScanResult Result;

    HANDLE Snapshot = CreateToolhelp32Snapshot(TH32CS_SNAPMODULE,
GetCurrentProcessId());
    if (Snapshot == INVALID_HANDLE_VALUE)
        return Result;

    MODULEENTRY32 ModuleEntry;
    ModuleEntry.dwSize = sizeof(MODULEENTRY32);

    if (Module32First(Snapshot, &ModuleEntry))
    {
        do
        {
            FString ModuleName = FString(ModuleEntry.szModule).ToLower();

            if (ModuleName.Contains(TEXT("cheat")) ||
                ModuleName.Contains(TEXT("inject")) ||
                ModuleName.Contains(TEXT("trainer")) ||
                ModuleName.Contains(TEXT("mod")))
            {
```

```
            Result.SuspiciousModules.Add(ModuleName);
        }
    }
    while (Module32Next(Snapshot, &ModuleEntry));
  }

  CloseHandle(Snapshot);
  return Result;
}
```

Module scanning provides a reliable method for detecting injected code, forming a cornerstone of runtime security.

Timing-Based Anti-debugging Techniques

Timing-based detection methods help identify debugging activity that is invisible to direct API checks. They detect how long execution takes between two points in time. Breakpoints, especially hardware breakpoints, pause execution while the debugger gains control, causing measurable spikes in elapsed time.

Timing detectors are simple to implement, difficult to bypass, and effective even when kernel-level masking is used.

Debugger-Induced Frame Delays

Even single-step debugging adds noticeable timing gaps. If your game measures

- Frame-to-frame delta

- Execution time of internal loops

- Timestamps between predictable operations

then it can expose debugger interference.

Timestamp-Based Breakpoint Detection

The next listings expand the previous timing detector into a more modular, subsystem-based approach.

Listing 5-11 introduces a subsystem that monitors global timing anomalies.

- LastTimestamp stores the last known tick time.

- Threshold defines acceptable pause duration.

- CheckForBreakpointPause evaluates timing gaps.

- Implemented as a subsystem for global consistency.

Listing 5-11. TimingDebuggerDetector.h

```
#pragma once

#include "CoreMinimal.h"
#include "Subsystems/WorldSubsystem.h"
#include "TimingDebuggerDetector.generated.h"

UCLASS()
class UTimingDebuggerDetector : public UWorldSubsystem
{
    GENERATED_BODY()

private:
    float LastTimestamp;
    float Threshold;

public:
    virtual void Tick(float DeltaTime) override;
    virtual bool DoesSupportWorldType(EWorldType::Type WorldType) const
override { return true; }

private:
    bool CheckForBreakpointPause(float CurrentTime) const;
};
```

Listing 5-12 implements the subsystem and logs detected anomalies.

- Initializes threshold-based timing detection

- Captures world time each tick

- Logs when execution stalls exceed the expected threshold

- Adds side-channel protection that survives most debugger masking

Listing 5-12. TimingDebuggerDetector.cpp

```cpp
#include "TimingDebuggerDetector.h"

void UTimingDebuggerDetector::Tick(float DeltaTime)
{
    float CurrentTime = GetWorld()->GetTimeSeconds();

    if (LastTimestamp > 0.0f)
    {
        if (CheckForBreakpointPause(CurrentTime))
        {
            UE_LOG(LogTemp, Error, TEXT("Timing anomaly detected. Potential
            debugger breakpoint."));
        }
    }

    LastTimestamp = CurrentTime;
}

bool UTimingDebuggerDetector::CheckForBreakpointPause(float
CurrentTime) const
{
    float Delta = CurrentTime - LastTimestamp;
    return Delta > Threshold;
}
```

Timing detection complements other strategies by revealing intrusions that leave no memory or API traces.

Memory and Code Integrity Checks

While debugging and injection allow direct manipulation of logic, patching allows attackers to modify executable memory regions. Detecting changes to .text, .rdata, or VTable regions can identify malicious alterations.

These checks work by

- Hashing executable sections

- Comparing region boundaries

- Validating untouched VTable pointers

- Ensuring no unauthorized writeable/executable pages exist

Because full implementation requires platform-specific tooling, this chapter introduces conceptual integrity checks that integrate with other layers.

Delayed and Passive Countermeasures

A critical rule in security design is to avoid reacting immediately when tampering is detected. If attackers know exactly when your game identifies them, they can reverse-engineer your detection logic more easily.

Delayed responses instead

- Allow the game to gather more evidence

- Avoid revealing the exact detection moment

- Prevent attackers from brute-forcing bypasses

- Introduce subtle gameplay degradations rather than hard crashes

Examples include reducing XP gains silently, slowing resource accumulation, or disabling certain unlocks.

Dead-Code Guards and Hidden Integrity Points

Dead-code guards involve embedding integrity checks in places where attackers do not expect them. These hidden checks activate only when certain conditions are met, making them difficult to detect or disable during reverse engineering.

- Checked during rare execution paths

- Hidden behind gameplay states

- Placed in non-core functions to avoid predictability

- Cause no overhead but drastically increase attacker workload

These guards are a powerful, low-cost defensive technique.

Case Study 1: Debugger-Assisted Stealth Bypass in a Single-Player Stealth Game

In a commercially released stealth game, players discovered that nearly every detection check performed by enemy AI relied on simple Boolean evaluations inside Blueprint logic. Because the AI's line-of-sight calculations were processed each frame, attackers attached a debugger and paused execution at the exact moment the detection logic was evaluated. By stepping through the code manually, they forced the internal Boolean bPlayerDetected to remain false, regardless of the actual game situation.

This exploit allowed players to

- Walk directly in front of enemies without being seen

- Disable entire detection trees by forcing return values

- Observe and modify internal state transitions frame by frame

- Identify the precise Blueprint nodes that controlled visibility

Because there were no timing-based detectors, no thread monitors, and no indirect behavioral sensors, the debugger never triggered any defensive response. This example highlights how vulnerable Blueprint-driven logic becomes when it can be paused or stepped through without resistance. Even minimal timing analysis or hidden integrity guards would have exposed these abnormal pauses.

Case Study 2: Injection-Based Input Hijacking Through a Custom DLL

In another example, a popular trainer used standard DLL injection to hook into a game's APlayerController::ProcessInput routine. The injected module intercepted all input commands before Unreal processed them. The trainer added auto-parry behavior by rewriting button press intervals and introduced instant dodge macros by sending artificial input events at precise timings.

The attack succeeded because

- The game performed no module scanning at runtime

- There were no checks for anomalous threads created by the injected DLL

- No VTable or function pointer validation existed

- The input handler lacked secondary verification layers

This type of injection completely bypassed in-game logic, letting the attacker insert new gameplay behaviors without modifying assets or variables. A simple module enumeration pass, like the one introduced earlier in this chapter, would have immediately identified the unauthorized DLL.

Lessons Learned Across Both Cases

These two case studies highlight different ends of the tampering spectrum, debugger-based manipulation and code injection–based hijacking. Yet they share the same underlying weaknesses. In both cases, the game trusted its runtime environment and assumed that internal logic would be executed as intended.

The key lessons include the following:

- Debuggers expose internal logic paths that were never meant to be inspected.

- DLL injectors gain access to entire gameplay systems without resistance.

- Without timing, thread, or module-based detectors, tampering remains silent.

- Defensive layers must be combined, not used in isolation.

- Even single-player titles suffer major gameplay degradation when unprotected.

These examples reinforce the need for multiple detection channels rather than relying on any single point of defense.

Conclusion

Anti-debugging and injection detection form a critical pillar of runtime protection. Debuggers allow attackers to freeze execution, inspect memory, and override logic at will, while injected DLLs introduce foreign code that can manipulate systems from inside the process itself. Throughout this chapter, we developed a layered approach built around direct detection functions, thread enumeration, module scanning, timing analysis, and behavioral inference.

These defenses make it significantly harder for attackers to pause your game, inject code, or patch functions without being observed. No single method guarantees complete protection, but together they disrupt most real-world techniques used by trainers, debuggers, and automated cheat frameworks.

The next chapter transitions naturally from runtime defense to data defense. Once an attacker fails to manipulate live memory, their next target is usually the game's save system. Chapter 6 begins by introducing key principles of save file encryption, integrity validation, and versioned hashing. This shift from active detection to data-centric protection continues with the layered security philosophy established throughout the book.

CHAPTER 6

Encrypting and Validating Save Data

Players often think of a save file as a simple snapshot of their progress. For developers, however, save data represents one of the most critical components of game integrity. In many single-player titles, the save file governs progression, reward distribution, unlock sequences, crafting systems, difficulty pacing, and economic balance. When these files are modified outside the game, attackers can skip intended progression, generate infinite resources, unlock gated content, or bypass difficulty systems.

A common scenario illustrates the problem clearly. A player discovers their save file inside the AppData directory and opens it using a hex editor. Inside the binary data they search for a familiar number, perhaps their current gold amount. They replace the value 450 with 999999, reload the game, and immediately disrupt the progression curve that designers carefully tuned over months of development. In other games, editing a single Boolean flag may unlock end-game content or enable abilities that were meant to be earned gradually.

These attacks require very little expertise. Players only need a hex editor, a trainer capable of modifying files, or a short online tutorial. As a result, save data becomes one of the most commonly exploited attack surfaces in single-player games.

This chapter focuses on the cryptographic foundations required to protect save files from modification and inspection. We explore the threat model, encryption mechanisms, key derivation techniques, validation metadata, and signature-based integrity verification required to secure persistent game data.

The behavioral traps and logic-based tamper detection mechanisms that analyze player actions belong to Chapter 7. This chapter focuses strictly on the cryptographic container that protects the save file itself.

© Sheikh Sohel Moon 2026
S. S. Moon, *Securing Single-Player Games in Unreal Engine*, https://doi.org/10.1007/979-8-8688-2833-1_6

Threat Modeling for Save Data

Before implementing encryption or validation systems, it is necessary to define the capabilities of the attacker. Cryptographic design depends heavily on the assumptions we make about adversaries and the tools available to them.

In the context of single-player games, save file attackers generally fall into three categories:

- Casual Editors

  These users search for obvious patterns like numbers representing coins or experience. They modify raw bytes without understanding how values are encoded.

- Tools-Assisted Modifiers

  These attackers use trainers or hex editors with structure-aware features. Some tools can search for known data formats, decompress sections, or interpret Unreal object layouts.

- Determined Reverse Engineers

  These individuals analyze the save file format, reverse-engineer the read and write logic, and build automated scripts to manipulate the data. They may also hook the serialization pipeline, emulate save workflow, and rebuild the file entirely.

A secure save system should resist the first two categories and reliably detect tampering attempts made by the third. In practice, this means designing a system that protects several core security properties.

The secure save system therefore focuses on the following objectives:

- Confidentiality

  Preventing attackers from reading sensitive data (e.g., exact XP, unlock states, narrative progression markers)

- Integrity

  Ensuring that any unauthorized modification is detectable when the file is loaded

- Authenticity

  Verifying that the save file was generated by the game and not
  constructed externally

- Version Compatibility

  Ensuring that encrypted or signed structures survive updates
  and patches

The remainder of this chapter builds upon these foundational pillars.

Cryptographic Principles for Game Save Security

Protecting save files in a single-player game differs from traditional enterprise security
environments. In a typical PC game scenario:

- The attacker owns the machine.

- The attacker can fully inspect the binary.

- The attacker can read or modify files at will.

- There is no secure execution environment.

Because of this, real-world cryptographic best practices must be adapted to a higher-
threat environment. We cannot rely on secret-keeping alone. Instead, we must rely
on a combination of encryption, metadata, validation structures, and tamper-evident
envelopes.

Because of these conditions, conventional assumptions about secret storage do
not apply. Developers cannot rely solely on hiding keys or obscuring file formats.
Instead, security must rely on cryptographic protection combined with tamper-evident
structures.

For this reason, save systems must use encryption, validation of metadata, and
authenticated containers that make modification detectable even if attackers understand
the file format.

This chapter introduces a cryptographic container called the **save envelope**, which
protects gameplay data using both encryption and integrity verification. Figure 6-1
illustrates the structure of the cryptographic save envelope and the sequence of
transformations that protect gameplay data before it is written to disk.

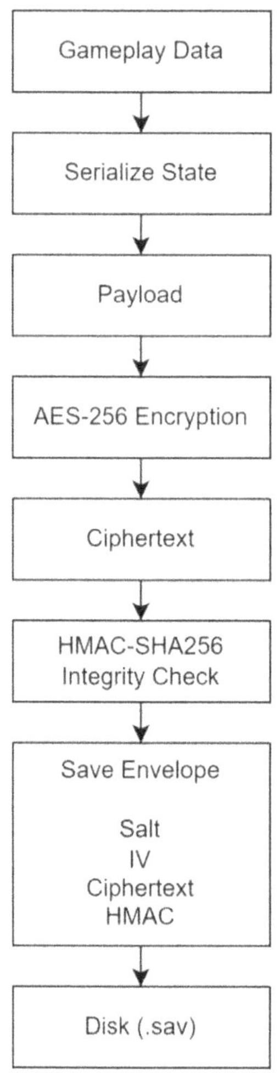

Figure 6-1. *Structure of the cryptographic save envelope showing serialization, encryption, and integrity verification before data is written to disk*

Introducing the Cryptographic Save Envelope

The first building block of a secure save system is a container that wraps gameplay data with cryptographic metadata. This container, called the save envelope, ensures that raw gameplay values are never written directly to disk.

Instead, the save envelope protects gameplay data through a combination of cryptographic mechanisms:

- AES-256 encryption for confidentiality

- HMAC-SHA256 for integrity and authenticity

- Nonce-based randomization to prevent replay

- Version identifiers for forward compatibility

Listing 6-1 defines the structures required to store encrypted save payloads. It separates plaintext data, ciphertext buffers, initialization vectors (IVs), and integrity signatures. The envelope functions are not implemented yet; they will be filled in later listings.

- Payload: Raw JSON or binary data representing the actual gameplay state before encryption

- Ciphertext: AES-encrypted form of the payload

- IV (Initialization Vector): A random byte sequence required for CBC (Cipher Block Chaining) or CTR encryption modes

- HMAC: SHA-256 based signature ensuring that ciphertext has not been modified

- Version: An integer identifying the serialization and envelope format version

- Serialize()/Deserialize(): Methods responsible for preparing the envelope for disk storage

Listing 6-1. SaveEnvelope.h

```cpp
#pragma once

#include "CoreMinimal.h"
#include <vector>

struct FSaveEnvelope
{
    // Raw gameplay data before encryption
    TArray<uint8> Payload;

    // AES-encrypted data
    TArray<uint8> Ciphertext;
```

```
// Initialization Vector used for encryption
TArray<uint8> IV;

// HMAC-SHA256 signature of the Ciphertext
TArray<uint8> HMAC;

// Envelope version for compatibility
int32 Version = 1;

// Serialization helpers
TArray<uint8> Serialize() const;
void Deserialize(const TArray<uint8>& InBytes);
};
```

The envelope creates a strict boundary between plaintext gameplay data and cryptographically protected storage.

Deriving Cryptographic Keys Securely

Before encryption can occur, the system must derive a cryptographic key that is unpredictable and unique to the installation. Hardcoding encryption keys inside the binary is a common mistake in indie projects. Attackers can extract such keys through static analysis, making every save file instantly decryptable.

To avoid this weakness, the system derives encryption keys dynamically at runtime. In this approach the final AES key never appears in plaintext form inside the binary. Instead, it is reconstructed through a combination of several inputs.

Listing 6-2 defines the interface used to derive cryptographic keys.

- GenerateSalt(): Creates a random cryptographic salt used to produce diversified keys

- GetMachineSecret(): A placeholder representing any installation-unique value (e.g., config UUID)

- DeriveKey(): Combines the salt and machine secret into a final hashed key

- OutputKey: The final 32-byte AES-256 key used by the encryption system

Listing 6-2. SaveKeyDerivation.h

```cpp
#pragma once

#include "CoreMinimal.h"
#include <vector>

struct FSaveKeyDerivation
{
    // Generates a fresh random salt for each save
    static TArray<uint8> GenerateSalt(int32 Size = 32);

    // Acquires a machine-unique secret (pseudo-unique fallback shown here)
    static TArray<uint8> GetMachineSecret();

    // Combines MachineSecret + Salt into a final 32-byte key
    static TArray<uint8> DeriveKey(const TArray<uint8>& Salt);
};
```

This interface separates key generation from encryption logic and ensures that save encryption always relies on dynamically derived keys rather than static secrets embedded in the binary.

Listing 6-3 defines how salts are generated and how the final 32-byte key is constructed.

- KeyBuffer: Holds the final 32-byte value used by AES-256 encrypt/ decrypt operations

Listing 6-3. SaveKeyDerivation.cpp

```cpp
#include "SaveKeyDerivation.h"
#include "Misc/SecureHash.h"
#include "HAL/PlatformMisc.h"

TArray<uint8> FSaveKeyDerivation::GenerateSalt(int32 Size)
{
    TArray<uint8> Salt;
    Salt.SetNum(Size);

    for (int32 i = 0; i < Size; ++i)
    {
```

```cpp
        Salt[i] = FMath::Rand() % 256;
    }

    return Salt;
}

TArray<uint8> FSaveKeyDerivation::GetMachineSecret()
{
    FString MachineId = FPlatformMisc::GetLoginId();
    FTCHARToUTF8 Converter(*MachineId);

    TArray<uint8> Secret;
    Secret.Append((uint8*)Converter.Get(), Converter.Length());
    return Secret;
}

TArray<uint8> FSaveKeyDerivation::DeriveKey(const TArray<uint8>& Salt)
{
    TArray<uint8> MachineSecret = GetMachineSecret();

    TArray<uint8> Combined;
    Combined.Append(Salt);
    Combined.Append(MachineSecret);

    FSHA256Hash Hash = FSHA256::HashBuffer(Combined.GetData(),
    Combined.Num());

    TArray<uint8> Key;
    Key.Append(Hash.Hash, 32); // AES-256 requires a 32-byte key
    return Key;
}
```

This implementation generates an encryption key that is both deterministic and installation specific. As a result, save files remain decryptable by the same installation while preventing attackers from using a globally extracted key across different systems.

AES Encryption of Save Data

A secure save system requires strong confidentiality, meaning that attackers should not be able to inspect internal gameplay values from the raw .sav file. Unreal Engine does not include built-in AES helpers for custom save logic, so we define our own.

Listing 6-4 declares a wrapper for AES-256 encryption and decryption. It abstracts away the raw cryptographic functions and allows our envelope to call Encrypt() and Decrypt() cleanly.

- Encrypt(): Takes plaintext, an AES key, and an IV, returning encrypted bytes

- Decrypt(): Reverses the operation

- GenerateIV(): Produces a fresh initialization vector for each encryption

- CipherMode: Defaults to CBC for simplicity, though CTR and GCM are alternative options

Listing 6-4. SaveAESCipher.h

```cpp
#pragma once

#include "CoreMinimal.h"
#include <vector>

struct FSaveAESCipher
{
    static TArray<uint8> Encrypt(
        const TArray<uint8>& Plaintext,
        const TArray<uint8>& Key,
        const TArray<uint8>& IV);

    static TArray<uint8> Decrypt(
        const TArray<uint8>& Ciphertext,
        const TArray<uint8>& Key,
        const TArray<uint8>& IV);

    static TArray<uint8> GenerateIV(int32 Size = 16);
};
```

This interface isolates encryption responsibilities inside a dedicated helper class. By separating cryptographic operations from gameplay logic, the save system remains easier to maintain and safer to evolve as encryption requirements change.

Listing 6-5 defines the AES encryption/decryption logic and IV generation.

- GenerateIV(): Creates a fresh 16-byte vector for AES-CBC

- Encrypt(): Performs AES encryption using a block cipher routine

- Decrypt(): Restores plaintext bytes using the same key and IV

Listing 6-5. SaveAESCipher.cpp

```cpp
#include "SaveAESCipher.h"
#include "Misc/AES.h"

TArray<uint8> FSaveAESCipher::GenerateIV(int32 Size)
{
    TArray<uint8> IV;
    IV.SetNum(Size);

    for (int32 i = 0; i < Size; ++i)
    {
        IV[i] = FMath::Rand() % 256;
    }

    return IV;
}

TArray<uint8> FSaveAESCipher::Encrypt(const TArray<uint8>& Plaintext,
                                      const TArray<uint8>& Key,
                                      const TArray<uint8>& IV)
{
    TArray<uint8> Output;
    Output.SetNum(Plaintext.Num());

    FAES::EncryptData(Output.GetData(), Plaintext.GetData(), Plaintext.
    Num(), Key.GetData(), IV.GetData());
    return Output;
}
```

```
TArray<uint8> FSaveAESCipher::Decrypt(const TArray<uint8>& Ciphertext,
                                      const TArray<uint8>& Key,
                                      const TArray<uint8>& IV)
{
    TArray<uint8> Output;
    Output.SetNum(Ciphertext.Num());

    FAES::DecryptData(Output.GetData(), Ciphertext.GetData(), Ciphertext.
    Num(), Key.GetData(), IV.GetData());
    return Output;
}
```

This implementation integrates Unreal Engine's built-in AES utilities with the custom save system. Each save operation generates a new initialization vector, ensuring that identical payloads produce different ciphertext outputs and preventing simple pattern-matching attacks.

Authenticating Save Data with HMAC

Encryption alone does not prevent attackers from modifying ciphertext. An attacker may flip bits in the encrypted file in the hope that the decrypted data produces useful results.

To defend against this risk, each encrypted payload is protected with an HMAC signature. When the game loads a save file, it recomputes the HMAC and compares it against the stored value. Any mismatch indicates that the file has been modified.

Listing 6-6 defines an HMAC-SHA256 helper used to sign arbitrary byte arrays. This helper provides the integrity verification layer for the save system.

- ComputeHMAC() calculates a 32-byte SHA-256 HMAC using the derived key.

- VerifyHMAC() compares a stored signature against a recomputed one.

- HMACSize specifies the fixed 32-byte output.

Listing 6-6. SaveHMAC.h

```cpp
#pragma once

#include "CoreMinimal.h"

struct FSaveHMAC
{
    static const int32 HMACSize = 32;

    static TArray<uint8> ComputeHMAC(
        const TArray<uint8>& Data,
        const TArray<uint8>& Key);

    static bool VerifyHMAC(
        const TArray<uint8>& Data,
        const TArray<uint8>& Key,
        const TArray<uint8>& ExpectedHMAC);
};
```

This interface defines the integrity verification layer used by the save system. It ensures that encrypted save data can be validated before it is accepted by the loader.

Listing 6-7 implements the SHA-256 HMAC calculation and validation.

- ComputeHMAC() uses UE's secure hashing to produce the signature.

- VerifyHMAC() recomputes the HMAC and performs a constant-time comparison.

- Constant-time comparison prevents attackers from fingerprinting timing differences.

- The computed HMAC is appended to the save envelope before the file is written to disk.

Listing 6-7. SaveHMAC.cpp

```cpp
#include "SaveHMAC.h"
#include "Misc/SecureHash.h"

TArray<uint8> FSaveHMAC::ComputeHMAC(
    const TArray<uint8>& Data,
```

```cpp
    const TArray<uint8>& Key)
{
    // Simple HMAC construction: Hash(Key || Data || Key)
    TArray<uint8> Combined;
    Combined.Append(Key);
    Combined.Append(Data);
    Combined.Append(Key);

    FSHA256Hash Hash = FSHA256::HashBuffer(Combined.GetData(),
Combined.Num());

    TArray<uint8> Result;
    Result.Append(Hash.Hash, 32);
    return Result;
}

bool FSaveHMAC::VerifyHMAC(
    const TArray<uint8>& Data,
    const TArray<uint8>& Key,
    const TArray<uint8>& ExpectedHMAC)
{
    TArray<uint8> Computed = ComputeHMAC(Data, Key);
    if (Computed.Num() != ExpectedHMAC.Num())
        return false;

    // Constant-time compare
    bool bMatches = true;
    for (int32 i = 0; i < Computed.Num(); ++i)
    {
        bMatches &= (Computed[i] == ExpectedHMAC[i]);
    }
    return bMatches;
}
```

This implementation allows the game to verify that encrypted save data has not been modified between the time it was written and the time it is loaded.

Designing a Complete Crypto Envelope

To store encrypted save data safely, the save system requires a structured container capable of holding several cryptographic components.

The envelope must include the following elements:

- A diversified key (via salt)

- A random IV for encryption

- Encrypted payload bytes

- An HMAC signature verifying correctness

This combination forms the cryptographic envelope, an authenticated container defining how save data is stored and validated. It ensures that even if attackers know the file format, modifying any byte will invalidate the HMC signature.

Listing 6-8 defines a data structure encapsulating all cryptographic components saved to disk.

- Salt: Diversifies the key derivation per save

- IV: Ensures encryption randomness even with identical data

- Ciphertext: Holds encrypted JSON/binary payload bytes

- HMAC: Verifies that the ciphertext and metadata remain untouched

- ToBytes(): Serializes the envelope into a disk-ready array

- FromBytes(): Reconstructs the envelope during loading

Listing 6-8. SaveEnvelope.h

```
#pragma once

#include "CoreMinimal.h"

struct FSaveEnvelope
{
    TArray<uint8> Salt;
    TArray<uint8> IV;
    TArray<uint8> Ciphertext;
    TArray<uint8> HMAC;
```

```
TArray<uint8> ToBytes() const;
static bool FromBytes(const TArray<uint8>& RawData, FSaveEnvelope&
OutEnvelope);
};
```

This structure defines the standardized on-disk representation used by the save system. By grouping the salt, IV, ciphertext, and HMAC together, the envelope ensures that all cryptographic metadata required for validation travels with the encrypted payload.

Listing 6-9 serializes and deserializes cryptographic envelope data.

- ToBytes(): Writes lengths + raw bytes in sequence for safe reconstruction.

- FromBytes(): Parses RawData back into envelope sub-blocks.

- The routine includes validity checks and prevents malformed input from crashing the parser.

- Length-based reconstruction protects against buffer overreads and corrupted disk data.

Listing 6-9. SaveEnvelope.cpp

```
#include "SaveEnvelope.h"

TArray<uint8> FSaveEnvelope::ToBytes() const
{
    TArray<uint8> Out;

    auto AppendArray = [&](const TArray<uint8>& Arr)
    {
        int32 Size = Arr.Num();
        Out.Append((uint8*)&Size, sizeof(int32));
        Out.Append(Arr);
    };

    AppendArray(Salt);
    AppendArray(IV);
    AppendArray(Ciphertext);
```

```cpp
    AppendArray(HMAC);

    return Out;
}

bool FSaveEnvelope::FromBytes(const TArray<uint8>& RawData, FSaveEnvelope&
OutEnvelope)
{
    int32 Offset = 0;

    auto ReadArray = [&](TArray<uint8>& Arr) -> bool
    {
        if (Offset + sizeof(int32) > RawData.Num()) return false;

        int32 Size = 0;
        FMemory::Memcpy(&Size, RawData.GetData() + Offset, sizeof(int32));
        Offset += sizeof(int32);

        if (Offset + Size > RawData.Num()) return false;

        Arr.SetNum(Size);
        FMemory::Memcpy(Arr.GetData(), RawData.GetData() + Offset, Size);
        Offset += Size;

        return true;
    };

    return ReadArray(OutEnvelope.Salt)
        && ReadArray(OutEnvelope.IV)
        && ReadArray(OutEnvelope.Ciphertext)
        && ReadArray(OutEnvelope.HMAC);
}
```

These functions ensure that encrypted save data can be reconstructed when
loading the file. By storing explicit lengths before each field, the system protects against
corrupted or malformed input and guarantees that envelope parsing remains safe.

Writing Encrypted Save Files

With the cryptographic envelope defined, writing a save file follows a structured sequence of operations:

1. Serialize gameplay data (JSON or binary).

2. Generate salt and derive the AES key.

3. Generate a random IV.

4. Encrypt the payload.

5. Compute the HMAC over (Salt ‖ IV ‖ Ciphertext).

6. Write the envelope to disk.

Listing 6-10 declares the writer class responsible for producing authenticated encrypted save files. This class coordinates the encryption pipeline and ensures that gameplay data is transformed into a secure envelope before being written to disk.

- WriteEncryptedSave(): Orchestrates the entire encryption and signing process

- SerializeGameplayState(): Converts gameplay structures into raw bytes

- BuildEnvelope(): Assembles salt, IV, ciphertext, and HMAC

- SaveToDisk(): Performs the actual disk write

Listing 6-10. SecureSaveWriter.h

```
#pragma once

#include "CoreMinimal.h"
#include "SaveEnvelope.h"

struct FSecureSaveWriter
{
    static bool WriteEncryptedSave(
        const FString& SlotName,
        const TArray<uint8>& GameplayData);
```

```
private:
    static bool SaveToDisk(
        const FString& SlotName,
        const TArray<uint8>& Raw);
};
```

This interface defines the entry point used by gameplay systems when writing secure save files. By isolating encryption and validation logic inside a dedicated writer class, the rest of the game interacts with the save system through a single high-level function.

Listing 6-11 defines the writer workflow used by FSecureSaveWriter. The function follows the encryption pipeline described earlier in the chapter.

- Key derivation uses the salt from the envelope.

- AES encryption produces the ciphertext.

- HMAC creation validates the ciphertext on load.

- Envelope serialization generates the final on-disk buffer.

- SaveToDisk() writes the data into the standard UE save directory.

Listing 6-11. SecureSaveWriter.cpp

```
#include "SecureSaveWriter.h"
#include "SaveKeyDerivation.h"
#include "SaveAESCipher.h"
#include "SaveHMAC.h"
#include "Misc/FileHelper.h"
#include "Misc/Paths.h"

bool FSecureSaveWriter::WriteEncryptedSave(
    const FString& SlotName,
    const TArray<uint8>& GameplayData)
{
    // 1. Prepare Salt and Keys
    TArray<uint8> Salt = FSaveKeyDerivation::GenerateSalt();
    TArray<uint8> Key = FSaveKeyDerivation::DeriveKey(Salt);

    // 2. Generate IV
    TArray<uint8> IV = FSaveAESCipher::GenerateIV();
```

```cpp
    // 3. Encrypt
    TArray<uint8> Ciphertext = FSaveAESCipher::Encrypt(GameplayData,
    Key, IV);

    // 4. Prepare HMAC input
    TArray<uint8> HMACInput;
    HMACInput.Append(Salt);
    HMACInput.Append(IV);
    HMACInput.Append(Ciphertext);

    // 5. Compute signature
    TArray<uint8> Signature = FSaveHMAC::ComputeHMAC(HMACInput, Key);

    // 6. Build envelope
    FSaveEnvelope Envelope;
    Envelope.Salt = Salt;
    Envelope.IV = IV;
    Envelope.Ciphertext = Ciphertext;
    Envelope.HMAC = Signature;

    TArray<uint8> Raw = Envelope.ToBytes();

    return SaveToDisk(SlotName, Raw);
}

bool FSecureSaveWriter::SaveToDisk(
    const FString& SlotName,
    const TArray<uint8>& Raw)
{

    FString Path = FPaths::ProjectSavedDir() / (SlotName + TEXT(".sav"));
    return FFileHelper::SaveArrayToFile(Raw, *Path);
}
```

This implementation converts gameplay data into a cryptographically protected envelope before writing it to disk. By combining encryption, key derivation, and HMAC validation in a single pipeline, the save system ensures that any modification to the stored file will be detected during loading.

Loading and Validating Encrypted Save Files

Saving data securely is only half of the process. The game must also validate save files when loading them to ensure that corrupted or tampered data cannot enter gameplay systems.

The loader reverses the operations performed by the writer. It parses the envelope, recomputes the HMAC, and decrypts the payload.

Loader Threat Model

A secure loader must be prepared to handle several categories of corrupted or malicious input.

- Save files modified by hex editors

- Files partially overwritten by corrupted disk sectors

- Files rolled back manually to bypass progression

- Ciphertext modified to alter decrypted gameplay values

- Replaced save files from another player's machine

- Any attempt to bypass or forge the HMAC

Implementing the Secure Loader

To safely reconstruct gameplay data, the loader follows a strict verification sequence:

1. Read the raw bytes from disk.

2. Parse them into an FSaveEnvelope instance.

3. Recompute the HMAC from (Salt ‖ IV ‖ Ciphertext).

4. Derive the AES key using the salt.

5. Compare computed HMAC against stored HMAC.

6. Decrypt the ciphertext.

7. Deserialize gameplay data.

This section implements the entire process in a structured Unreal-friendly format.

Listing 6-12 defines the loader interface and its responsibilities. This class performs the reverse operations of the save writer by validating and decrypting stored save data before it is returned to gameplay systems.

- LoadEncryptedSave(): Orchestrates the envelope validation and decryption

- LoadFromDisk(): Retrieves the raw save bytes

- ReconstructEnvelope(): Deserializes the encrypted envelope

- VerifyIntegrity(): Checks the HMAC signature

- DecryptPayload(): Returns the decrypted gameplay data

Listing 6-12. SecureSaveLoader.h

```cpp
#pragma once

#include "CoreMinimal.h"
#include "SaveEnvelope.h"

struct FSecureSaveLoader
{
    static bool LoadEncryptedSave(
        const FString& SlotName,
        TArray<uint8>& OutGameplayData);

private:
    static bool LoadFromDisk(
        const FString& SlotName,
        TArray<uint8>& OutRaw);

    static bool ReconstructEnvelope(
        const TArray<uint8>& Raw,
        FSaveEnvelope& OutEnvelope);

    static bool VerifyIntegrity(
        const FSaveEnvelope& Envelope,
        const TArray<uint8>& Key);
```

```cpp
static bool DecryptPayload(
    const FSaveEnvelope& Envelope,
    const TArray<uint8>& Key,
    TArray<uint8>& OutDecrypted);
};
```

This interface defines the loading pipeline used by the save system. It ensures that encrypted data is validated and decrypted through controlled steps before it is passed back into gameplay logic.

Listing 6-13 implements the secure loading process end-to-end. The loader reverses the operations performed by the save writer and ensures that only valid encrypted data is accepted.

- LoadEncryptedSave(): The main entry point used by gameplay systems

- LoadFromDisk(): Loads the raw file into memory

- ReconstructEnvelope(): Parses the salt, IV, ciphertext, and HMAC

- VerifyIntegrity(): Recomputes the HMAC to validate the envelope

- DecryptPayload(): Performs the AES decryption using the derived key

Listing 6-13. SecureSaveLoader.cpp

```cpp
#include "SecureSaveLoader.h"
#include "SaveKeyDerivation.h"
#include "SaveAESCipher.h"
#include "SaveHMAC.h"
#include "Misc/FileHelper.h"
#include "Misc/Paths.h"

bool FSecureSaveLoader::LoadEncryptedSave(
    const FString& SlotName,
    TArray<uint8>& OutGameplayData)
{
    // 1. Load Raw
    TArray<uint8> Raw;
```

```cpp
    if (!LoadFromDisk(SlotName, Raw))
        return false;

    // 2. Reconstruct envelope
    FSaveEnvelope Envelope;
    if (!ReconstructEnvelope(Raw, Envelope))
        return false;

    // 3. Derive Key
    TArray<uint8> Key = FSaveKeyDerivation::DeriveKey(Envelope.Salt);

    // 4. Verify HMAC
    if (!VerifyIntegrity(Envelope, Key))
        return false;

    // 5. Decrypt
    if (!DecryptPayload(Envelope, Key, OutGameplayData))
        return false;

    return true;
}

bool FSecureSaveLoader::LoadFromDisk(
    const FString& SlotName,
    TArray<uint8>& OutRaw)
{
    FString Path = FPaths::ProjectSavedDir() / (SlotName + TEXT(".sav"));
    return FFileHelper::LoadFileToArray(OutRaw, *Path);
}

bool FSecureSaveLoader::ReconstructEnvelope(
    const TArray<uint8>& Raw,
    FSaveEnvelope& OutEnvelope)
{
    return FSaveEnvelope::FromBytes(Raw, OutEnvelope);
}

bool FSecureSaveLoader::VerifyIntegrity(
    const FSaveEnvelope& Envelope,
```

```cpp
    const TArray<uint8>& Key)
{
    TArray<uint8> HMACInput;
    HMACInput.Append(Envelope.Salt);
    HMACInput.Append(Envelope.IV);
    HMACInput.Append(Envelope.Ciphertext);

    return FSaveHMAC::VerifyHMAC(
        HMACInput,
        Key,
        Envelope.HMAC);
}

bool FSecureSaveLoader::DecryptPayload(
    const FSaveEnvelope& Envelope,
    const TArray<uint8>& Key,
    TArray<uint8>& OutDecrypted)
{
    OutDecrypted = FSaveAESCipher::Decrypt(
        Envelope.Ciphertext,
        Key,
        Envelope.IV);

    return OutDecrypted.Num() > 0;
}
```

This implementation ensures that every save file is validated before decryption occurs. If the HMAC verification fails, the loader rejects the file immediately, preventing corrupted or tampered data from entering the game state.

Handling Save Integrity Failures

When validation fails, the game must decide how to respond. Different projects may choose different strategies depending on design goals.

Possible responses include

- *Soft Fallback*: Load a default empty save.

- *Alert-Only*: Show a message that the save is corrupted.

- *Partial Recovery*: Load gameplay progress but reset currencies.

- *Full Block*: Refuse to load any corrupted data.

- *Telemetry Ping* (if your game uses analytics).

The key design principle is simple: never load unverified data, even partially. Any corrupted or forged block compromises the game's internal logic.

Case Study 1: The RPG Skill Tree Corruption Incident

In a mid-sized single-player RPG released by an indie studio, players quickly discovered that the save file stored the entire skill tree as a clear JSON block inside the .sav file. Attributes such as SkillPoints, UnlockedNodes, and XPProgression appeared without any obfuscation, encryption, or integrity metadata. One player leaked a tutorial showing how to unlock every skill in the tree by changing a handful of numbers in Notepad++, and the technique spread across forums within hours.

At first, the developers assumed this would have little impact because the game was offline and single player. The community reaction proved otherwise. Because players could instantly unlock every skill intended to be gradually earned across 30–40 hours of gameplay, the entire difficulty curve collapsed. The game's economy, damage scaling, and enemy design all depended on controlled XP growth and progressive unlocking.

This incident created several issues:

- Many players accidentally broke their save files, causing corrupt states.

- Others intentionally bypassed progression and then reviewed the game as "too easy."

- Some legitimate players complained they felt forced to cheat because "everyone else had all skills unlocked already."

- YouTube channels amplified the exploit, reducing the game's perceived depth.

If even a minimal cryptographic envelope had been used, a sealed structure containing encrypted data and an HMAC validation step, the exploit would not have spread. Players modifying the file would have caused the loader to reject it rather than silently accept corrupted logic states. This incident highlights how saving critical gameplay values in cleartext can collapse an entire progression system.

Case Study 2: The Sandbox Construction Game Rollback Exploit

A popular voxel-based construction sandbox game used a conventional binary save format that serialized world state and player inventory directly through Unreal's USaveGame mechanism. However, the game implemented no integrity checks, no timestamps, and no validation logic. When players performed high-risk crafting actions like merging rare materials, attempting difficult upgrades, or gambling resources for randomized perks, the game would overwrite the existing save slot.

Players quickly realized that by making a copy of the save file before attempting a risky upgrade, performing the upgrade, and then restoring the old save file if the outcome was unfavorable, they could infinitely retry resource-intensive actions. This rollback technique was widely shared and became the dominant way to interact with the crafting system.

The impact was severe:

- The rarest materials in the game lost all meaning.

- Resource scarcity, one of the game's core balancing pillars, evaporated.

- The late-game crafting curve was trivialized.

- Community guides openly recommended rollback as the "optimal playstyle."

- Post-launch analytics showed players skipping major portions of the intended loop.

A lightweight cryptographic envelope by itself (as implemented in this chapter) would have elevated the difficulty but not fully prevented the rollback exploit. What was required is the dual-layer defense model for save files:

1. Cryptographic validation to prevent silent byte modification

2. Behavioral and metadata validation to detect rollback patterns using timestamp and save counter logic

This layered approach is exactly how Chapter 6 and Chapter 7 interact. Chapter 6 provides the sealed container. Chapter 7 adds the behavioral interpretation that identifies illegitimate save sequences. The rollback exploit above demonstrates why a cryptographic system must be paired with metadata tracking to create a resilient save ecosystem.

Conclusion

Save data represents the accumulated progress, decisions, and investment a player has made in a game. When these files can be modified freely, core progression systems can collapse, and the intended gameplay experience quickly breaks down.

This chapter introduced a cryptographic framework that protects save files through encryption, key derivation, integrity verification, and authenticated containers. Together, these mechanisms ensure that save data written by the game can be validated reliably when it is loaded.

While this cryptographic layer ensures that raw data cannot be modified silently, it does not yet interpret what those values represent. The next chapter expands this system by introducing behavioral validation techniques that detect rollback abuse, implausible progression patterns, and other semantic forms of tampering.

CHAPTER 7

Protecting Save Files Against Tampering

Save data forms the backbone of a single-player experience. It records everything the player earns, discovers, unlocks, or changes throughout the game world. Because of this, the save file effectively becomes the persistent memory of the entire progression system.

Chapter 6 introduced cryptographic protections that secure save files through encryption, key derivation, and integrity verification. These mechanisms ensure that the data stored on disk cannot be modified silently at the byte level.

However, cryptographic protection alone does not guarantee that the information inside a save file represents a legitimate gameplay state.

A determined attacker may still produce logically impossible but cryptographically valid saves. For example, they may restore older saves, duplicate resources, manipulate runtime values before saving, or copy modified data from external tools.

This chapter introduces behavioral, structural, temporal, and semantic validation systems that detect tampering even when the encrypted save file itself appears valid.

Why Save Tampering Requires Behavioral and Structural Defenses

Even when cryptographic protections prevent direct modification of the save structure, attackers can still manipulate the surrounding gameplay process. These manipulations typically occur before a save is written, or after a legitimate save has been duplicated.

Common manipulation techniques include the following:

- Restoring old saves to reverse mistakes

- Duplication of item-rich saves before major purchases

S. S. Moon, *Securing Single-Player Games in Unreal Engine*, https://doi.org/10.1007/979-8-8688-2833-1_7

- Editing memory *before* the save occurs (runtime cheating → persisted cheating)

- Creating impossible stat combinations through progression skips

- Using external tools to modify values and then re-encrypting

- Injecting debug flags left by developers during production

These manipulations allow attackers to bypass intended progression rules even when the save file itself remains cryptographically valid.

Layered Model of Save Security

To defend against these attacks, save security must operate across several complementary layers. Each layer focuses on a different type of manipulation and together they form a defense-in-depth model.

A robust save protection system typically includes the following layers:

- *Cryptographic Integrity (Chapter 6)*: Ensures the file has not been altered at the byte level

- *Behavioral Integrity*: Ensures values evolve according to normal gameplay rules

- *Structural Integrity*: Ensures fields maintain logical relationships with one another

- *Temporal Integrity*: Ensures save timestamps from a consistent timeline

- *Semantic Integrity*: Ensures stats follow expected patterns (XP curves, unlock timelines, etc.)

- *Decoy Defenses*: Uses fake variables to detect tampering attempts

- *Reputation Systems*: Creates save slot histories that track trustworthiness

Figure 7-1 illustrates the layered tampering detection pipeline applied after cryptographic validation, where multiple validation systems analyze save data to determine whether a save state is trustworthy.

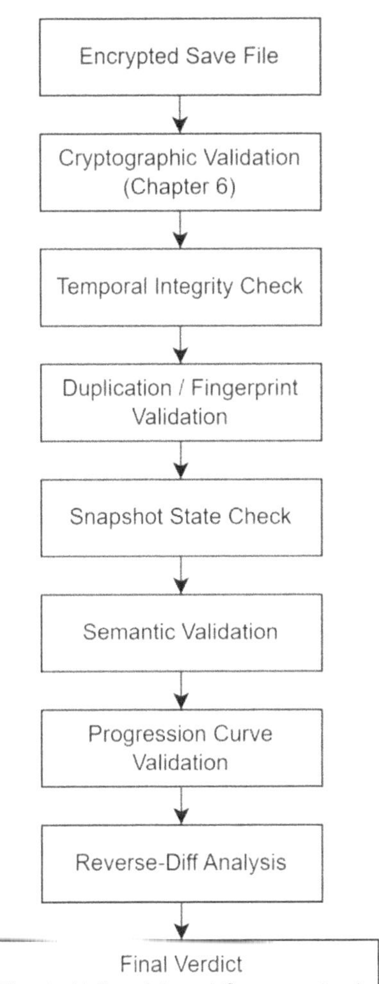

Figure 7-1. *Layered save tampering detection pipeline combining temporal validation, fingerprint analysis, semantic checks, and reputation scoring*

Trap Variables As Early Detection Mechanisms

Trap variables, also known as honeypots or decoy save entries, are artificial values that look meaningful but serve no gameplay purpose. Their only job is to indicate tampering when found in an unexpected state.

Developers often leave debug toggles or developer flags in save data by accident. Cheaters search for these values because they resemble cheat switches. Properly designed trap values exploit this behavior by presenting tempting targets that no legitimate player will trigger.

Listing 7-1 introduces the trap-variable pattern. The listing establishes decoy values, a detection method, and encapsulated logic to test abnormalities during load.

- *FakeXPBoost* simulates an important numeric modifier, encouraging tamper attempts.

- *bDebugGodMode* resembles a cheat flag used during development.

- *HasTriggeredTrap()* analyzes these fields during load and flags manipulation.

Listing 7-1. SaveWithTraps.h

```cpp
UCLASS()
class USaveWithTraps : public USaveGame
{
    GENERATED_BODY()

public:
    UPROPERTY()
    float FakeXPBoost = 0.0f;

    UPROPERTY()
    bool bDebugGodMode = false;

    bool HasTriggeredTrap()
    {
        return FakeXPBoost != 0.0f || bDebugGodMode != false;
    }
};
```

This structure introduces values that appear meaningful to attackers but serve no gameplay purpose. If these fields change unexpectedly, the loader immediately knows that the save file has been manipulated or runtime values were altered prior to saving.

Detecting Implausible Save States

Not all tampering occurs through trap variables. More commonly, attackers modify legitimate fields to produce states that could never occur naturally during gameplay.

The following examples illustrate common contradictions that appear in manipulated save files:

- PlayerLevel = 3 but Gold = 1,200,000

- XP = 0 but AllSkillsUnlocked = true

- WorldCompletion = 95% after only 10 minutes of play

- DifficultyLevel = "Nightmare" but DamageTaken = 0

- InventoryCapacity = 30 but ItemCount = 473

These contradictions serve as semantic fingerprints of tampering. Unlike cryptographic checks, implausibility detection evaluates *meaning*, not bytes.

Listing 7-2 demonstrates a save structure containing fields whose relationships can be validated using domain logic.

- *PlayerLevel* represents natural character progression.

- *Gold* reflects in-game economy accumulation.

- *bAllSkillsUnlocked* indicates full skill tree completion.

- *IsImplausible()* checks relationships, not raw values.

- Thresholds and rules reflect the intended balance of the game.

Listing 7-2. ImplausibilityCheck.h

```
UCLASS()
class USaveSanity : public USaveGame
{
    GENERATED_BODY()

public:
    UPROPERTY()
    int32 PlayerLevel = 1;
```

```cpp
    UPROPERTY()
    int32 Gold = 0;

    UPROPERTY()
    bool bAllSkillsUnlocked = false;

    bool IsImplausible()
    {
        return (PlayerLevel <= 2 && Gold > 100000) ||
                (PlayerLevel < 5 && bAllSkillsUnlocked);
    }
};
```

This validation logic evaluates relationships between fields rather than individual values. By verifying progression rules and value dependencies, the system can detect tampering even when the encrypted save file itself remains structurally valid.

Temporal Integrity and Rollback Detection

Cryptographic validation ensures that a save file is structurally intact and unmodified at the byte level, but this does not protect against time-based manipulation, such as rolling back to an earlier save to reverse costly decisions or duplicating save files to farm rare items.

Temporal integrity ensures that the timeline of saved progress is consistent with normal gameplay behavior. This layer focuses not on the values themselves but on when and how they were produced.

Rollback detection is critical because it is one of the most common forms of offline cheating in single-player games and requires no technical skill. A player can simply copy a save file before a major purchase or outcome, restore it afterward, and repeatedly benefit from events that were intended to be irreversible.

Temporal Consistency Through Metadata Tracking

Every save file should carry internal metadata that helps reconstruct its chronological position in the player's progression timeline. Typical metadata includes

- SaveTimestamp: When the save was produced

- SessionID: Which gameplay session created it

- SaveIndex: The nth save in a chain

- PlaytimeSeconds: How long the player has been in the game

- LastKnownCheckpoint: Progress anchor

While none of these fields alone prove tampering, collectively they allow the engine to detect

- Saves that travel backward in time

- Saves produced too frequently or too rapidly

- Saves whose playtime does not align with world-state changes

- Chains of saves with broken ancestry

Temporal patterns are one of the strongest indicators of illegitimate manipulation.

Listing 7-3 introduces UTemporalMetadataSave, which embeds timestamp and progression metadata for chronological validation.

- *SaveTimestamp*: Records the real-world time a save was created

- *PlaytimeSeconds*: Captures cumulative in-game playtime

- *SaveIndex*: Increments with each successful save

- *IsRollback()*: Determines if the save regresses in time or sequence

Listing 7-3. TemporalMetadataSave.h

```
UCLASS()
class UTemporalMetadataSave : public USaveGame
{
    GENERATED_BODY()

public:
    UPROPERTY()
    FString SaveTimestamp;

    UPROPERTY()
    int32 PlaytimeSeconds = 0;
```

```
UPROPERTY()
int32 SaveIndex = 0;

bool IsRollback(const UTemporalMetadataSave* PreviousSave) const
{
    if (!PreviousSave) return false;

    bool TimeWentBackwards =
        SaveTimestamp < PreviousSave->SaveTimestamp;

    bool IndexWentBackwards =
        SaveIndex < PreviousSave->SaveIndex;

    bool PlaytimeRegressed =
        PlaytimeSeconds < PreviousSave->PlaytimeSeconds;

    return TimeWentBackwards || IndexWentBackwards || PlaytimeRegressed;
}
};
```

These checks ensure that save progression follows a consistent timeline. If a save appears to move backward in time or sequence, the system can flag it as a potential rollback attempt.

Save Duplication and Device Fingerprinting

Save duplication occurs when players copy files and reuse them later to repeat outcomes or reverse losses. Even with encryption in place, duplication can still enable infinite retries or resource farming loops.

Detecting duplication requires metadata that ties the save file to the environment in which it was created. Device fingerprints and save lineage information allow the engine to recognize when files have been copied.

Listing 7-4 introduces UFingerprintSave, which tracks device identity and save lineage to expose duplication.

- *MachineHash*: Represents a hashed hardware or OS identifier

- *SaveUUID*: Uniquely identifies this specific save instance

- *ParentUUID*: Links this save to its predecessor to form a lineage chain

- *IsDuplicated()*: Compares machine identity and lineage to detect external copying

Listing 7-4. FingerprintSave.h

```
UCLASS()
class UFingerprintSave : public USaveGame
{
    GENERATED_BODY()

public:
    UPROPERTY()
    FString MachineHash;

    UPROPERTY()
    FString SaveUUID;

    UPROPERTY()
    FString ParentUUID;

    bool IsDuplicated(const UFingerprintSave* LastSave) const
    {
        if (!LastSave) return false;

        bool DifferentDevice =
            MachineHash != LastSave->MachineHash;

        bool MissingExpectedParent =
            ParentUUID != LastSave->SaveUUID;

        return DifferentDevice || MissingExpectedParent;
    }
};
```

After reconstruction, this metadata allows the engine to detect both cross-device copying and unexpected breaks in the save lineage chain. When combined with temporal metadata, device fingerprints provide strong evidence of duplication-based exploits.

Detecting Repeated, Identical Save States

Some exploits involve repeatedly loading the same save state until a desirable outcome occurs. This behavior can be detected by computing a lightweight hash of important gameplay values.

A strong tamper system must detect not only backward movement but also "stationary fraud."

This occurs when the player

- Creates a save before opening a loot chest

- Gets bad loot

- Reloads

- Repeats until top-tier items appear

Even cryptographically valid saves can be exploited this way. Identifying repeated identical snapshots allows the engine to recognize exploit loops. We can compute a hash of relevant gameplay fields (not the entire save payload) to generate a state signature. If this signature repeats too frequently, it suggests reload exploitation.

Listing 7-5 introduces USnapshotHashSave, which computes a lightweight state hash to detect repeated identical states.

- *StateHash*: Records a digest of key gameplay values

- *ComputeStateHash()*: Computes a deterministic signature

- *IsRepeatState()*: Checks whether a new save replicates a prior state too closely

Listing 7-5. SnapshotHashSave.h

```
UCLASS()
class USnapshotHashSave : public USaveGame
{
    GENERATED_BODY()

public:
    UPROPERTY()
    int32 PlayerLevel = 1;
```

```cpp
UPROPERTY()
int32 Gold = 0;

UPROPERTY()
FString StateHash;

void ComputeStateHash()
{
    FString Combined =
        FString::FromInt(PlayerLevel) + TEXT("|") +
        FString::FromInt(Gold);

    StateHash = FMD5::HashAnsiString(*Combined);
}

bool IsRepeatState(const USnapshotHashSave* PreviousSave) const
{
    if (!PreviousSave) return false;
    return StateHash == PreviousSave->StateHash;
}
};
```

State hashing provides a lightweight way to detect repeated gameplay states. Frequent repetition of identical snapshots often indicates exploit loops such as repeated loot rerolls.

Session-Level Correlation Checks

Certain tampering behaviors become visible only when comparing save data against session activity. By correlating gameplay statistics with save contents, the engine can detect values that exceed what the session could realistically produce.

Examples of session metrics include the following:

- Time played

- XP gained

- Items acquired

- Missions completed

- Movement through world checkpoints

We can derive whether the save file *fits* the session's observed behavior. If a player acquires a rare item during a session where no relevant events occurred, the session-to-save correlation fails.

Listing 7-6 introduces USessionSummarySave, which validates save contents against session-derived expectations.

- *ExpectedXP, ExpectedGold,* and *ExpectedMissionCount* reflect actual session activity.

- *ValidateAgainstSession()* ensures stored values do not exceed what was observed.

Listing 7-6. SessionSummarySave.h

```cpp
UCLASS()
class USessionSummarySave : public USaveGame
{
    GENERATED_BODY()

public:
    UPROPERTY()
    int32 StoredXP = 0;

    UPROPERTY()
    int32 StoredGold = 0;

    UPROPERTY()
    int32 StoredMissions = 0;

    bool ValidateAgainstSession(
        int32 ExpectedXP,
        int32 ExpectedGold,
        int32 ExpectedMissionCount) const
    {
        if (StoredXP > ExpectedXP) return false;
        if (StoredGold > ExpectedGold) return false;
        if (StoredMissions > ExpectedMissionCount) return false;
```

```
        return true;
    }
};
```

Session correlation prevents saves from introducing values that exceed what the player actually achieved during gameplay.

Cross-Field Semantic Validation

Even when temporal metadata and duplication fingerprints appear valid, a save file may still contain values that do not align with the natural structure of the game's progression. This kind of tampering is more subtle than extreme value injection and often appears legitimate unless examined mathematically or semantically.

A game's economy, XP systems, skill unlock trees, quest flags, and difficulty scaling are all interconnected. Attackers who manually edit values rarely maintain these relationships correctly.

For example:

- A player may have enough gold for a late-game weapon but no quests completed.

- XP may reflect 40 hours of play while the playtime counter shows 2 hours.

- A skill that requires Level 15 may be unlocked at Level 3.

- Item rarity may not match the area the player has reached.

- Boss defeat flags may be set while the associated rewards remain absent.

Semantic validation checks these internal relationships to detect contradictions that naturally arise from tampering.

Listing 7-7 introduces UCrossFieldValidator, which verifies structured relationships within the save data.

- *PlayerLevel, XP, SkillPoints, QuestsCompleted* represent a simplified progression framework.

- *PassesSemanticChecks()* tests dependencies between fields (XP $\leftrightarrow$ Level, Level $\leftrightarrow$ Skills).

- Ensures data remains coherent even after cryptographic validation.

- Designed to run right before the save is accepted into active gameplay.

Listing 7-7. CrossFieldValidator.h

```cpp
UCLASS()
class UCrossFieldValidator : public USaveGame
{
    GENERATED_BODY()

public:
    UPROPERTY()
    int32 PlayerLevel = 1;

    UPROPERTY()
    int32 XP = 0;

    UPROPERTY()
    int32 SkillPoints = 0;

    UPROPERTY()
    int32 QuestsCompleted = 0;

    bool PassesSemanticChecks() const
    {
        bool XPTooHigh = XP > PlayerLevel * 1500;
        bool TooManySkillPoints = SkillPoints > PlayerLevel * 2;
        bool TooManyQuests = QuestsCompleted > PlayerLevel * 3;

        return !(XPTooHigh || TooManySkillPoints || TooManyQuests);
    }
};
```

Cross-field validation maintains logical relationships between progression variables and ensures that save data remains consistent with the game's internal rules.

Progression Curve Modeling (XP, Gold, Difficulty)

Most games follow natural curves for progression. XP, gold accumulation, unlock timing, and difficulty scaling tend to follow predictable patterns.

Every progression-based game develops a natural "curve" for how a player accumulates

- XP

- Gold

- Items

- Unlocks

- Power tier

The curve does not need to be perfectly mathematical; even simple models identify deviations. A manipulated save tends to create spikes, flatlines, or jumps inconsistent with long-term play.

Using Regression Curves to Detect Abnormal Progression

You can model progression using

- Linear regression (simple trends)

- Polynomial regression (RPG difficulty curves)

- Logistic curves (skill trees and level caps)

This allows the engine to classify whether the accumulated values match expected ranges for a given playtime, level, area, or mission index.

Listing 7-8 introduces UProgressionCurveSave, which evaluates player XP against an expected mathematical curve.

- *PlayerLevel* indicates natural character strength.

- *XP* stores actual progression.

- *ExpectedXP()* computes the predicted amount based on your designed curve.

- *IsCurveViolation()* flags progression that deviates excessively from the expected range.

- Detects spikes introduced by manual editing or trainer usage.

Listing 7-8. ProgressionCurveSave.h

```
UCLASS()
class UProgressionCurveSave : public USaveGame
{
    GENERATED_BODY()

public:
    UPROPERTY()
    int32 PlayerLevel = 1;

    UPROPERTY()
    int32 XP = 0;

    int32 ExpectedXP() const
    {
        return PlayerLevel * PlayerLevel * 100;
    }

    bool IsCurveViolation(float ToleranceMultiplier = 2.0f) const
    {
        int32 Expected = ExpectedXP();
        int32 LowerBound = Expected / ToleranceMultiplier;
        int32 UpperBound = Expected * ToleranceMultiplier;

        return XP < LowerBound || XP > UpperBound;
    }
};
```

Progression curve validation detects abnormal spikes in player growth that often result from manual editing or trainer tools.

Reverse-Diff Tamper Reconstruction

Sometimes tampering is not visible directly in loaded values. Instead, you detect anomalies at load time and must determine which field likely caused the violation.

Reverse-diff reconstruction compares

- Saved values (current load)

- Previous validated values

- Expected behavioral deltas

This technique identifies the field most "responsible" for the contradiction.

Listing 7-9 introduces UReverseDiffSave, which identifies the field most likely affected by tampering through delta comparison.

- *StoredXP, StoredGold, StoredSkillPoints* represent key fields.

- *ComputeDiffs()* calculates magnitude differences from previous state.

- *IdentifySuspectField()* returns the field showing the abnormal spike.

- Helps classify tampering without rejecting the save entirely.

Listing 7-9. ReverseDiffSave.h

```
UCLASS()
class UReverseDiffSave : public USaveGame
{
    GENERATED_BODY()

public:
    UPROPERTY()
    int32 StoredXP = 0;

    UPROPERTY()
    int32 StoredGold = 0;

    UPROPERTY()
    int32 StoredSkillPoints = 0;

    FString IdentifySuspectField(const UReverseDiffSave* Previous) const
    {
```

```
    if (!Previous) return TEXT("None");

    int32 XPDelta = FMath::Abs(StoredXP - Previous->StoredXP);
    int32 GoldDelta = FMath::Abs(StoredGold - Previous->StoredGold);
    int32 SkillDelta = FMath::Abs(StoredSkillPoints - Previous-
    >StoredSkillPoints);

    int32 MaxDelta = FMath::Max3(XPDelta, GoldDelta, SkillDelta);

    if (MaxDelta == XPDelta) return TEXT("XP");
    if (MaxDelta == GoldDelta) return TEXT("Gold");
    return TEXT("SkillPoints");
  }
};
```

Reverse-diff analysis helps developers identify the field most responsible for suspicious changes, providing useful diagnostic insight.

Save Slot Reputation Scoring

Instead of immediately rejecting suspicious saves, the system can track long-term behavior using reputation scoring. Each anomaly slightly reduces a save slot's trust score.

Over time the save slot builds a trust profile. Possible responses include the following:

- Implausibility flags

- Rollback detections

- Curve violations

- Duplicated snapshots

- Triggered decoys

- Reverse-diff anomaly counts

- Session mismatch violations

Over time, each save slot forms a trust score, enabling soft and friendly responses such as

- Disabling achievements

- Reducing rare drops

- Storing "taint flags" internally

- Silently banning access to online leaderboards

- Enabling conversational warnings

- Reporting metrics for developer analytics

This is one of the most elegant methods of balancing security and player friendliness.

Implementing a Basic Reputation Model

Listing 7-10 introduces USaveReputationModel, which aggregates anomaly scores into a trust classification.

- *ReputationScore*: Accumulates penalties

- *RecordAnomaly()*: Adds incremental penalties

- *GetReputationTier()*: Maps numeric reputation to qualitative trust tiers

Listing 7-10. SaveReputationModel.h

```
UCLASS()
class USaveReputationModel : public USaveGame
{
    GENERATED_BODY()

public:
    UPROPERTY()
    int32 ReputationScore = 0;

    void RecordAnomaly(int32 Severity)
    {
        ReputationScore += Severity;
    }
```

```cpp
    FString GetReputationTier() const
    {
        if (ReputationScore < 10) return TEXT("Trusted");
        if (ReputationScore < 30) return TEXT("Suspicious");
        return TEXT("Compromised");
    }
};
```

Reputation scoring allows the game to respond proportionally to suspicious behavior rather than punishing players immediately.

Designing a Unified Save Tampering Detection Pipeline

Each validator, temporal, semantic, behavioral, or structural, catches a different class of anomaly. A unified detection pipeline integrates all layers into a single routine that runs after cryptographic validation (Chapter 6) but before the game world is loaded.

This ensures systematic, repeatable tamper evaluation and prevents contradictory actions across systems. A well-designed pipeline includes

- Cryptographic integrity verification (AES + HMAC from Chapter 6)

- Temporal metadata check

- Duplication and fingerprints validation

- Snapshot identity comparison

- Semantic relationship validation

- Progression curve modeling

- Reverse-diff reconstruction

- Reputation scoring

The goal is not to punish players harshly but to evaluate risk, categorize saves into "trust tiers," and decide how the gameplay should adapt.

Listing 7-11 introduces USaveTamperManager, which coordinates all validation layers and yields a structured detection result.

- *RunAllChecks()* invokes each validator sequentially.

- *Results* stores Boolean indicators for every detection category.

- *ComputeFinalVerdict()* determines whether the save is trusted, suspicious, or compromised.

- *ReputationModel* integrates anomaly scoring across checks.

Listing 7-11. SaveTamperManager.h

```
USTRUCT()
struct FSaveCheckResults
{
    GENERATED_BODY()

    bool bTemporalRollback = false;
    bool bDuplicatedSave = false;
    bool bRepeatSnapshot = false;
    bool bSemanticViolation = false;
    bool bCurveViolation = false;
    FString PrimarySuspectField;
};

UCLASS()
class USaveTamperManager : public UObject
{
    GENERATED_BODY()

public:
    UPROPERTY()
    USaveReputationModel* ReputationModel;

    FSaveCheckResults RunAllChecks(
        UTemporalMetadataSave* Temporal,
        UTemporalMetadataSave* PreviousTemporal,
        UFingerprintSave* Fingerprint,
        UFingerprintSave* PreviousFingerprint,
        USnapshotHashSave* Snapshot,
        USnapshotHashSave* PreviousSnapshot,
```

```cpp
    UCrossFieldValidator* Semantic,
    UProgressionCurveSave* Curve,
    UReverseDiffSave* Reverse,
    UReverseDiffSave* PreviousReverse
)
{
    FSaveCheckResults Results;

    Results.bTemporalRollback =
        Temporal->IsRollback(PreviousTemporal);

    Results.bDuplicatedSave =
        Fingerprint->IsDuplicated(PreviousFingerprint);

    Results.bRepeatSnapshot =
        Snapshot->IsRepeatState(PreviousSnapshot);

    Results.bSemanticViolation =
        !Semantic->PassesSemanticChecks();

    Results.bCurveViolation =
        Curve->IsCurveViolation();

    Results.PrimarySuspectField =
        Reverse->IdentifySuspectField(PreviousReverse);

    return Results;
}

FString ComputeFinalVerdict(const FSaveCheckResults& Results)
{
    int32 Severity = 0;

    if (Results.bTemporalRollback) Severity += 5;
    if (Results.bDuplicatedSave) Severity += 5;
    if (Results.bRepeatSnapshot) Severity += 3;
    if (Results.bSemanticViolation) Severity += 4;
    if (Results.bCurveViolation) Severity += 4;
```

```
    ReputationModel->RecordAnomaly(Severity);
    return ReputationModel->GetReputationTier();
  }
};
```

This manager coordinates all validation layers and produces a unified tamper verdict, simplifying integration into the save/load lifecycle.

Soft vs. Hard Countermeasures

A detection pipeline is only as effective as the **responses** that follow it. Countermeasures must be fair, proportional, player-friendly, and supportive of your game's design philosophy.

Soft Countermeasures (Preferred for Single-Player Games)

Soft countermeasures maintain player freedom while reducing exploit viability:

- Disable achievements for this session.

- Reduce drop rates subtly.

- Prevent access to hidden endings or challenge modes.

- Disable leaderboard submissions.

- Slow down save frequency.

- Increase autosave strictness.

- Force exclusive offline mode.

- Trigger developer analytics events.

- Mark save slot as "restricted."

Soft responses do not ruin the player's experience but make cheating less beneficial.

Hard Countermeasures (Use Only When Necessary)

Hard responses may be appropriate for egregious or repeated tampering:

- Refuse to load the save entirely.

- Load the save in "restricted mode" with limited functionality.

- Revert suspicious fields to last known valid values.

- Restore minimal baseline progression.

- Replace suspicious data with default parameters.

- Trigger in-game narrative consequences (story-friendly penalties).

Hard countermeasures should be rare, clearly justified, and used only when the detection certainty is high.

Integrating Detection Into Unreal's Save/ Load Lifecycle

Tampering detection should occur at predictable points in Unreal's lifecycle:

- Right after decrypting and verifying (Chapter 6)

- Before deserializing active gameplay structures

- Before applying world state changes

- During session initialization

- During autosave

- After major milestones (boss fights, mission completion)

- Before awarding achievements

This ensures that suspicious saves do not silently override important systems.

Case Study 1: Platformer Save Duplication Exploit

A 2D platformer shipped with a lightweight save system where the player's inventory and progress were stored without temporal metadata. Players discovered that by copying the save before entering a shop, they could

- Buy expensive items

- Restore the save

- Repeat the purchase infinitely

The cryptographic structure remained intact, so the game accepted the manipulated saves. However, if the developer had implemented

- SaveIndex and ParentUUID lineage

- Snapshot hashing

- Temporal metadata comparisons

the duplication loop would have been detected quickly. Even soft countermeasures like suppressing shop restocks or disabling rare items would have mitigated the exploit.

Case Study 2: Open-World RPG Stat Inflation via Save-State Injection

In a large open-world RPG developed in Unreal, players discovered a method to artificially inflate late-game stats by manipulating save states outside the game.

The exploit worked like this:

1. The player would begin a session with normal stats (Level 14, moderate XP).

2. They would use Cheat Engine to modify XP **only in memory**, not in the save file.

3. They would force an immediate save, embedding the inflated value.

4. They would reload a previous, legitimate save and **copy specific blocks** from the tampered file over it at byte boundaries they had discovered through experimentation.

5. Because the game only validated the save's AES + HMAC envelope (Chapter 6 concepts) and not the *semantic relationships* between fields, the manipulated fields were accepted without question.

The resulting save files contained

- Level values far too low for the XP stored

- Skill unlocks inconsistent with quest progress

- Item rarities that required regions the player had not visited

- Gold counts that exceeded the sum of all available quest rewards

Chapter 7's techniques would have detected the exploit:

- Cross-field semantic validation would flag XP exceeding the level's expected range.

- Progression curves would detect the mismatch between playtime and total accumulated XP.

- Reverse-diff reconstruction would identify the XP field as the anomalous source.

- Reputation scoring would classify the save slot as "suspicious" long before it caused balance issues.

This case demonstrates how memory-based stat manipulation becomes permanent when written to disk and how behavioral validation is essential even after cryptographic protection is applied.

Conclusion

Save file tampering remains one of the most accessible forms of cheating because it requires very little technical expertise. Players can duplicate files, revert progress, or manipulate gameplay values using simple tools. Chapter 6 introduced cryptographic protections that secure the save file at the byte level. This chapter expanded that foundation by introducing behavioral, temporal, structural, and semantic validation systems.

Together, these mechanisms transform the save system from passive storage into an active defense layer capable of recognizing and responding to suspicious behavior.

In Chapter 8, we shift our focus from save data to another important attack surface: Blueprint-based exploits.

CHAPTER 8

Avoiding Blueprint-Based Exploits

Blueprints provide developers with an expressive and highly accessible visual environment for building gameplay systems, prototyping mechanics, defining UI interaction rules, creating state machines, wiring player input, and binding events to functional behavior. This accessibility makes them extremely valuable for rapid iteration and experimentation during development.

However, the same accessibility also introduces a significant security liability. Every function exposed to the Blueprint virtual machine, every variable marked visible to the scripting layer, every Event Dispatcher, and every `BlueprintCallable` annotation creates a possible pathway for an attacker to modify or trigger logic outside its intended context.

In many shipped single-player games, these pathways become the earliest and most easily abused entry points for cheat trainers, memory editors, and even casual players exploring extracted assets.

Blueprint tampering, unlike binary manipulation or runtime injection, does not require sophisticated tooling. Tools that unpack content archives can expose Blueprint bytecode, metadata, function names, property lists, and default values. Attackers do not need to understand your C++ code or reverse engineer assembly instructions to cause damage.

In many cases they only need to call an exposed function such as

- `AwardXP`

- `UnlockSkill`

- `GiveKeyItem`

- `OpenPortal`

Developers frequently underestimate the degree of introspection available into Blueprint assets and the ease with which callable functions can be misused.

This chapter focuses on transforming how you design, annotate, and structure Blueprints so that even if attackers extract or inspect your assets, your core logic remains difficult or impossible to exploit.

The Blueprint Reflection Surface

Blueprint assets are not opaque or sealed by packaging. They compile into bytecode representations stored inside .uasset files, which can be inspected, decompiled, analyzed, and sometimes modified.

The reflection system that powers Blueprint interoperability with C++ provides structured metadata fields, function descriptors, property descriptors, and annotations. While extremely useful for development, this reflection surface exposes information that attackers can leverage.

The reflection system exposes several types of information:

- UClass metadata describing Blueprint-visible functions, interfaces, and inheritance hierarchies

- UFunction metadata describing callability, replication behavior, and execution context

- UProperty metadata describing visibility, serialization, and mutability

- Default variable values stored in Blueprint assets

- Kismet bytecode, which can reveal node-level logic

- Blueprint-generated class layouts that reveal system boundaries

Blueprints should therefore be treated not as protected compiled code, but as front-end scripting logic whose internal structure is frequently visible to anyone who extracts your game archives.

Exposure Vectors in Blueprint Assets

Blueprint exploitation generally arises from a small set of exposure vectors. Understanding these vectors provides a theoretical framework for auditing and securing Blueprint assets.

Several common exposure vectors appear repeatedly across vulnerable projects:

- *Callable Surface Exposure*: Functions reachable via BlueprintCallable or exec can be invoked by external tools even if you never intended them to be called outside controlled contexts.

- *Property Exposure*: Variables marked BlueprintReadWrite or EditAnywhere often leak game state that should remain internal, including progress flags, currency counts, or debug toggles.

- *Trigger Exposure*: Events that open doors, grant rewards, or manipulate quest states can be triggered without validation.

- *Widget Graph Exposure*: UI Blueprints frequently expose sensitive logic because developers assume UI is inherently safe or ephemeral.

- *Interface and Dispatcher Exposure*: Blueprint Interfaces and Event Dispatchers can be misused by trainers to simulate gameplay events.

Reducing these exposure surfaces is one of the most effective ways to limit Blueprint exploitation.

The Five Practical Blueprint Exploit Families

When attackers exploit Blueprint systems through trainers or scripting tools, their behavior typically falls into five predictable exploit families. Understanding these patterns helps developers design targeted defenses.

Common Blueprint exploit families include

- *Direct Function Invocation*: Calling a BlueprintCallable method such as AddXP, UnlockLevel, or GiveItem with arbitrarily large or invalid values

- *State Injection*: Modifying BlueprintReadWrite variables that act as gates for unlocking features or skipping progression

- *Event Spoofing*: Triggering events such as OnBossDefeated or OnQuestCompleted without completing the underlying tasks

- *Widget Event Hijacking*: Overriding or simulating UI button presses to trigger debug actions left behind in the project

- *Constructor or Default Value Abuse*: Exploiting default values of variables defined in Blueprint class defaults to grant capabilities never intended for release

Blueprint hardening must address each exploit category directly.

Restricting BlueprintCallable Surfaces

BlueprintCallable is not inherently unsafe, but it becomes dangerous when used without constraints. Any function annotated with BlueprintCallable becomes visible to the Blueprint virtual machine and may be discovered through reflection tables. Trainers can search for these functions and call them directly. Sensitive operations such as granting XP or unlocking skills should always pass through validation layers.

Listing 8-1 introduces a safe XP update procedure by separating the publicly exposed entry point from the internal logic. The BlueprintCallable entry point performs strict input validation and delegates to a private C++ implementation. The breakdown includes

- AddXP_Internal(int32 XPAmount): Implements the true XP update and is never exposed to the Blueprint layer

- AddXP(int32 XPAmount): Exposed to Blueprints and externally visible, but applies strict bounds validation

- Private Access Modifiers: Hide sensitive logic from the Blueprint reflection layer

- BlueprintCallable Annotation: Leaves the function visible but within a controlled pipeline

Listing 8-1. SecureXPWrapper.cpp

```cpp
UCLASS()
class AMyCharacter : public ACharacter
{
    GENERATED_BODY()

private:
    void AddXP_Internal(int32 XPAmount);

public:
    UFUNCTION(BlueprintCallable)
    void AddXP(int32 XPAmount)
    {
        if (XPAmount > 0 && XPAmount < 2000)
        {
            AddXP_Internal(XPAmount);
        }
    }
};
```

This pattern separates public entry points from the internal implementation. The Blueprint layer calls the validated wrapper, while the true gameplay logic remains hidden inside the private C++ function.

Blueprint Metadata and Unsafe Annotations

Metadata annotations determine how functions and properties are exposed to the Blueprint system. Developers frequently underestimate how these annotations change visibility boundaries.

Several annotations require careful consideration:

- BlueprintReadWrite: Allows Blueprints to modify the variable. Should be avoided for critical values.

- BlueprintReadOnly: Safer, but still exposes internal state unnecessarily.

- EditAnywhere: Appears in defaults and can leak debug values.

- Exec: Allows invocation through the console. Must be removed from shipping builds.

- BlueprintAssignable: Event Dispatchers can be subscribed to by external entities.

- CallInEditor: Should never appear in a shipping build.

- SaveGame: Causes values to be stored in save files, making them vulnerable outside this chapter's subject.

Careful annotation analysis is an essential component of Blueprint hardening.

Auditing Blueprint Graphs for Exploitability

Blueprint graphs can create exploit surfaces even without explicit annotations. A structured audit process reveals flaws before attackers find them.

A comprehensive audit examines

- *All Variables Stored in Defaults*: Ensure no debug flags remain.

- *All BlueprintCallable Functions*: Remove or restrict them.

- *All Custom Events*: Ensure they require state validation.

- *All Widget Blueprint Functions*: Check for hidden debug or cheat actions.

- *All References to* ExecuteConsoleCommand: Remove them.

- *All Event Dispatchers*: Ensure subscription boundaries are tight.

- All timelines or latent actions that control gameplay progression.

- All flows that immediately modify critical state without checks.

Hardening efforts begin with identifying these patterns and then restructuring them to rely on internal C++ logic where appropriate.

Escalating Critical Logic to C++

Blueprints should orchestrate gameplay, not govern core rules. Logic that governs economy values, health, skill unlocks, inventory modification, or progression prerequisites must be implemented in C++. Blueprint events should request state changes from C++, and C++ should validate and execute those changes. This ensures that no one can bypass essential game rules by manipulating Blueprint values or graphs.

Listing 8-2 introduces a secure item unlock system by delegating validation to a C++ method that checks inventory state, progression requirements, and preconditions that cannot be bypassed. The BlueprintCallable method performs only minimal role verification.

- UnlockItem_Internal(FName ItemID): Implements validation and logic

- UnlockItem(FName ItemID): Exposed but restricted method

- Internal Validation: Prevents external calls from bypassing requirements

- Strong Type Usage: Reduces misuse from string injections

Listing 8-2. SecureUnlockWrapper.cpp

```cpp
UCLASS()
class AMyInventoryManager : public AActor
{
    GENERATED_BODY()

private:
    bool UnlockItem_Internal(const FName& ItemID);

public:
    UFUNCTION(BlueprintCallable)
    bool UnlockItem(const FName& ItemID)
    {
        if (!ItemID.IsNone())
        {
```

```
        return UnlockItem_Internal(ItemID);
    }
    return false;
  }
};
```

In this architecture, Blueprint access remains possible while the underlying unlock logic stays protected within internal C++ code.

Hardening Widget Blueprints and UI Event Graphs

Widget Blueprints are among the most frequently exploited assets in Unreal Engine games because developers assume that UI has little impact on game systems. In practice, UI graphs often contain functions that call BlueprintCallable methods, grant items, unlock features, adjust player state, or expose console commands for debugging. Attackers who extract UI Blueprints can inspect button bindings, exposed variables, and event flows. They can simulate interaction with these UI bindings even if the UI is not visible or not intended to be active.

A secure design treats Widget Blueprints as high-risk surfaces. Buttons should never directly change game state. Instead, UI elements should request state changes from C++ endpoints that enforce validation, verification, and permission checks. This rule becomes essential in preventing attackers from calling UI functions through trainers or from triggering them indirectly.

Creating a Secure Input Gateway for UI Interaction

To prevent UI from directly modifying critical game state, every button or interactive element should call into a C++ handler that enforces validation. Blueprint does not have the capability to perform secure, context-sensitive checks without exposing too much state. You must consolidate all UI-triggered gameplay actions into one or more secure handlers.

In Listing 8-3, we introduce a secure UI action gateway that centralizes the handling of critical player actions coming from any Widget Blueprint. The secure gateway verifies the sender, checks the validity of the request, enforces game rules, and prevents UI graphs from bypassing essential progression logic.

- HandleUIAction_Internal(FName ActionName): Contains the actual logic and cannot be accessed from Blueprints.

- HandleUIAction(FName ActionName): BlueprintCallable wrapper that restricts input to a set of approved actions.

- Whitelist Validation: Ensures that only recognized UI actions are processed.

- Separation of UI and Logic: Widget Blueprints never contain real gameplay rules.

Listing 8-3. SecureUIActionGateway.cpp

```cpp
UCLASS()
class AMyUIActionGateway : public AActor
{
    GENERATED_BODY()

private:
    bool HandleUIAction_Internal(const FName& ActionName);

public:
    UFUNCTION(BlueprintCallable)
    bool HandleUIAction(const FName& ActionName)
    {
        static const TSet<FName> AllowedActions = {
            TEXT("OpenInventory"),
            TEXT("ToggleMap"),
            TEXT("ShowQuestLog")
        };

        if (AllowedActions.Contains(ActionName))
        {
            return HandleUIAction_Internal(ActionName);
        }
```

```
        return false;
    }
};
```

By validating action names and routing logic through C++, this gateway prevents UI graphs from executing unauthorized gameplay operations.

Hardening Event Dispatchers and Global Triggers

Event Dispatchers can be powerful tools for decoupling systems, but they introduce an exploitable mechanism. Any external caller, including trainers or modified classes, can bind to dispatchers if they are exposed. Similarly, dispatchers that broadcast critical events such as boss defeats, level transitions, or unlock events can be triggered without validation.

Dispatchers that must remain callable from Blueprints require strict state validation in C++. Only C++ can reliably ensure that the conditions for triggering a dispatcher match the rules of progression.

In Listing 8-4, we create a secure dispatcher wrapper that prevents unauthorized event broadcasts. The C++ layer verifies prerequisites before allowing a dispatcher to fire.

- OnBossDefeated_Internal: The actual dispatcher that broadcasts the event

- OnBossDefeated: BlueprintAssignable but only triggered internally

- TriggerBossDefeat(): Validates real combat state before firing

- Private Gating: Prevents Blueprints from calling internal triggers directly

Listing 8-4. SecureBossDispatcher.h

```
UCLASS()
class ABossEventManager : public AActor
{
    GENERATED_BODY()

public:
    DECLARE_DYNAMIC_MULTICAST_DELEGATE(FBossDefeatEvent);
```

```cpp
    UPROPERTY(BlueprintAssignable)
    FBossDefeatEvent OnBossDefeated;

private:
    void OnBossDefeated_Internal()
    {
        OnBossDefeated.Broadcast();
    }

public:
    UFUNCTION(BlueprintCallable)
    void TriggerBossDefeat()
    {
        if (VerifyCombatConditions())
        {
            OnBossDefeated_Internal();
        }
    }

private:
    bool VerifyCombatConditions() const
    {
        return CurrentBossHealth <= 0 && bCombatPhaseCompleted;
    }

    int32 CurrentBossHealth = 0;
    bool bCombatPhaseCompleted = true;
};
```

This ensures the event can only fire when legitimate combat conditions are satisfied.

Detecting Blueprint Variable Tampering Through State Fingerprinting

Variables defined inside Blueprints often include default values stored in class defaults. These values can be modified unexpectedly if attackers alter Blueprints or manipulate save data. Because Blueprints are not cryptographically protected, developers must use behavioral and structural detection techniques to identify tampering.

State fingerprinting creates signatures based on variable combinations expected at key points in progression. Even if individual variables look valid, a combined fingerprint may reveal tampering.

In Listing 8-5, we introduce a lightweight state fingerprint validator designed to check whether the combination of Blueprint variables matches valid progression patterns. The fingerprint is derived from multiple variables that normally evolve together.

- Expected Progression Windows: Defines permissible ranges for state

- CheckProgressionFingerprint(): Validates the internal consistency of states

- Deterministic Fingerprinting: Flags any mismatch between expected variables

- Non-cryptographic: Behavioral detection instead of cryptography

Listing 8-5. ProgressionFingerprint.h

```
USTRUCT()
struct FProgressionFingerprint
{
    GENERATED_BODY()

    UPROPERTY()
    int32 PlayerLevel;

    UPROPERTY()
    int32 StoryChapter;

    UPROPERTY()
    int32 SkillPointsUnlocked;

    bool CheckProgressionFingerprint() const
    {
        if (PlayerLevel < 3 && SkillPointsUnlocked > 10)
        {
            return false;
        }
```

```
    if (StoryChapter < 2 && PlayerLevel > 20)
    {
        return false;
    }
    return true;
  }
};
```

Blueprints should never be trusted to store critical state without deeper consistency checks.

Securing Blueprint Interfaces and Preventing Unauthorized Implementations

Blueprint Interfaces can quietly create dangerous bypasses in your gameplay systems. When an interface is implemented by an actor, any Blueprint or trainer capable of obtaining a reference to that actor can call exposed interface functions. Developers often use interfaces for quest systems, AI communication, door interactions, or world events. However, if these interface functions are designed without security considerations, attackers may trigger them directly.

A secure design treats interface calls as request signals rather than authoritative commands. Each interface call routed through Blueprint should hand control to a C++ guardian function. This guardian function validates whether the call is legitimate, based on internal game state rather than the caller's identity.

In Listing 8-6, we introduce a secure Blueprint Interface implementation where the public interface handler does not directly perform the sensitive action. Instead, it delegates to a private C++ method protected by strict validation rules. This architecture prevents malicious call sequences or spoofed interface invocations.

- ISecureInteractInterface: Declares the interface method visible to Blueprints

- HandleInteraction_Internal: Private implementation guarded by validation logic

- HandleInteraction(): BlueprintCallable entry point that performs minimal pre-checks

- Caller-Agnostic Design: Prevents direct actor-to-actor spoofing

Listing 8-6. SecureInteractInterface.cpp

```
UINTERFACE(BlueprintType)
class USecureInteractInterface : public UInterface
{
    GENERATED_BODY()
};

class ISecureInteractInterface
{
    GENERATED_BODY()

public:
    UFUNCTION(BlueprintCallable)
    virtual void HandleInteraction() = 0;
};

UCLASS()
class ASecureDoor : public AActor, public ISecureInteractInterface
{
    GENERATED_BODY()

private:
    bool HandleInteraction_Internal();

public:
    virtual void HandleInteraction() override
    {
        if (CanPlayerInteract())
        {
            HandleInteraction_Internal();
        }
    }
```

```
private:
    bool CanPlayerInteract() const
    {
        return bHasKey && !bIsLocked;
    }

    bool bHasKey = false;
    bool bIsLocked = true;
};
```

The interface method is now harmless on its own, since all significant logic is isolated in the internal implementation.

Blueprint Construction Script Abuse and Default Value Leakage

Blueprint Construction Scripts (CSs) execute when an object is placed in the editor or when a dynamically spawned Blueprint is initialized. While developers often use Construction Scripts to set initial values or spawn helper components, these scripts can introduce unexpected vulnerabilities when default values store debug flags or unchecked state initialization.

Construction Scripts are compiled into Blueprint bytecode and may reveal hidden configuration logic when extracted. Attackers analyzing the script can read values such as hidden debug variables, temporary editor-only flags, or hardcoded shortcuts. Any variable stored as EditAnywhere or BlueprintReadWrite may be visible in extracted assets.

The safest approach is to prevent Construction Scripts from setting any sensitive state. Instead, move logic to C++ constructors or BeginPlay and guard it appropriately. Construction Scripts should contain only non-sensitive initialization, such as setting mesh references or adjusting materials.

In Listing 8-7, we demonstrate a safe pattern where initialization of sensitive Blueprint-related state is deferred to internal C++ logic rather than stored in the Blueprint Construction Script. Listing 8-7 highlights a secure initialization pipeline that replaces Blueprint CS logic with protected native code.

- Blueprint Construction Script Disabled: Sensitive state initialization removed

- Initialize_Internal(): C++ method that performs secure initialization

- BeginPlay(): Ensures initialization occurs only in runtime conditions

- Avoids Storing Sensitive Defaults in Assets: Prevents leakage through extraction

Listing 8-7. SecureInitialization.cpp

```cpp
UCLASS()
class ASecureActor : public AActor
{
    GENERATED_BODY()

public:
    ASecureActor()
    {
        bReplicates = false;
    }

protected:
    virtual void BeginPlay() override
    {
        Super::BeginPlay();
        Initialize_Internal();
    }

private:
    void Initialize_Internal()
    {
        Health = 100;
        bIsBossRoomUnlocked = false;
        bDebugShortcutEnabled = false;
    }
```

```
    int32 Health;
    bool bIsBossRoomUnlocked;
    bool bDebugShortcutEnabled;
};
```

Any value potentially used for unlocking content or testing functionality should never appear in the defaults of a Blueprint asset.

Preventing Exploits Through Blueprint-Callable Console Commands

Developers sometimes use ExecuteConsoleCommand in Blueprints for debugging, quick testing, or administrative controls. In shipping builds, these nodes become a serious vulnerability. Trainers and Cheat Engine scripts can invoke these Blueprint nodes through function calls or forced event paths. Even if the command is benign, the ability to execute arbitrary console commands indirectly can lead to security violations.

Your production-grade Blueprints should never contain ExecuteConsoleCommand. Instead, sensitive commands should be encapsulated in C++ methods, and these methods should have guard conditions or be removed entirely from shipping builds.

In Listing 8-8, we create a secure command execution wrapper in C++ that filters allowable console commands and rejects dangerous or unintended inputs. By restricting the list of commands, you prevent Blueprint abuse while preserving flexibility during development.

- ExecuteCommand_Internal(FName Command): Core command logic not visible to Blueprints

- ExecuteCommand(FName Command): Public callable wrapper with validation

- AllowedCommands Whitelist: Prevents arbitrary command injection

- Removes dependency on ExecuteConsoleCommand Blueprint node

Listing 8-8. SecureConsoleWrapper.cpp

```cpp
UCLASS()
class AConsoleSecureWrapper : public AActor
{
    GENERATED_BODY()

private:
    void ExecuteCommand_Internal(const FString& Command);

public:
    UFUNCTION(BlueprintCallable)
    void ExecuteCommand(const FName Command)
    {
        static const TSet<FName> AllowedCommands = {
            TEXT("ToggleMap"),
            TEXT("OpenInventory")
        };

        if (AllowedCommands.Contains(Command))
        {
            ExecuteCommand_Internal(Command.ToString());
        }
    }
};
```

This technique eliminates the need for direct Blueprint console invocation and removes the risk of unexpected or dangerous commands running in shipped builds.

Securing Blueprint-Exposed Variables and Default Properties

Variables marked with BlueprintReadWrite or EditAnywhere can be manipulated by external tools if they are not isolated behind validation logic. Even BlueprintReadOnly variables can leak meaningful state if extracted. Variables governing progression, unlocking, difficulty, or rewards should never be directly exposed.

Blueprint variables should fall into one of three categories:

- *Purely Visual Variables*: Safe to expose (UI displays, cosmetic toggles, non-essential values)

- *State Request Variables*: Used to request changes but not authoritative (must pass through C++ validation)

- *Protected State Variables*: Not exposed at all and stored only in C++

In Listing 8-9, we create a secure wrapper around Blueprint-exposed variables by implementing setter functions that validate input before applying state changes. The Blueprint layer never directly sets protected values.

- SetDifficulty_Internal(int32 Level): Internal setter with trusted logic

- SetDifficulty(int32 Level): BlueprintCallable setter with validation

- DifficultyLevel: Stored in native code, hidden from Blueprints

- Preconditions: Prevent invalid or exploitable values

Listing 8-9. SecureDifficultySetter.cpp

```cpp
UCLASS()
class AMyDifficultyManager : public AActor
{
    GENERATED_BODY()

private:
    int32 DifficultyLevel = 1;

    void SetDifficulty_Internal(int32 Level)
    {
        DifficultyLevel = Level;
    }

public:
    UFUNCTION(BlueprintCallable)
    void SetDifficulty(int32 Level)
    {
        if (Level >= 1 && Level <= 5)
```

```
        {
            SetDifficulty_Internal(Level);
        }
    }
};
```

This separation ensures that even if Blueprint values are manipulated externally, the underlying game state remains protected.

Hardening Blueprint Graph Flow Against Direct Trigger Paths

Blueprint graphs contain flow control such as branch nodes, sequence nodes, custom events, and timelines. If any graph begins with a publicly callable event, attackers can bypass game rules by calling it directly. Every event chain must begin with a state validation step implemented in C++ or with checks driven by facts that cannot be externally modified.

The easiest design is to treat all Blueprint events as visual or presentation-driven flows rather than as authoritative logic bodies. Each event that results in a gameplay change must forward the request to validated C++ logic before performing any mutation.

In Listing 8-10, we illustrate a secure approach where a Blueprint event requests a critical action, but the action can only proceed if a C++-controlled state validator confirms the request.

- Blueprint Event RequestOpenChest: Never authoritative

- OpenChest_Internal(): Trusted implementation

- ValidateChestOpenState(): Prevents exploitation by checking internal conditions

- Separation of Event and Logic: Prevents direct Blueprint event spoofing

Listing 8-10. SecureChestEvent.cpp

```cpp
UCLASS()
class ASecureChest : public AActor
{
    GENERATED_BODY()

public:
    UFUNCTION(BlueprintCallable)
    void RequestOpenChest()
    {
        if (ValidateChestOpenState())
        {
            OpenChest_Internal();
        }
    }

private:
    bool ValidateChestOpenState() const
    {
        return !bHasBeenOpened && bPlayerNearby;
    }

    void OpenChest_Internal()
    {
        bHasBeenOpened = true;
        SpawnLoot();
    }

    bool bHasBeenOpened = false;
    bool bPlayerNearby = false;
};
```

This architecture ensures that external manipulations cannot force critical events without concurrence from trusted C++ code.

Creating Blueprint Honeypots and Tamper Traps

Blueprints can incorporate trap variables, fake functions, or decoy events designed to catch unauthorized manipulation. Unlike fully secured C++ logic, Blueprint graphs are traceable, making well-placed honeypots effective against amateur cheaters.

Decoy variables may include

- Fake unlock toggles

- Debug flags

- Misleading function names

- Meaningless integers or floats

If attackers modify these values or call decoy functions, the game can log the incident or trigger soft countermeasures. The purpose is not to stop expert attackers but to detect unsophisticated tampering early.

In Listing 8-11, we introduce a simple decoy function implemented in Blueprint but validated in C++. If this function is ever invoked, the C++ handler marks the profile as suspicious.

- FakeGodModeToggle: BlueprintCallable decoy.

- OnHoneypotTriggered(): Internal handler for tamper detection.

- TamperFlag: Set when honeypot is triggered.

- Passive Detection: No gameplay changes required.

Listing 8-11. BlueprintHoneypot.cpp

```cpp
UCLASS()
class ABlueprintHoneypot : public AActor
{
    GENERATED_BODY()

private:
    bool bTamperDetected = false;

    void OnHoneypotTriggered()
    {
```

```
        bTamperDetected = true;
    }

public:
    UFUNCTION(BlueprintCallable)
    void FakeGodModeToggle()
    {
        OnHoneypotTriggered();
    }

    bool HasTamperOccurred() const
    {
        return bTamperDetected;
    }
};
```

If attackers trigger this function while exploring assets, the game can record tampering behavior.

Blueprint Latent Actions and Exploit Timing Windows

Latent actions such as delays, timelines, async nodes, and latent Blueprint functions introduce timing windows that can be exploited. Attackers can manipulate memory to alter latent behavior or force certain latent nodes to complete instantly. Additionally, any gameplay-critical logic placed immediately after latent actions becomes vulnerable, because the latent execution point can be triggered from trainers or modified Blueprint calls without the intended sequencing.

Critical systems such as reward distribution, unlocking progression, transitioning levels, awarding experience, and handling death-state transitions must not depend solely on Blueprint latent nodes. If the continuation of a latent sequence represents a significant gameplay change, its execution must be barricaded behind C++ state validation.

In Listing 8-12, we illustrate a secure pattern that protects a latent-driven loot drop sequence. The Blueprint event initiates a cinematic delay, but the actual gameplay action is approved only after C++ re-validates combat and state conditions, ensuring no bypass is possible even if attackers accelerate or modify the latent path.

- RequestDropLoot(): Blueprint event initiating the flow

- OnLootDropSequenceCompleted(): Latent callback

- DropLoot_Internal(): Trusted final action

- ValidateDropState(): Ensures state legitimacy before executing drop logic

Listing 8-12. SecureLatentFlow.cpp

```
UCLASS()
class ASecureLootManager : public AActor
{
    GENERATED_BODY()

public:
    UFUNCTION(BlueprintCallable)
    void RequestDropLoot()
    {
        // Blueprint drives cinematic delay or visual sequence.
    }

    UFUNCTION(BlueprintCallable)
    void OnLootDropSequenceCompleted()
    {
        if (ValidateDropState())
        {
            DropLoot_Internal();
        }
    }

private:
    bool ValidateDropState() const
    {
```

```
    return bBossDefeated && !bRewardClaimed;
}

void DropLoot_Internal()
{
    bRewardClaimed = true;
    SpawnLoot();
}

bool bBossDefeated = true;
bool bRewardClaimed = false;
};
```

This pattern mitigates latent exploit timing vulnerabilities by requiring a second, validated approval before proceeding.

Protecting Blueprint Data Assets and Data Tables

Data Assets, CurveTables, and DataTables in Unreal Engine are heavily used to store game-balancing values, progression definitions, loot tiers, narrative bindings, or skill trees. While these tools increase flexibility, they also become a major exploit surface when extracted from packaged content.

Attackers can

- Modify loot probabilities

- Change XP requirements

- Unlock skills prematurely

- Adjust difficulty scaling

- Remove cost restrictions

- Modify enemy stats

Blueprint-driven systems often rely on these assets without validating whether the values remain within expected ranges. Data integrity must be enforced in C++, especially during runtime loading.

In Listing 8-13, we introduce a secure Data Asset wrapper where the C++ layer verifies values as they are retrieved. This method allows developers to catch tampering even if Data Asset files have been modified, corrupted, or replaced by attackers.

- LoadSkillData(): Loads data and applies validation

- ValidateSkillData(): Ensures data remains within expected parameters

- SkillDataTable: Stored securely in project content but checked per use

- Fallback Logic: Prevents invalid data from being used

Listing 8-13. SecureDataAssetWrapper.cpp

```cpp
UCLASS()
class USecureSkillLoader : public UObject
{
    GENERATED_BODY()

public:
    UPROPERTY(EditAnywhere)
    UDataTable* SkillDataTable;

    bool LoadSkillData(FName RowName, FSkillData& OutData)
    {
        if (!SkillDataTable) return false;

        FSkillData* Row = SkillDataTable->FindRow<FSkillData>(RowName,
TEXT(""));
        if (!Row) return false;

        if (ValidateSkillData(*Row))
        {
            OutData = *Row;
            return true;
        }

        return false;
    }
```

```
private:
    bool ValidateSkillData(const FSkillData& Data) const
    {
        if (Data.RequiredLevel < 1 || Data.RequiredLevel > 100)
        {
            return false;
        }
        if (Data.Cost < 0 || Data.Cost > 100000)
        {
            return false;
        }
        return true;
    }
};
```

This protects against DataTable tampering by ensuring that unsafe modifications are detected before they influence gameplay.

Encrypting Blueprint Parameter Channels Without Cryptography

While cryptography belongs in Chapter 6, Blueprint-safe design relies on an alternative technique: **semantic obfuscation**. Semantic obfuscation does not encrypt values, but it reduces the predictability and interpretability of parameters passed through Blueprint graphs.

For example, rather than passing raw XP values directly through Blueprint nodes, developers can pass abstracted tokens or enumerations that represent categories of XP awards. These tokens are resolved in C++ using secure logic.

In Listing 8-14, we create a safe XP awarding interface where Blueprint passes an enumerated token rather than an integer. This reduces the attack surface by preventing attackers from passing arbitrary XP amounts.

- EXPAwardType: Enumerated categories instead of free integers.

- AwardXP_Internal(EXPAwardType): Internal logic determines real XP values.

- AwardXP(EXPAwardType): BlueprintCallable interface.

- Prevents Arbitrary Overrides: Attackers cannot inject unrealistic values.

Listing 8-14. SecureAwardToken.cpp

```cpp
UENUM(BlueprintType)
enum class EXPAwardType : uint8
{
    Small,
    Medium,
    Large
};

UCLASS()
class AExperienceManager : public AActor
{
    GENERATED_BODY()

private:
    void AwardXP_Internal(EXPAwardType AwardType)
    {
        int32 Amount = 0;

        switch (AwardType)
        {
            case EXPAwardType::Small: Amount = 10; break;
            case EXPAwardType::Medium: Amount = 50; break;
            case EXPAwardType::Large: Amount = 200; break;
        }

        CurrentXP += Amount;
    }

public:
    UFUNCTION(BlueprintCallable)
    void AwardXP(EXPAwardType AwardType)
    {
```

```
        AwardXP_Internal(AwardType);
    }
private:
    int32 CurrentXP = 0;
};
```

This technique greatly reduces the risk of arbitrary value injection through Blueprint.

Refactoring Blueprint State Machines for Security

Blueprint state machines, especially Animation Blueprints or Gameplay Ability state graphs, often contain exposed transition rules and conditions. Attackers can manipulate variables to force illegal transitions or skip necessary prerequisites. These manipulations might bypass cooldowns, unlock abilities prematurely, or cause the player to activate otherwise restricted states.

To secure Blueprint state machines:

- Move key transition conditions to C++.

- Use C++ to validate prerequisites for each critical state.

- Expose only visual or UI-safe flags to Blueprints.

- Ensure animation-driven logic remains presentation-only.

- Prevent abilities from activating solely based on Blueprint checks.

In Listing 8-15, we provide a secure ability activation handler where Blueprint requests an ability activation, but C++ enforces cooldowns, costs, and prerequisites before approving the transition.

- CanActivateAbility_Internal(): Verifies all rules

- RequestActivateAbility(): Blueprint entry point

- Ability Activation: Performed only after validation

- Prevents state machine bypasses

Listing 8-15. SecureAbilityActivation.cpp

```cpp
UCLASS()
class AAbilityManager : public AActor
{
    GENERATED_BODY()

public:
    UFUNCTION(BlueprintCallable)
    void RequestActivateAbility(FName AbilityName)
    {
        if (CanActivateAbility_Internal(AbilityName))
        {
            ActivateAbility_Internal(AbilityName);
        }
    }

private:
    bool CanActivateAbility_Internal(const FName& AbilityName) const
    {
        const bool bOffCooldown = !Cooldowns.Contains(AbilityName);
        const bool bHasCost = AbilityCosts.Contains(AbilityName) &&
        CurrentResource >= AbilityCosts[AbilityName];
        const bool bUnlocked = UnlockedAbilities.Contains(AbilityName);

        return bOffCooldown && bHasCost && bUnlocked;
    }

    void ActivateAbility_Internal(const FName& AbilityName)
    {
        CurrentResource -= AbilityCosts[AbilityName];
        Cooldowns.Add(AbilityName);
    }

    int32 CurrentResource = 100;
    TSet<FName> UnlockedAbilities;
    TMap<FName, int32> AbilityCosts;
    TSet<FName> Cooldowns;
};
```

This approach ensures that even if state machines reveal gameplay structure, attackers cannot invoke transitions without satisfying rules.

Case Study 1: Exposed Skill Unlock Paths in an Indie RPG

An independently developed RPG shipped with all skill unlock logic implemented in a single large Blueprint graph. Each skill node checked only the player level and a Boolean flag representing whether the skill had been previously unlocked. Unfortunately, both values were stored in Blueprint defaults and directly modifiable through trainer calls.

Attackers discovered the Blueprint node names by extracting .uasset files and began calling methods such as UnlockSkill without validation. The game had no internal validation, no C++ gating, and no progression-level fingerprinting. Players gained full access to all skills within minutes of game launch.

This case demonstrates how even well-structured Blueprint graphs can be compromised if critical logic remains in an exposed scripting layer.

Case Study 2: UI Button Exploits in a Survival Game

A survival-focused title left several debug-only UI buttons inside Widget Blueprints. These buttons invoked BlueprintCallable functions that granted resources, skipped weather cycles, and teleported the player. The developers disabled the debug UI in shipping builds but did not remove the underlying functions or separate the debug paths from the production paths.

When attackers extracted the UI assets, they discovered button-bound function names such as GiveWood, GiveFood, and TeleportHome. They then invoked these functions directly through trainers. The debug UI was hidden, but the callable Blueprint functions remained accessible.

This reinforces the need for C++ gating around all UI-facing functions and the avoidance of persistent debug functions in shipping builds.

Conclusion

Blueprints are powerful tools for rapid development and visual logic control, but they also reveal much of a game's internal structure. Attackers can analyze Blueprint scripts, modify exposed variables, invoke dangerous functions, and bypass intended logic by exploiting reflection metadata and callable surfaces. Securing Blueprints requires a layered architectural approach where scripting serves only as a front-end, while authoritative logic and core state changes reside exclusively in C++ under strict validation. When Blueprint exposure is treated as a legitimate security threat, developers gain tighter control over gameplay integrity and provide players with a fairer, more stable experience.

In the next chapter, we will examine another often-overlooked attack surface: the Unreal Engine developer console and configuration system.

CHAPTER 9

Disabling Console and Developer Access

Unreal Engine provides a powerful set of internal tools for developers, including the in-game console, debug CVars, exec functions, and configuration overrides. These tools are invaluable during development because they allow rapid iteration, state inspection, profiling, and temporary manipulation of gameplay conditions.

In a shipping build, however, these same tools become significant liabilities. Attackers quickly learn to exploit developer-facing systems that were never meant for player access, using them as entry points to bypass rules, alter systems, or force internal states that would never occur naturally.

A key principle of game security is simple: **any surface exposed to the player can eventually be controlled by the player**, even if the developer never intended that exposure. This applies not only to commands accessed through the tilde (~) console, but also to hidden developer commands, engine CVars that change gameplay behavior, and configuration files that allow debug-level overrides.

These surfaces collectively form a high-value attack vector because they were originally designed to modify game behavior.

Once a trainer or modding tool discovers how to route calls through these interfaces, entire categories of gameplay logic become vulnerable. To secure a single-player game effectively, developers must systematically disable or harden all developer interfaces. This includes

- Removing the console subsystem

- Restricting or locking CVars

- Sanitizing exec functions

© Sheikh Sohel Moon 2026

S. S. Moon, *Securing Single-Player Games in Unreal Engine*, https://doi.org/10.1007/979-8-8688-2833-1_9

- Validating configuration files

- Removing developer modules from builds

The following sections explain how the Unreal console works, why CVars are dangerous, how exec functions expose vulnerabilities, and how these systems can be hardened.

Understanding the Console and CVar Attack Surface

Unreal Engine's console is not just a UI; it is a routing mechanism. Behind the scenes, the console is implemented primarily through the UConsole class, which processes incoming commands, resolves them to console variables or exec functions, and executes the results. The console itself is typically created by UGameViewportClient, meaning that even if the player never sees a visible console window, its machinery may still exist.

When the user presses the tilde key (~), the viewport routes the input event to UConsole, which then interprets the typed command. However, the far more serious issue is that **external tools can call console commands even when the user cannot see the console UI at all**. Cheat frameworks can inject these commands silently through internal engine routes or by simulating input directly on the viewport or player controller. For this reason, simply hiding the console screen is not enough; the system must be disabled at a deeper architectural level.

Why CVars Are Dangerous in Shipping Builds

Console variables (CVars) power a significant portion of the engine. Many of Unreal's internal systems depend heavily on dynamic configuration, which is why CVars exist in categories such as

- **r.** (rendering)

- **sg.** (scalability presets)

- **ai.** (AI debugging and simulation)

- **net.** (network behavior and replication simulation)

- **p.** (physics and collision)

- **wp.** (weapon or world partition, depending on project conventions)

In development, these variables support testing and fine-tuning. In a shipping build, however, they give attackers direct read/write control over critical subsystems. For example:

- Changing ai.debug flags can affect how AI senses the player.

- Modifying physics CVars can disable recoil or fall damage.

- Adjusting rendering CVars can reveal occluded enemies.

- Enabling network profiling CVars can expose gameplay timing.

Even worse, some CVars affect **damage application, character movement, and stamina drain**, allowing players to modify combat or progression without touching memory.

Exec Functions and Hidden Cheat Entry Points

Any function marked with UFUNCTION(Exec) becomes callable from the console, regardless of whether it is publicly documented. This is often used for debugging or internal testing:

- Teleporting

- Giving items

- Unlocking levels

- Modifying player stats

- Triggering events

- Enabling freecam or debug camera

Trainers can enumerate all exec functions by scanning the object registry or analyzing UFunction metadata. This means that even a single forgotten debug exec command can become a complete game-breaker.

For example:

```
UFUNCTION(Exec)
void GodMode();
```

If this survives into the shipping build, it is an invitation to cheat. Securing Exec commands therefore requires both discovery and restriction.

Disabling the Console in Shipping Builds

The Unreal Engine console is one of the most powerful developer utilities available, but it becomes one of the most dangerous attack vectors when included in a shipping build. Even if the visible console UI is hidden, the command-execution pipeline may still exist internally.

Attackers can exploit this hidden pipeline to re-enable debug commands or modify gameplay variables. To eliminate this attack surface, developers must prevent the console from being created at all.

Unreal Engine relies on the **viewport client** to instantiate the console subsystem. Specifically, `UGameViewportClient` creates the `UConsole` object responsible for command routing.

By replacing the viewport client with a custom implementation that does not create a console object, developers can disable the console at its root.

This approach has four major benefits:

- It removes console creation entirely, not just hiding UI access.

- It ensures external tools cannot silently invoke console commands, because the underlying processor does not exist.

- It blocks exec command routing, since those depend on console parsing.

- It prevents accidental re-enablement if some other subsystem tries to spawn a console.

The following listings define a minimal but robust override of the default viewport client to remove console instantiation.

Listing 9-1 introduces UNoConsoleViewportClient, a viewport client that blocks all console-related creation paths.

- UNoConsoleViewportClient: Replaces Unreal's default viewport client

- ViewportConsole property overridden to nullify console allocation

- CreateConsole Override: Ensures no console object is ever instantiated

- Safe for Shipping Builds: No dependency on editor features or debug modules

Listing 9-1. UNoConsoleViewportClient.h

```
#pragma once

#include "Engine/GameViewportClient.h"
#include "NoConsoleViewportClient.generated.h"

UCLASS()
class UNoConsoleViewportClient : public UGameViewportClient
{
    GENERATED_BODY()

public:
    virtual void CreateConsole() override;
};
```

This header defines a custom viewport client that overrides the default console creation path.

Listing 9-2 implements the override that permanently blocks console instantiation.

- CreateConsole() Override Left Intentionally Empty: Prevents the engine from spawning a console component

- ViewportConsole = nullptr: Ensures no residual references remain

- Fully Functional in Shipping Builds: Does not affect any non-console engine systems

- Stops external trainers from routing hidden console requests

Listing 9-2. UNoConsoleViewportClient.cpp

```
#include "NoConsoleViewportClient.h"

void UNoConsoleViewportClient::CreateConsole()
{
    // Block console creation entirely
    ViewportConsole = nullptr;
}
```

This implementation prevents the engine from spawning a console object, ensuring that no console command routing system exists at runtime.

Build-Level Removal of Console Bindings

While removing UConsole at runtime is essential, developers should also ensure that the build pipeline does not unintentionally restore console components. Certain engine modules contain debug UI systems, console overlays, or editor-mode features that attempt to create or reference console objects. Removing or disabling these modules for shipping builds ensures that no back-paths to console creation remain.

Typical modules to avoid:

- DeveloperSettings

- DevMenu

- CrashDebugHelper

- EditorStyle/EditorWidgets

- EditorScriptingUtilities

Although some of these modules may not create consoles directly, they often keep latent hooks that reference console systems or debug CVars. The safest strategy is to explicitly unregister or blacklist modules not required for shipping builds.

Input Routing Protection

Even when the console subsystem is removed, some attacks attempt to exploit input events in order to simulate console opening behavior. The tilde key (~) used for toggling the console is particularly targeted. Certain cheats or injected code may try to intercept input events and re-activate console-like behavior through alternative routes.

To prevent this, the player controller or input subsystem can block the tilde key globally in shipping configurations. This ensures that no matter what external tools attempt, the game never treats the tilde key as a privileged debug action.

Typical input protections include

- Overriding PlayerController to swallow the tilde key

- Blocking console-toggle key events at the input mapping layer

- Strip any remaining input bindings referencing console commands

- Removing debug camera and advanced editor bindings introduced during development

These protections ensure that even if a malicious trainer injects key events into the game, no internal system will treat them as console-relevant commands.

Hardening the CVar System

Console variables are registered dynamically and exposed globally through Unreal's console manager. Because they can influence rendering, AI, physics, and gameplay subsystems, CVars must be restricted carefully in shipping builds.

A hardened CVar security model typically includes several protections. Developers should

- Restrict write access for most CVars

- Allow only a small whitelist of safe variables

- Block runtime overrides from console or command-line sources

- Monitor suspicious modifications

To enforce these rules, the following manager class centralizes CVar security behavior.

Making Non-Whitelisted CVars Read-Only

Unreal Engine assigns each CVar a data structure containing its current value, access flags, and modification history. By controlling write access to these variables, developers can define which CVars are allowed to change at runtime and which must remain immutable. To enforce this cleanly, we introduce a small manager that

1. Stores a list of whitelisted CVar names

2. Walks through the registered console objects at startup

3. Marks every non-whitelisted CVar as read-only

Listing 9-3 declares FCVarSecurityManager, a utility responsible for whitelisting and protection of CVars at startup.

- FCVarSecurityManager: A small manager type that owns the whitelist and protection logic

- WhitelistedNames: A set of CVar names that are allowed to be modified at runtime

- AddWhitelistName: Lets you register additional safe CVars

- Initialize: Entry point to configure and then lock protected CVars

- ProtectAllCVars: Iterates through console objects and applies restrictions

- ProtectCVar: Sets read-only flags for a single CVar

- IsWhitelisted: Normalizes CVar names and checks against the whitelist

Listing 9-3. FCVarSecurityManager.h

```
#pragma once

#include "CoreMinimal.h"

class IConsoleVariable;

/**
 * FCVarSecurityManager
 *
 * A lightweight manager that enforces security policies on console
variables.
 * It collects a whitelist of safe CVars and forces all other CVars into
 * read-only mode in Shipping builds.
 */
struct FCVarSecurityManager
{
private:
    /** Names of CVars that are allowed to be modified at runtime. */
    TSet<FString> WhitelistedNames;
```

```
public:
    FCVarSecurityManager();

    /** Adds a single CVar name to the whitelist (case-insensitive). */
    void AddWhitelistName(const FString& Name);

    /**
     * Initializes the manager and applies protection rules.
     * Should be called once during startup, ideally in a game instance
     * or a custom subsystem.
     */
    void Initialize();

private:
    /** Returns true if the given CVar name is allowed to be modified. */
    bool IsWhitelisted(const FString& Name) const;

    /** Iterates over all console objects and protects non-whitelisted
    CVars. */
    void ProtectAllCVars() const;

    /** Applies read-only protection to a single CVar. */
    void ProtectCVar(IConsoleVariable* Var, const FString& Name) const;
};
```

This header defines a manager responsible for tracking a whitelist of safe console variables and applying security restrictions to all others.

Listing 9-4 implements the CVar security logic by traversing console objects and applying read-only flags to non-whitelisted entries.

- Constructor: Initializes the whitelist with a small set of known-safe CVars

- AddWhitelistName: Normalizes and inserts names into the whitelist set

- Initialize: Calls ProtectAllCVars after any project-specific whitelist entries are added

- ProtectAllCVars: Uses IConsoleManager to iterate over console objects and locate CVars

- ProtectCVar: Uses the CVar's own flag API to enforce read-only behavior for dangerous entries

- IsWhitelisted: Normalizes names to lowercase and checks membership in the whitelist

Listing 9-4. FCVarSecurityManager.cpp

```cpp
#include "FCVarSecurityManager.h"
#include "HAL/IConsoleManager.h"

FCVarSecurityManager::FCVarSecurityManager()
{
    // Register a minimal safe set here.
    // Project-specific CVars can be added from game code before
        Initialize() is called.
    AddWhitelistName(TEXT("r.ScreenPercentage"));
    AddWhitelistName(TEXT("sg.ViewDistanceQuality"));
}

void FCVarSecurityManager::AddWhitelistName(const FString& Name)
{
    WhitelistedNames.Add(Name.ToLower());
}

void FCVarSecurityManager::Initialize()
{
    ProtectAllCVars();
}

bool FCVarSecurityManager::IsWhitelisted(const FString& Name) const
{
    return WhitelistedNames.Contains(Name.ToLower());
}

void FCVarSecurityManager::ProtectAllCVars() const
{
    IConsoleManager& ConsoleMgr = IConsoleManager::Get();
```

```cpp
    // Visit every console object currently registered with the console
        manager.
    ConsoleMgr.ForEachConsoleObject(
        FConsoleObjectVisitor::CreateLambda(
            [this](const TCHAR* Name, IConsoleObject* Object)
            {
                if (IConsoleVariable* Var = Object->AsVariable())
                {
                    const FString VarName(Name);

                    if (!IsWhitelisted(VarName))
                    {
                        ProtectCVar(Var, VarName);
                    }
                }
            }));
}

void FCVarSecurityManager::ProtectCVar(IConsoleVariable* Var, const
FString& Name) const
{
    if (Var == nullptr)
    {
        return;
    }

    // Retrieve current flags and add read-only + cheat markers.
    EConsoleVariableFlags Flags = Var->GetFlags();

    Flags = (EConsoleVariableFlags)(Flags | ECVF_ReadOnly | ECVF_Cheat);

    Var->SetFlags(Flags);

    // Optionally, you could log which CVars have been locked for auditing:
    // UE_LOG(LogTemp, Verbose, TEXT("Protected CVar '%s' as read-
        only."), *Name);
}
```

This implementation iterates through the engine's console variable registry and marks non-whitelisted variables as read-only, preventing runtime manipulation.

CVar Category Restrictions

While name-based whitelisting offers precise control, some CVar categories are too dangerous to allow any runtime modification, regardless of individual entries. Categories such as ai.* and p.* (physics) fundamentally affect gameplay behavior. Rendering categories like r.* and sg.* can reveal occluded actors, disable vision-related effects, or alter the readability of combat encounters.

Typical high-risk categories include

- ai.*: AI behavior, sensing, perception, pathfinding, and decision making

- p.*: Physics simulation, collision behavior, and gravity

- Custom Gameplay Prefixes: Project-specific namespaces such as g., wp., or game.

- r.*: Rendering flags that can reveal hidden geometry or masked enemies

- sg.*: Scalability groups that directly change visual feedback and clarity

A robust security layer should combine **per-name whitelisting** with **prefix-level blocking.** In practice, that means treating any CVar that begins with a forbidden prefix as non-whitelisted by definition and forcing it into read-only mode, even if it was accidentally added to the whitelist.

You can extend FCVarSecurityManager with a small list of protected prefixes and modify IsWhitelisted to reject any CVar whose name starts with those prefixes. This produces a compact but powerful rule set that eliminates entire cheat classes while remaining easy to reason about and maintain.

Preventing Runtime CVar Overrides

Console commands are not the only way to modify CVars. Unreal Engine also supports modifications via

- Command-line arguments passed to the executable

- INI file entries in configuration files such as DefaultGame.ini or Engine.ini

- In-game console commands triggered via bindings or external injection

- Direct C++ calls issued by injected DLLs or trainer code

Each CVar stores information about its modification source through internal flags that distinguish between changes made by code, console, command line, or configuration systems. Attackers exploit this by

- Passing custom command-line arguments like -cheatsEnabled=1 or -ForceDebugView

- Dropping extra INI files that re-enable debug CVars or developer-only options

- Injecting DLLs that call SetByCode on sensitive CVars

A well-designed CVar security system must therefore combine

- **Startup stripping of unsafe command-line arguments** before CVars see them

- **Protection of CVars so that SetByConsole and SetByCommandLine are ignored** for non-whitelisted variables

- **Monitoring patterns of SetByCode writes** to detect suspicious modification behavior

Together with FCVarSecurityManager, these techniques transform the CVar system from an open configuration mechanism into a tightly controlled surface that no longer grants easy advantages to attackers.

Sanitizing Exec Functions

Exec functions are one of the most frequently overlooked security risks in Unreal Engine. Any function marked with UFUNCTION(Exec) becomes callable through the in-game console. While this is intended for debugging during development, it creates a silent, powerful attack surface in shipping builds.

Attackers benefit from exec functions because

- Exec functions bypass normal gameplay logic

- Exec functions accept arbitrary user input

- Exec functions can modify actor properties instantly

- Exec functions are visible to reflection, allowing enumeration

- Exec functions can be invoked *even if the visible console UI is disabled*

If a trainer or DLL injection script gains access to UGameViewportClient, APlayerController, or command routing structures, it can call any registered exec function silently. This makes sanitizing exec functions a mandatory step in any anti-cheat pipeline.

To address this problem, we take a two-layer approach:

1. **Discover all exec functions at startup** (so you know what is exposed).

2. **Restrict or disable dangerous exec functions** based on your security policy.

The following listings show how to scan the entire reflection system for exec functions and classify them for restriction.

Detecting All Exec Functions at Startup

Before restricting exec commands, developers must first know which ones exist. The Unreal reflection system makes it possible to scan all loaded classes and detect functions flagged with the FUNC_Exec specifier.

We start by building a scanner capable of walking through all UFUNCTIONs in all UClasses loaded into the reflection system. Every exec function is detected by checking for the appropriate function flags. This information can then be logged, filtered, or restricted.

This scanning process allows developers to audit the entire runtime environment and discover unexpected debug commands.

Listing 9-5 defines FExecScanner, which iterates through reflected types to find all exec functions.

- ExecFunctions: Stores the names of functions found with the exec flag

- ScanAll: Walks every loaded class in memory

- ScanClass: Inspects a single UClass and extracts exec-tagged functions

- IsExecFunction: Identifies a UFunction with the FUNC_Exec flag

- DumpToLog: Optional helper for debugging or auditing during development

Listing 9-5. FExecScanner.h

```cpp
#pragma once

#include "CoreMinimal.h"

class UClass;
class UFunction;

/**
 * FExecScanner
 *
 * Scans the Unreal reflection system to identify every Exec function
 * currently registered in the runtime environment. This enables developers
 * to audit which commands are exposed in packaged builds.
 */
struct FExecScanner
{
private:
    /** All discovered exec functions (ClassName.FunctionName format). */
    TArray<FString> ExecFunctions;
```

```cpp
public:
    /** Scans every loaded class to discover exec functions. */
    void ScanAll();

    /** Writes the collected exec functions to the log (optional). */
    void DumpToLog() const;

    /** Returns the results for external processing and filtering. */
    const TArray<FString>& GetResults() const { return ExecFunctions; }
private:
    /** Scans a single class for Exec functions. */
    void ScanClass(UClass* Class);

    /** Checks whether a function has the Exec flag. */
    bool IsExecFunction(UFunction* Func) const;
};
```

This header defines a clean, minimal scanning utility that can run at startup and gather all exposed exec functions.

Listing 9-6 implements the exec scanning logic using reflection and function flag inspection.

- ScanAll: Uses TObjectIterator<UClass> to iterate through all loaded class types.

- ScanClass: Walks the function list for each class.

- IsExecFunction: Checks the function flag mask for FUNC_Exec.

- Exec functions are appended in "Class.Function" naming format for clarity.

- DumpToLog: Emits the discovered functions into the UE log for auditing.

Listing 9-6. FExecScanner.cpp

```cpp
#include "FExecScanner.h"
#include "UObject/Class.h"
#include "UObject/UObjectIterator.h"
```

```cpp
#include "UObject/UnrealType.h"
#include "Engine/Engine.h"

void FExecScanner::ScanAll()
{
    ExecFunctions.Empty();

    for (TObjectIterator<UClass> It; It; ++It)
    {
        ScanClass(*It);
    }
}

void FExecScanner::ScanClass(UClass* Class)
{
    if (!Class)
    {
        return;
    }

    for (TFieldIterator<UFunction> FuncIt(Class, EFieldIteratorFlags::Inclu
    deSuper); FuncIt; ++FuncIt)
    {
        UFunction* Func = *FuncIt;

        if (IsExecFunction(Func))
        {
            const FString Entry = Class->GetName() + TEXT(".") + Func->
            GetName();
            ExecFunctions.Add(Entry);
        }
    }
}

bool FExecScanner::IsExecFunction(UFunction* Func) const
{
    if (!Func)
    {
```

```
        return false;
    }

    return Func->HasAllFunctionFlags(FUNC_Exec);
}

void FExecScanner::DumpToLog() const
{
    UE_LOG(LogTemp, Warning, TEXT("=== Exec Functions Discovered ==="));

    for (const FString& Entry : ExecFunctions)
    {
        UE_LOG(LogTemp, Warning, TEXT("%s"), *Entry);
    }
}
```

This implementation iterates through all loaded classes and records functions marked with the Exec flag, allowing developers to audit exposed commands. This scanner gives you complete visibility into every exec command active in your project. It forms the foundation for deeper sanitization.

Restricting Sensitive Exec Commands

Once you know which exec functions are present, the next step is to selectively restrict or disable the dangerous ones. This is especially important when

- Designers accidentally leave debug commands in production classes

- Blueprint-exposed exec nodes allow manipulation of internal states

- Editor-only utilities end up inside packaged builds

- Debug camera, stat commands, or cheat-enabling functions are left exposed

A proper restriction pass allows you to

- Whitelist only functions that are safe (such as screenshot utilities)

- Block functions that alter gameplay state

- Block any exec function whose class lives inside an "Editor" module

- Block exec bindings that affect rendering, physics, or networking

To perform restriction, we introduce a complementary manager that compares the scanned exec list against a whitelist.

Configuration File Attacks and Protection

Configuration files (DefaultGame.ini, Engine.ini, Scalability.ini, etc.) are one of the most overlooked attack surfaces in Unreal Engine. Even if your console is disabled and exec functions are locked down, a cheater who modifies your INI files can still enable cheats, adjust gameplay variables, modify rendering behavior, or bypass developer restrictions.

In single-player games, INI manipulation is one of the *most common* ways players defeat restrictions because

- INI files are plain text

- They load **before gameplay begins**, giving attackers influence early

- Unreal automatically merges config layers (Default → Project → User → Device profiles)

- Many sensitive properties are exposed directly in config

This section shows how to sanitize the configuration layer and prevent cheaters from modifying it to gain unfair advantages.

Sanitizing INI Files in Shipping Builds

Before hardening anything at runtime, developers must ensure the packaged project doesn't include unsafe or developer-only configuration flags. Many games accidentally ship with

- bEnableCheats=true

- AllowDebugViewmodes=1

- r.SetRes=1920x1080f

- p.NetShowCorrections=1

- vr.DebugCommands=1

Attackers can also inject these into the user's %AppData% or Saved/Config/Windows directory.

To prevent this, we introduce a lightweight ruleset similar to the exec rules file.

Listing 9-7 defines the sanitization rules for config files.

- [ForbiddenKeys]: List of config entries that must *never* appear

- [ForbiddenSections]: Entire categories blocked from loading

- [WhitelistOnly]: Optional mode that only allows explicitly listed keys

- Allows fast auditing for each release

- Loaded by the FConfigValidator class at startup

Listing 9-7. INISecurityRules.txt

```
[ForbiddenKeys]
[/Script/Engine.GameSession].bAllowCheats
[/Script/Engine.RendererSettings].r.AllowOcclusionQueries
[/Script/Engine.Engine].bUseFixedFrameRate
[/Script/Engine.InputSettings].ConsoleKeys
[/Script/Engine.Engine].bEnableOnScreenDebugMessages

[ForbiddenSections]
[/Script/UnrealEd.EditorEngine]
[/Script/Engine.DebugCameraController]
[/Script/Engine.Console]

[WhitelistOnly]
; Optional:
; If enabled, only whitelisted config entries are allowed.
; Disabled by default.
Enabled=false
```

This rule file defines forbidden configuration entries and sections that should never appear in a shipping build.

Config Validation System

To enforce the rules, we introduce FConfigValidator, which

- Loads rules from INISecurityRules.txt

- Iterates through all loaded config files

- Detects forbidden keys, forbidden sections, or user-modified values

- Rejects or resets invalid entries before gameplay begins

- Logs violations for telemetry or anti-tampering monitoring

Listing 9-8 declares FConfigValidator, which scans config entries against all rule sets.

- ForbiddenKeys: Fully qualified property names

- ForbiddenSections: Entire config categories

- bWhitelistMode: Optional strict mode

- LoadRules(): Reads INISecurityRules.txt

- ValidateAllConfigs(): Scans all config layers

- ValidateEntry(): Core logic for enforcing rules

- StripForbiddenKeys(): Removes invalid entries before gameplay

Listing 9-8. FConfigValidator.h

```cpp
#pragma once

#include "CoreMinimal.h"

/**
 * FConfigValidator
 *
 * Validates configuration files before they affect gameplay.
 * Enforces forbidden-key rules and removes unsafe config entries.
 */
```

```cpp
struct FConfigValidator
{
private:
    TArray<FString> ForbiddenKeys;
    TArray<FString> ForbiddenSections;
    bool bWhitelistMode = false;

public:
    void LoadRules();
    void ValidateAllConfigs();

private:
    bool IsForbiddenSection(const FString& Section) const;
    bool IsForbiddenKey(const FString& FullyQualifiedKey) const;
    void StripForbiddenKeys(const FString& IniFilename) const;
};
```

This header defines a validator responsible for loading rule sets and scanning configuration files.

Listing 9-9 implements the validator, scanning all config layers and removing unsafe entries before the game reads them.

- Reads the rule file

- Determines which INI sections or keys are unsafe

- Iterates through all config files found in the runtime directory

- Calls StripForbiddenKeys() to remove invalid entries

- Prevents debug-cheat flags from taking effect in packaged builds

Listing 9-9. FConfigValidator.cpp

```cpp
#include "FConfigValidator.h"
#include "Misc/FileHelper.h"
#include "Misc/Paths.h"
#include "Misc/ConfigCacheIni.h"
```

```cpp
void FConfigValidator::LoadRules()
{
    ForbiddenKeys.Empty();
    ForbiddenSections.Empty();
    bWhitelistMode = false;

    FString RulesPath = FPaths::ProjectContentDir() / TEXT("Security/
    INISecurityRules.txt");
    TArray<FString> Lines;

    if (!FFileHelper::LoadFileToStringArray(Lines, *RulesPath))
    {
        UE_LOG(LogTemp, Warning, TEXT("INISecurityRules.txt not found."));
        return;
    }

    enum class ESection { None, ForbiddenKeys, ForbiddenSections,
    WhitelistOnly };
    ESection Current = ESection::None;

    for (const FString& Line : Lines)
    {
        if (Line.StartsWith(TEXT("[ForbiddenKeys]")))
        {
            Current = ESection::ForbiddenKeys;
        }
        else if (Line.StartsWith(TEXT("[ForbiddenSections]")))
        {
            Current = ESection::ForbiddenSections;
        }
        else if (Line.StartsWith(TEXT("[WhitelistOnly]")))
        {
            Current = ESection::WhitelistOnly;
        }
        else if (!Line.TrimStartAndEnd().IsEmpty())
        {
            if (Current == ESection::ForbiddenKeys)
```

```cpp
            {
                ForbiddenKeys.Add(Line.TrimStartAndEnd());
            }
            else if (Current == ESection::ForbiddenSections)
            {
                ForbiddenSections.Add(Line.TrimStartAndEnd());
            }
            else if (Current == ESection::WhitelistOnly)
            {
                const bool bEnable = Line.Contains(TEXT("Enabled=true"));
                if (bEnable)
                {
                    bWhitelistMode = true;
                }
            }
        }
    }
}

bool FConfigValidator::IsForbiddenSection(const FString& Section) const
{
    return ForbiddenSections.Contains(Section);
}

bool FConfigValidator::IsForbiddenKey(const FString&
FullyQualifiedKey) const
{
    return ForbiddenKeys.Contains(FullyQualifiedKey);
}

void FConfigValidator::StripForbiddenKeys(const FString& IniFilename) const
{
    FConfigFile Config;
    if (!Config.Read(IniFilename))
    {
        return;
    }
```

```cpp
for (auto SectionIt = Config.CreateConstIterator(); SectionIt;
++SectionIt)
{
    const FString& SectionName = SectionIt->Key;

    if (IsForbiddenSection(SectionName))
    {
        UE_LOG(LogTemp, Warning, TEXT("Removing forbidden section:
        %s"), *SectionName);
        Config.Remove(SectionName);
        continue;
    }

    const FConfigSection& Section = SectionIt->Value;

    for (const auto& Pair : Section)
    {
        const FString FullyQualified = SectionName + TEXT(".") + Pair.
        Key.ToString();

        if (IsForbiddenKey(FullyQualified))
        {
            UE_LOG(LogTemp, Warning, TEXT("Stripping forbidden key:
            %s"), *FullyQualified);
            Config.RemoveKey(SectionName, Pair.Key.ToString());
        }
    }
}

Config.Write(IniFilename);
}

void FConfigValidator::ValidateAllConfigs()
{
    // Validate DefaultGame.ini, GameUserSettings.ini, and platform
        config layers.
    TArray<FString> IniFiles;
```

```cpp
FPaths::FindFilesRecursive(
    IniFiles,
    *(FPaths::ProjectDir() / TEXT("Saved/Config")),
    TEXT("*.ini"),
    true
);

for (const FString& Ini : IniFiles)
{
    StripForbiddenKeys(Ini);
}
}
```

This implementation scans all configuration files and removes forbidden entries before gameplay systems read them.

Build Pipeline Hardening

Even with runtime protections in place, developer tools can still appear in packaged builds if the build pipeline is not configured carefully.

Unreal Engine includes many editor-only modules that should never ship with a final game. Attackers often search packaged files for debug menus, developer tools, or hidden UI elements.

To prevent this, the build system must explicitly remove unnecessary modules.

Removing Developer Modules at Build Time

Unreal Engine includes many editor-only modules that should never be compiled into a shipping build. If left enabled, attackers can

- Re-enable editor features

- Trigger debugging tools

- Access development menus

- Call hidden debug UI panels

- Load internal commands

To prevent this, we strip modules across

- .uproject > Modules

- .Build.cs file flags

- Required/optional build dependencies

We introduce a simple, centralized module blacklist to help ensure nothing unsafe ever compiles.

Listing 9-10 defines a blacklist for modules that should never ship in a packaged build.

- ForbiddenModules: Module names that must not be loaded

- StripModules(): Removes invalid entries at build time

- Integrates into your project's Target.cs

Listing 9-10. DeveloperModuleBlacklist.txt

```
# These modules must never appear in a shipping build.
UnrealEd
EditorStyle
EditorWidgets
DeveloperSettings
DeveloperToolSettings
Persona
BlueprintGraph
KismetCompiler
FunctionalTesting
GameplayDebugger
AutomationController
ViewportInteraction
EditorFramework
```

This file defines modules that should never appear in a shipping build.

Listing 9-11 declares FModuleStripper, which inspects the module list for forbidden entries.

- Loads blacklist from text file

- Scans the list of modules included in the target

- Logs warnings for any module that must be removed

- Supports integration into both .Build.cs and Target.cs

Listing 9-11. FModuleStripper.h

```cpp
#pragma once

#include "CoreMinimal.h"

/**
 * FModuleStripper
 *
 * Removes forbidden editor/developer modules from Shipping targets.
 */
struct FModuleStripper
{
private:
    TArray<FString> ForbiddenModules;

public:
    void LoadBlacklist();
    void StripModules(TArray<FString>& ModuleList);
};
```

This header declares a module-filtering utility used during the build process.

Listing 9-12 implements the stripper, removing unsafe modules before the build is generated.

- Reads blacklist file

- Compares each module name

- Removes matching entries

- Logs every removal for auditing

- Prevents accidental inclusion of dev-only features

Listing 9-12. FModuleStripper.cpp

```cpp
#include "FModuleStripper.h"
#include "Misc/FileHelper.h"
#include "Misc/Paths.h"

void FModuleStripper::LoadBlacklist()
{
    ForbiddenModules.Empty();

    const FString Path = FPaths::ProjectContentDir() / TEXT("Security/
    DeveloperModuleBlacklist.txt");

    TArray<FString> Lines;
    if (!FFileHelper::LoadFileToStringArray(Lines, *Path))
    {
        UE_LOG(LogTemp, Warning, TEXT("DeveloperModuleBlacklist.txt not
        found."));
        return;
    }

    for (const FString& Line : Lines)
    {
        const FString Clean = Line.TrimStartAndFnd();
        if (!Clean.IsEmpty() && !Clean.StartsWith(TEXT("#")))
        {
            ForbiddenModules.Add(Clean);
        }
    }
}

void FModuleStripper::StripModules(TArray<FString>& ModuleList)
{
    for (int32 i = ModuleList.Num() - 1; i >= 0; --i)
    {
```

```
    const FString& Module = ModuleList[i];

    if (ForbiddenModules.Contains(Module))
    {
        UE_LOG(LogTemp, Warning, TEXT("Stripping forbidden module:
        %s"), *Module);
        ModuleList.RemoveAt(i);
    }
  }
}
```

This implementation removes developer modules from the build configuration before packaging.

Removing Debug Commands from PAK Files

Even if modules are removed, leftover debug widgets or console UI fragments may remain inside your .pak files. Tools like FModel allow cheaters to browse through UI assets and find

- Debug menus

- Cheat buttons

- Editor-only widgets

- Test maps

- Developer console panels

To prevent this, we provide a simple blacklist of filenames and directory patterns. Listing 9-13 defines a PAK blacklist to filter assets during packaging.

- Rejects debug UI assets

- Blocks editor-only materials and widgets

- Ensures maps and content prefixed with "Dev_", "Test_", etc., are excluded

- Works with UnrealPak's -create=... rules

Listing 9-13. PakBlacklist.txt

```
# Forbidden folders
/Content/Dev/
/Content/Debug/
/Content/Editor/
/Content/Test/

# Forbidden asset name patterns
*DebugMenu*
*DevMenu*
*TestMap*
*EditorWidget*
*DebugPanel*
*CheatUI*
```

This blacklist prevents debug UI assets and developer maps from being packaged into the final build.

Unsafe Build Flags That Must Be Removed

Unreal's build configuration system includes several flags that completely destroy security if enabled in shipping builds. These must be *disabled*:

- bCompileICU=true (causes huge debug symbols)

- bUseLoggingInShipping=true (exposes console)

- bAllowConsoleInShipping=true

- bBuildDeveloperTools=true

- bCompileAgainstEngine=true (can expose internal headers)

- bUseChecksInShipping=true (debug checks become exploitable)

Below is the corrected configuration.

Listing 9-14 shows the recommended shipping build target settings.

- Fully disables console and dev tools

- Removes editor support

- Ensures no debug flags slip into packaged builds

Listing 9-14. YourGame.Target.cs (Shipping Safe Version)

```
using UnrealBuildTool;
using System.Collections.Generic;

public class YourGameTarget : TargetRules
{
    public YourGameTarget(TargetInfo Target) : base(Target)
    {
        Type = TargetType.Game;
        DefaultBuildSettings = BuildSettingsVersion.V2;
        IncludeOrderVersion = EngineIncludeOrderVersion.Unreal5_1;

        bUsesSteam = false;
        bBuildDeveloperTools = false;
        bUseLoggingInShipping = false;
        bAllowConsoleInShipping = false;

        ExtraModuleNames = new List<string> { "YourGame" };
    }
}
```

This configuration disables console access, developer tools, and debug logging in the shipping build.

Platform-Specific Rules

Unreal Engine targets many platforms, but each platform exposes a different set of debugging interfaces, developer backdoors, and command channels that attackers can abuse. Even if your console and CVar systems are fully locked down, platform-level behavior can reintroduce vulnerabilities through external tools.

This section describes how to harden your shipping build across **Windows**, **Linux**, and **Android**, which are the most common platforms for single-player titles. Each platform requires specialized treatment because each one exposes unique debugging surfaces.

Windows Shipping Considerations

Windows provides the richest and most mature debugging ecosystem. Tools such as x64dbg, Cheat Engine, Process Hacker, and DLL injectors rely on Windows APIs that interact directly with your game process. It is critical to harden your build against these platform-level risks.

The biggest threats on Windows are

- Debug pipe attachment (DebugActiveProcess)

- DLL search path hijacking

- Console window exposure

- Side-channel debugging via pause events

- Easy command-line tampering

- External module injection

Below we examine each and outline recommended protections.

Preventing Console Window Exposure

Some packaged Unreal builds still spawn a console window if

- The build was compiled with any leftover debug flags

- The -log parameter is injected

- The application inherits a subsystem that still expects a console

Revealing a console is dangerous because it creates a direct feedback loop that reveals engine logs, CVar behavior, memory failures, and module status.

To ensure no console is spawned:

- Set the project's Windows subsystem to "Windows" (not "Console").

- Remove any accidental UE_BUILD_DEVELOPMENT checks that enable the logging window.

- Sanitize command-line arguments early (as implemented in the previous part).

Harden DLL Search Paths

Windows loads DLLs using a search order that can be manipulated by attackers. If your game attempts to load SomeDependency.dll, Windows will search in

1. The game's directory

2. The system directory

3. The Windows directory

4. The PATH chain

Attackers exploit this by dropping **malicious DLLs** in your game folder. Mitigation:

- Use **absolute paths** for all manually loaded DLLs.

- Use LoadLibraryEx with the LOAD_LIBRARY_SEARCH_ APPLICATION_DIR flag.

- Never rely on PATH directories.

- Package dependent DLLs inside Paks if possible.

This increases resistance to DLL preloading attacks.

Disable Debug Pipes

Windows debuggers attach via DebugActiveProcess, which communicates through a series of internal pipes. If your build does not explicitly deny such attachments, any debugger running with the same user permissions can attach.

Mitigation techniques:

- Monitor debug events via CheckRemoteDebuggerPresent.

- Use periodic internal breakpoint detection (covered in Chapter 5's timing based anti-debugging section).

- Ensure your shipping config defines bDisableDebugWindow = true.

These do not completely prevent kernel-level debuggers, but they stop most user-mode attachments.

Protect Against Remote Thread Injection

Most Windows cheat tools inject cheats by creating a remote thread in your process via

- CreateRemoteThread

- NtCreateThreadEx

- QueueUserAPC

While you cannot reliably block these calls from user space, you *can* detect the side effects:

- Unexpected new threads appearing with suspicious module start addresses

- Threads starting inside memory regions that do not belong to your executable

- Thread names that do not match Unreal Engine conventions

This is handled in your thread scanner (Listings 5-5 and 5-6), but Windows rules reinforce why those detectors are necessary.

Linux Shipping Considerations

Linux exposes different debugging and injection pathways than Windows. Tools like gdb, lldb, and ptrace are the primary methods attackers use to tamper with the game process.

Because ptrace is the core debugging interface, you must start by controlling it.

Locking Down ptrace

By default, Linux allows any process owned by the same user to use ptrace to debug another process. This means attackers can attach to your game using

```
gdb --pid=<yourpid>
```

or

```
strace -p <yourpid>
```

To mitigate this

- Disallow ptrace using prctl(PR_SET_DUMPABLE, 0).

- Use /proc/sys/kernel/yama/ptrace_scope to limit ptrace access.

- Ship with hardened kernel parameters if possible.

These measures prevent most standard attach attempts on Linux.

Minimal Logging and stdout/stderr Suppression

Many Linux builds leak internal engine logs through stdout or stderr, even when you disable logging inside Unreal. External tools can capture this output stream to reverse-engineer internal behavior.

Mitigation:

- Route stdout to /dev/null in shipping builds.

- Use Unreal's internal log suppression flags.

- Disable or sanitize print statements in game code and plugins.

Shared Object Injection Risks

Linux cheat tools often abuse LD_PRELOAD to inject malicious .so libraries before the game even starts.

An attacker might launch

```
LD_PRELOAD=./hack.so ./YourGame-Linux-Shipping
```

This is extremely dangerous because the injected library can override any system function.

Mitigation:

- Always unset LD_PRELOAD during your launch script.

- Validate environment variables on startup.

- Use early integrity checks to detect function patching.

These add meaningful friction to injection on Linux systems.

Android Shipping Considerations

Android has its own set of risks due to its sandbox model and the prevalence of modded APKs, repackaged assets, and runtime hooking libraries like Frida, Xposed, and GameGuardian.

Because Android builds are frequently attacked by single-player cheaters, shipping security is crucial.

Minimizing logcat Exposure

Android's logcat system can leak

- CVar names

- Internal debug strings

- Engine errors

- Network information

- Binding hints

Attackers use logcat to locate the exact events or C++ functions they want to hook. Mitigation:

- Set logcat filtering to suppress everything except fatal errors.

- Disable engine log categories in shipping builds.

- Strip verbose logging at compile time.

Blocking JNI Debug Entry Points

Android apps can be debugged using JDWP or certain JNI flags. Cheaters who inject Frida scripts or Xposed modules often rely on these debug entry points.

To mitigate

- Disable JDWP in the manifest.

- Remove all native debug symbols.

- Use secure loading flags for .so libraries.

APK Repacking and Tampered Asset Detection

APK modding is the most common form of Android single-player cheating.
Attackers often

- Extract the APK

- Modify Paks

- Repack the APK

- Re-sign it

Your game must detect this.
Mitigation strategies:

- Validate your signing certificate on startup.

- Hash your Paks and compare them against known values.

- Check for mismatched package names.

- Guard against stripped or modified assets.

This mirrors your Pak protection logic (coming in Chapter 12), but applied to
Android's ecosystem.

Case Study 1: Runtime Console Exploitation Unlocks All Debug Commands in a UE Shooter

This incident occurred in a commercially released single-player shooter where certain
debug commands were unintentionally included in the shipping build. The developers
assumed that the console would not be accessible, but attackers quickly discovered that
the console subsystem had been compiled into the viewport client.
Attackers found that

- Pressing the tilde key revealed a hidden debug console

- god, fly, ghost, and allammo were still compiled in

- Several internal commands such as DebugGiveWeapon were still
  marked as exec

- Many rendering CVars remained writable, enabling wallhack-style graphics adjustments

- The UI contained a debug stats binding that was still active

Using these primitives, players were able to

- Enable invincibility

- Teleport through collision

- Skip boss encounters

- Force unlock all weapons

- Print internal actor lists to the console

This drastically reduced the difficulty of the game and spread quickly through forums that shared "command lists" and "cheat walkthroughs."

If exec commands are exposed, they will be enumerated. If CVars remain writable, they will be abused. The case highlights why the sections on disabling the console in Shipping builds, hardening the CVar system, and sanitizing Exec functions must be treated as mandatory security work rather than optional hardening.

- Developer console subsystem was not disabled.

- Exec functions were shipped without sanitization.

- No whitelist of safe CVar categories.

- Rendering CVars such as r.Fog and r.PostProcessAAQuality remained writable.

Case Study 2: INI Injection Unlocks Hidden God Mode and Developer Cheats

In this case, a single-player RPG shipped with a number of hidden debugging toggles embedded in its configuration files. The developers believed that because these flags were only referenced in C++ during early development and were never exposed to the UI, they posed no risk.

However, the .ini files told a different story.

Players extracted the game's INI files and discovered settings such as

```
bEnableDevCheats=true
bGodModeAllowed=true
DebugStartLevel=5
SkipAllCinematics=true
```

Even though these flags were not exposed to Blueprints or menus, Unreal's configuration hierarchy dutifully loaded them at runtime. By placing modified .ini entries in the MyGame/Saved/Config/Windows/ directory, players bypassed core gameplay systems.

The result was

- Automatic god mode

- Ability unlocks without criteria

- Cinematic skipping that broke story pacing

- Forced debug start levels that skipped early progression

Never assume configuration values are private. If Unreal can read them, attackers can write them. The sections on sanitizing INI files in Shipping builds and building a config validation system exist specifically to prevent this type of exploit.

- The game trusted configuration input from user-modifiable directories.

- No signature or validation was applied to configuration files.

- DefaultGame.ini overrides were not sanitized.

- Sensitive flags were left in the final build.

Conclusion

The developer console, CVar system, exec commands, configuration files, and build pipeline together form one of the largest attack surfaces in Unreal Engine. These systems were designed to empower developers during production, but if they remain accessible in shipping builds, they grant attackers the same capabilities.

By disabling the console, restricting CVars, sanitizing exec functions, validating configuration files, and stripping developer modules, developers can eliminate a large category of runtime exploits. However, attackers rarely stop when these systems are removed.

When console and configuration entry points disappear, cheaters often turn to automation tools such as macros, input scripting, and bot frameworks. The next chapter examines these behavioral automation attacks and how to detect them through runtime analysis and pattern recognition.

CHAPTER 10

Preventing Trainer and Macro Exploits

Modern single-player games face a different category of attacks than those discussed in earlier chapters. Instead of attaching debuggers, modifying memory, or injecting code, many attackers now rely on automation tools that simulate player input. These tools behave like extremely efficient robotic players capable of repeating actions perfectly for long periods of time.

Trainer tools and macro frameworks manipulate gameplay indirectly by controlling the player's inputs. They press keys faster than a human can react, repeat actions without fatigue, and exploit deterministic gameplay systems such as farming loops, cooldown timers, or menu interactions.

This chapter focuses on **behavior-based automation attacks** and explains how to detect and discourage them using lightweight gameplay-level systems rather than intrusive anti-cheat software.

The core idea is simple. Even if memory protection, debugger detection, and save file validation are perfectly implemented, an automated player can still break progression by controlling the game externally.

The goal of this chapter is to detect and neutralize that behavior.

Why Macro Automation Is Fundamentally Different from Debugging

Instead of modifying values such as health, gold, or experience points, automation tools influence the game indirectly through highly precise input control. These tools simulate actions that appear legitimate to the engine but occur with speeds and patterns that no human could realistically sustain.

Typical macro behavior includes the following:

- Press buttons at inhuman speeds

- Create loops that never fatigue

- Automate repetitive actions perfectly

- Exploit predictable cooldown timers

- Manipulate camera and movement with robotic precision

- Abuse shop menus, crafting loops, and farming mechanics

Because these tools generate legitimate input events, traditional anti-cheat systems that monitor memory integrity cannot detect them. The detection strategy therefore shifts from protecting game state to analyzing player behavior.

Why Single-Player Games Attract Macro-Based Cheating

Single-player environments lack competitive matchmaking and server-side authority systems. As a result, many players believe automation causes no harm. Developers also tend to underestimate how quickly repetitive mechanics can be exploited.

Several characteristics of single-player design unintentionally encourage macro abuse:

- There is no matchmaking or fairness requirement.

- Many players believe "it hurts no one."

- Developers often underestimate automation abuse.

In grinding-heavy genres such as RPGs, ARPGs, survival crafting, and strategy games, attackers use macros to

- Farm resources while away from keyboard (AFK)

- Repeat menu actions hundreds of times per minute

- Skip crafting or upgrade delays

- Perform impossible precision in combat

- Cancel reload animations with frame-perfect timing

Even relatively simple automation can destabilize progression balance and invalidate core gameplay systems.

Overview of Modern Trainer Ecosystems

Automation tools have evolved significantly over the past decade. Many trainers now include scripting environments that simulate player input rather than editing memory directly.

The modern automation ecosystem includes several widely used frameworks. Common examples include

- *WeMod*: Executes hotkeys, toggles infinite cooldowns through input hooks

- *AutoHotkey*: Simulates custom macros, loops, pixel-based recognition

- *Python Automation*: Uses libraries such as PyAutoGUI to click menus and simulate motion

- *Cheat Engine Trainers*: Includes Lua-based automation tools on top of its memory editor

- *Arduino/Hardware Macros*: External USB devices emulating perfect human input

- *Frida/Xposed Automation (Android)*: Runtime hooking to trigger input and events

These tools produce activity that looks like a legitimate input stream. They never need to attach a debugger or open your memory.

How Input Simulation Bypasses Traditional Anti-cheat Assumptions

Traditional anti-cheat systems are built around the assumption that cheating requires tampering with the game process.

Automation tools violate this assumption by interacting with the game from the outside. These tools simulate input events such as

- Keyboard key presses

- Mouse movement deltas

- Controller axis values

- Pointer events

- Virtual HID device signals

Because Unreal Engine treats all input events equally, simulated events appear identical to real player's actions. The only reliable detection strategy is therefore behavioral analysis.

Key Threat Categories in Macro Automation

Automation tools typically target three main domains inside a game. Understanding these domains helps guide the design of behavioral detectors and informs the defensive systems introduced later in this chapter.

Input System Attack Surface

Attackers manipulate the input system by producing impossible timing patterns and excessive frequency.

- Repeated keypresses at intervals below human reaction capacity

- Mouse movement deltas that form perfect geometric patterns

- Input sequences that occur identically for hours

- Axis updates without natural jitter or noise

Gameplay Logic Attack Surface

Certain systems are easier to exploit with automation:

- Menu actions that repeat predictable economic patterns

- Farming loops in large maps

- No-cooldown attacks caused by fast animation-cancel macros

- Auto-aim or auto-pathing driven by input scripting rather than memory edits

Timing-Based Attack Surface

Most games rely on cooldown windows, stamina drains, or cast times that assume variability in human input. Macros exploit this by

- Firing actions at perfect minimum intervals

- Using millisecond-level timing accuracy

- Never making mistakes

- Never hesitating or delaying

Figure 10-1 illustrates the layered macro-detection pipeline used throughout this chapter. Multiple behavioral signals are analyzed, aggregated into a composite score, and then routed through delayed-response and soft-penalty systems.

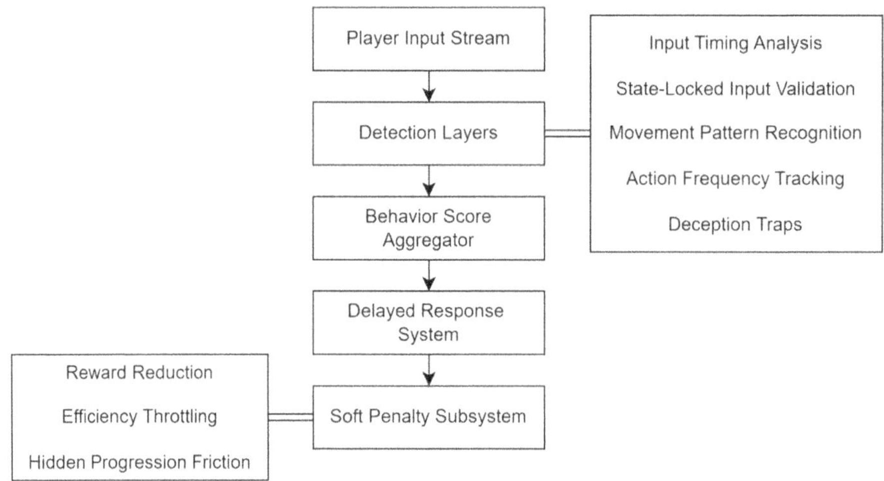

Figure 10-1. *Behavioral macro-detection pipeline combining input timing analysis, movement pattern recognition, deception traps, composite behavior scoring, delayed response, and soft-penalty enforcement*

How Automation Tools Attack Unreal Games

Before we can design meaningful detection systems, we must understand how trainers and macros interact with the engine at a technical level. Unlike memory editors or debuggers, which modify the internal state of the process, automation tools exploit Unreal Engine's **input system**, **gameplay loops**, and **timing assumptions**. These tools behave like an "idealized player" who performs actions with perfect timing, infinite patience, and no human inconsistencies.

This section analyzes the three core attack surfaces used by automation tools: the input pipeline, gameplay systems, and timing-based systems. Understanding these surfaces informs the detectors designed later in the chapter.

The Input System Attack Surface

Unreal Engine's input system treats all keypresses, mouse movements, controller actions, and virtual HID devices equally. From the engine's perspective, simulated inputs are indistinguishable from physical inputs unless you deliberately add logic to spot the difference.

Automation tools leverage this by injecting perfectly timed or artificially precise events that cannot be produced by a human.

Simulated Keyboard and Mouse Events

Most trainer macros simulate keyboard presses through operating-system-level input APIs, such as

- SendInput() (Windows)

- X11 XTestFakeKeyEvent (Linux)

- input tap, input keyevent (Android)

- USB HID spoofing through hardware devices

These tools allow attackers to send

- Thousands of actions per minute

- Input patterns with no jitter

- Frame-perfect rotations and targeting

- Sustained loops that run for hours

By default, Unreal Engine does not differentiate between

- A key pressed by a human

- A key fired by an AutoHotkey script

- A key injected by a WeMod trainer

- A key coming from a virtual keyboard device

This creates an open vector for macro exploitation.

Virtual Device Injection

Some advanced tools create fake HID devices that Unreal treats as real gamepads, mice, or keyboards. These devices can be programmed to

- Move analog sticks with inhuman precision

- Provide perfect circular or grid-shaped movement

- Output exact, repeatable acceleration curves

- Manipulate camera control down to fractional degrees

This becomes especially dangerous in genres where camera or movement sensitivity impacts combat, traversal, or speedrunning routes.

Repeated Input Pulses and Flooding

Attackers often exploit

- Repeated key down/up cycles

- Instantaneous tapping

- Multi-key chains executed sequentially

These create behavior such as

- Attacks fired in mathematically perfect intervals

- Dodge rolls repeated without human delay

- Menu skipping at impossible speed

- Frame-perfect animation cancels

Your input layer must be able to detect and deny unrealistic input frequency if you want to prevent automation.

Unlimited-Rate Input Attacks

Some engines attempt to cap input rates implicitly. Unreal Engine generally does not impose strict limits unless developers implement them explicitly.

This allows strategies such as

- Reload-cancelling through frame-perfect macro loops

- Canceling stamina regeneration delays

- Spamming shop or inventory actions to exploit value multipliers

- Overriding cooldowns through precise sequence timing

This forms the first major category of macro attack behavior.

The Gameplay Logic Attack Surface

Even if input appears normal, automation may target gameplay loops. Many single-player systems have inherent vulnerabilities when faced with robotic repetition.

Farming Loops

In open-world, ARPG, and procedural games, macros frequently automate progression loops:

- Resource gathering routes

- Enemy farming cycles

- Infinite XP loops

- Crafting-reselling cycles

- Time-based system exploitation (e.g., day-night resets)

Because the macro behaves like a "perfect farmer," it can execute cycles more efficiently than any human.

Auto-Aim and Camera-Control Macros

Some macros move the camera with pixel-perfect precision:

- Smooth camera rotations with unnatural consistency

- Snap-aim movements executed without human jitter

- Oscillation-free tracking

These patterns can be identified by logging mouse deltas and analyzing trajectory shape over time.

Menu and UI Automation

Menu systems are often the easiest surface to exploit:

- Automated shop selling/buying

- Crafting loops repeated thousands of times

- Skipping cutscenes or dialogues instantly

- Navigating inventory screens with precise coordinates

If your UI triggers gameplay-affecting actions, such as purchases or upgrades, macros can exploit those more easily than any in-world mechanic.

Frame-Step Abuse

Some tools simulate single-frame advancement by sending alternating input pulses. This lets them

- Cancel animations

- Skip cooldown windows

- Break stamina systems

- Exploit loopable combos

This category overlaps with timing exploits, which are covered next.

The Timing-Based Attack Surface

Human input contains natural delays, reaction-time variability, and inconsistency. Macros do not.

Attackers exploit your game's reliance on timing assumptions.

Microsecond Macro Pulses

Human input arrives at a granularity of tens of milliseconds. Automation tools operate in microseconds.

This allows

- Perfect combo chains

- Zero-delay dodge rolling

- Instant reaction to events

- Infinite perfect parries

If your game's timing systems assume human constraints, macros can bypass them entirely.

Impossible Timing Sequences

Examples of unrealistic timing:

- 12 perfectly spaced attacks every second

- Zero-variance delays between dodge inputs

- Continuous circular camera movement without jitter

- Identical frame timing for hours

Unreal Engine logs and input events make these patterns detectable, but only if you build analysis tools.

Exploiting Predictable Cooldown Systems

Predictable cooldown systems invite automation:

- Refreshing abilities exactly at cooldown end

- Refreshing stamina at perfect thresholds

- Exploiting integer division or rounding boundaries

- Tight resource loops executed flawlessly

Cool down–driven macros exploit deterministic logic at the edge of system transitions.

Detecting Unnatural Input Patterns

Behavior-based automation detection begins with identifying input sequences that are unlikely to be produced by a human player. Humans naturally exhibit timing variation in their actions. Even experienced speed runners cannot maintain perfectly consistent intervals for extended periods of time.

Therefore, the only reliable way to recognize automation is to measure human constraints and highlight deviations from them. This part introduces two detection systems:

1. Input Timing Analysis

2. State-Locked Input Validation

Both systems operate independently but can be combined for extremely high accuracy in detecting macro behavior.

Input Timing Analysis

Humans have irregular timing. Even veteran speed runners cannot press a button at exactly the same interval repeatedly. This natural variance becomes a rich source of data for detecting macro use. If attackers produce intervals so precise that they fall outside known human jitter ranges, the system can classify the behavior as suspicious.

The following system measures input intervals and analyze patterns over time.

Input Interval Detection

The engine's input layer is capable of recording keypress timestamps and comparing them across events. If an input arrives

- Too frequently

- Too consistently

- With nearly zero deviation

- Beyond human reaction potential

then it is likely driven by automation.

This requires collecting timing samples and computing variance. A human player has high variance. A macro has low variance.

Burst Frequency Analysis

Another suspicious pattern is repeated bursts of keypresses at impossible rates. Typical human input bursts are

- Irregular

- Short

- Noisy

Whereas macro bursts

- Contain dozens or hundreds of input events

- Occur perfectly at fixed frequencies

- Repeat identically for long periods

Listing 10-1 introduces a timing analyzer used to identify input intervals that are suspiciously consistent. Automated scripts often produce extremely regular input timing, while human input naturally contains small variations.

- UInputTimingAnalyzer represents the object responsible for evaluating input timing patterns.

- RecentInputs stores a rolling history of timestamp values for recent inputs.

- MaxSamples limits how many timing samples are retained for analysis.

- RecordInput() records each new input timestamp.

- ComputeIntervalVariance() calculates how much the spacing between inputs varies.

- IsUnnaturallyConsistent() determines whether the measured variance falls below a threshold that suggests macro behavior.

Listing 10-1. UInputTimingAnalyzer.h

```
#pragma once

#include "CoreMinimal.h"
#include "UObject/Object.h"
#include "InputTimingAnalyzer.generated.h"

UCLASS()
class UInputTimingAnalyzer : public UObject
{
    GENERATED_BODY()

private:
    TArray<float> RecentInputs;
    int32 MaxSamples;

public:
    UInputTimingAnalyzer();

    void RecordInput(float Timestamp);
```

```
    float ComputeIntervalVariance() const;
    bool IsUnnaturallyConsistent(float VarianceThreshold = 0.0008f) const;
};
```

After integrating this analyzer into the input processing layer, every input event contributes to a timing history that can be evaluated in real time. Over time, the variance calculations reveal input patterns that are too regular to originate from normal player interaction.

Listing 10-2 implements the timing analysis system introduced previously. The implementation records timestamps, converts them into intervals, and calculates statistical variance to determine whether the pattern resembles human input.

- Constructor initializes the timing sample window and prepares the buffer.

- RecordInput() maintains a rolling list of timestamp samples.

- ComputeIntervalVariance() converts timestamps into interval measurements and computes variance.

- IsUnnaturallyConsistent() compares the calculated variance against a detection threshold.

Listing 10-2. UInputTimingAnalyzer.cpp

```cpp
#include "InputTimingAnalyzer.h"
#include "Math/UnrealMathUtility.h"

UInputTimingAnalyzer::UInputTimingAnalyzer()
{
    MaxSamples = 20;
    RecentInputs.Reserve(MaxSamples);
}

void UInputTimingAnalyzer::RecordInput(float Timestamp)
{
    if (RecentInputs.Num() >= MaxSamples)
    {
        RecentInputs.RemoveAt(0);
```

```cpp
    }
    RecentInputs.Add(Timestamp);
}

float UInputTimingAnalyzer::ComputeIntervalVariance() const
{
    if (RecentInputs.Num() < 3)
    {
        return 0.f;
    }

    float Mean = 0.f;
    TArray<float> Intervals;

    for (int32 i = 1; i < RecentInputs.Num(); ++i)
    {
        Intervals.Add(RecentInputs[i] - RecentInputs[i - 1]);
    }

    for (float Delta : Intervals)
    {
        Mean += Delta;
    }
    Mean /= Intervals.Num();

    float Variance = 0.f;
    for (float Delta : Intervals)
    {
        Variance += FMath::Pow(Delta - Mean, 2);
    }
    Variance /= Intervals.Num();

    return Variance;
}

bool UInputTimingAnalyzer::IsUnnaturallyConsistent(float
VarianceThreshold) const
```

```
{
    return ComputeIntervalVariance() < VarianceThreshold;
}
```

When connected to gameplay input events, this implementation continuously evaluates player timing behavior. Consistent intervals over many samples strongly suggest automation rather than natural human input.

State-Dependent Input Validation

Timing alone does not detect all automation. Some macros only activate in menus or specific gameplay states. To catch these, inputs must be validated against the current gameplay context.

For example:

- Opening the shop exactly every 500 ms

- Clicking the same UI element repeatedly

- Activating abilities before cooldown completion

- Executing actions during invalid character states

This section introduces a state-aware component that restricts actions unless the player is in a valid game state.

Why State Validation Matters

State validation catches

- Shop automation

- Crafting automation

- Inventory exploit loops

- Cooldown bypass attempts

- Movement-in-menu exploitation

By verifying that each input aligns with the player's legitimate state, macro abuse becomes significantly harder.

Listing 10-3 introduces a component that validates input actions against the player's current gameplay state. This mechanism prevents automation scripts from executing actions in contexts where they should not occur.

- EGameInputState defines the different gameplay contexts that influence input permissions.

- UStateLockedInputComponent manages validation of player input against these contexts.

- CurrentState tracks the player's current interaction state.

- AllowedStates stores the set of states in which input is accepted.

- SetState() updates the active gameplay context.

- CanAcceptInput() determines whether input should be processed.

- RejectInput() provides a mechanism for logging or handling invalid actions.

Listing 10-3. UStateLockedInputComponent.h

```cpp
#pragma once

#include "CoreMinimal.h"
#include "Components/ActorComponent.h"
#include "StateLockedInputComponent.generated.h"

UENUM()
enum class EGameInputState : uint8
{
    Normal,
    Menu,
    Shop,
    Dialogue,
    Disabled
};
```

```cpp
UCLASS(ClassGroup=(Security))
class UStateLockedInputComponent : public UActorComponent
{
    GENERATED_BODY()

private:
    EGameInputState CurrentState;
    TSet<EGameInputState> AllowedStates;

public:
    UStateLockedInputComponent();

    void SetState(EGameInputState NewState);
    bool CanAcceptInput() const;
    void RejectInput(const FString& ActionName) const;
};
```

This component allows gameplay systems to reject input attempts when the player is not in a valid interaction state. Such validation prevents macros from abusing menu interactions, shop loops, or dialogue systems.

Listing 10-4 provides the implementation for the state validation component. The logic ensures that gameplay actions are accepted only when the current state matches an allowed context.

- Constructor initializes the default gameplay state and allowed state set.

- SetState() updates the internal state used during validation.

- CanAcceptInput() verifies whether the current state is permitted.

- RejectInput() records suspicious attempts for diagnostic or detection purposes.

- The component is designed for integration with player input handlers.

Listing 10-4. UStateLockedInputComponent.cpp

```cpp
#include "StateLockedInputComponent.h"
#include "Engine/Engine.h"

UStateLockedInputComponent::UStateLockedInputComponent()
{
    PrimaryComponentTick.bCanEverTick = false;

    AllowedStates = {
        EGameInputState::Normal,
        EGameInputState::Dialogue
    };

    CurrentState = EGameInputState::Normal;
}

void UStateLockedInputComponent::SetState(EGameInputState NewState)
{
    CurrentState = NewState;
}

bool UStateLockedInputComponent::CanAcceptInput() const
{
    return AllowedStates.Contains(CurrentState);
}

void UStateLockedInputComponent::RejectInput(const FString&
ActionName) const
{
    UE_LOG(LogTemp, Warning, TEXT("Rejected automated input attempt: %s"),
    *ActionName);
}
```

With this implementation active, automated systems that attempt to trigger
actions outside valid gameplay contexts can be detected or blocked before they affect
game logic.

Detecting Macro Patterns in Player Behavior

Input timing analysis is a powerful first layer. However, many sophisticated macros deliberately introduce tiny amounts of jitter or randomization to appear more human. To detect these improved scripts, the game must observe broader behavioral patterns that involve **movement, spatial repetition, and event frequency**.

This section introduces two behavioral detection systems:

1. Movement Pattern Recognition

2. Action Frequency and Heatmap Analysis

These tools identify repetitive or robotic gameplay loops that are unlikely to be produced by a human. While human behavior is noisy and context driven, macro behavior tends to be geometrically consistent, highly repetitive, and statistically stable.

Movement Pattern Recognition

A macro's greatest weakness is that it often follows the same path repeatedly. Whether farming a spawn zone, running a loot route, or circling a crafting station, automated players tend to repeat spatial trajectories with extreme precision.

Human movement, even when trying to repeat a route, contains

- Drift

- Overshooting

- Corrective turns

- Hesitation

- Irregularity

A macro contains none of these. Looping paths often take the shape of

- Circles of identical radius

- Perfect rectangles

- Repeated line segments

- Triangular enemy-to-enemy loops

- Identical harvesting circles

By periodically sampling the player's location and comparing it against previously stored positions, the system can identify suspiciously consistent trajectories.

Using a Movement Window for Detection

Movement pattern detection requires

- A buffer of recent player positions

- A method for computing path similarity

- A way to detect repeated shapes over time

The following component implements a lightweight movement analyzer suitable for real-time use.

Listing 10-5 introduces the movement analyzer that samples positions and computes geometric pattern consistency.

- RecentPositions holds a fixed window of historical locations.

- RecordPosition() inserts new observations.

- ComputePathRepetitionScore() measures how close paths are to prior loops.

- IsLoopingPattern() determines macro-level looping behavior.

Listing 10-5. UMovementPatternAnalyzer.h

```cpp
#pragma once

#include "CoreMinimal.h"
#include "UObject/Object.h"
#include "MovementPatternAnalyzer.generated.h"

UCLASS()
class UMovementPatternAnalyzer : public UObject
{
    GENERATED_BODY()

private:
    TArray<FVector> RecentPositions;
    int32 MaxSamples;
```

```
public:
    UMovementPatternAnalyzer();

    void RecordPosition(const FVector& Pos);
    float ComputePathRepetitionScore() const;
    bool IsLoopingPattern(float Threshold = 0.85f) const;
};
```

This header defines a movement analysis component that records recent player positions for behavioral evaluation. By tracking movement history, the system can later determine whether the player is following suspiciously repetitive or deterministic paths.

Listing 10-6 implements the geometric comparison logic, generating a repetition score from multiple samples.

- Constructor sets the default sample window.

- RecordPosition() maintains a rolling buffer.

- ComputePathRepetitionScore() compares distances between matched points.

- IsLoopingPattern() returns true if movement is overly similar to past movement.

- Designed for continuous gameplay monitoring.

Listing 10-6. UMovementPatternAnalyzer.cpp

```
#include "MovementPatternAnalyzer.h"
#include "Math/UnrealMathUtility.h"

UMovementPatternAnalyzer::UMovementPatternAnalyzer()
{
    MaxSamples = 60;  // roughly a few seconds of movement data
    RecentPositions.Reserve(MaxSamples);
}

void UMovementPatternAnalyzer::RecordPosition(const FVector& Pos)
{
    if (RecentPositions.Num() >= MaxSamples)
    {
```

```cpp
        RecentPositions.RemoveAt(0);
    }
    RecentPositions.Add(Pos);
}

float UMovementPatternAnalyzer::ComputePathRepetitionScore() const
{
    if (RecentPositions.Num() < 10)
    {
        return 0.f;
    }

    float Score = 0.f;
    int32 Count = 0;

    for (int32 i = 0; i < RecentPositions.Num() - 10; ++i)
    {
        float Dist = FVector::Dist(RecentPositions[i],
        RecentPositions[i + 10]);

        if (Dist < 30.f)
        {
            Score += 1.f;
        }

        Count++;
    }

    return Count > 0 ? (Score / Count) : 0.f;
}

bool UMovementPatternAnalyzer::IsLoopingPattern(float Threshold) const
{
    return ComputePathRepetitionScore() >= Threshold;
}
```

This implementation compares movement samples to determine whether the player's path forms repeating geometric patterns. Such patterns often indicate farming macros or scripted movement loops, which rarely occur in natural human gameplay.

Action Frequency and Heatmap Analysis

Beyond movement, macros frequently target **actions** such as attacking, harvesting, crafting, or interacting. While humans perform these actions with irregular timing and intent, macros do so with machine precision at extremely high frequencies.

You can detect this by tracking

- Action counts

- Action frequency per second

- Repeated sequences

- Heatmap intensity of interactable objects

This can be implemented using a simple tracker.

Tracking Unrealistic Rates of Input Actions

Humans cannot perform actions such as

- 20 attacks per second

- 300 interactions per minute

- Identical sequences repeated without mistakes

But macros can. This system records each action and its timestamp, allowing the engine to identify patterns incompatible with human play.

Listing 10-7 introduces the action frequency tracker with a rolling time window.

- Timestamps store recent action timestamps.

- RecordAction() adds new entries.

- ComputeActionsPerSecond() evaluates rates.

- IsFrequencySuspicious() detects macro-level speeds.

Listing 10-7. UActionFrequencyTracker.h

```
#pragma once

#include "CoreMinimal.h"
#include "UObject/Object.h"
#include "ActionFrequencyTracker.generated.h"
```

```cpp
UCLASS()
class UActionFrequencyTracker : public UObject
{
    GENERATED_BODY()

private:
    TArray<float> Timestamps;
    int32 MaxSamples;

public:
    UActionFrequencyTracker();

    void RecordAction(float Timestamp);
    float ComputeActionsPerSecond(float CurrentTime) const;
    bool IsFrequencySuspicious(float Threshold = 8.f) const;
};
```

This class tracks the frequency of gameplay actions over time using a rolling timestamp buffer. By monitoring how often certain actions occur, the system can detect input speeds that exceed realistic human limits.

Listing 10-8 implements the frequency evaluation logic.

- Constructor sets the rolling sample size.

- RecordAction() manages the sliding window.

- ComputeActionsPerSecond() calculates density.

- IsFrequencySuspicious() flags impossible action rates.

Listing 10-8. UActionFrequencyTracker.cpp

```cpp
#include "ActionFrequencyTracker.h"

UActionFrequencyTracker::UActionFrequencyTracker()
{
    MaxSamples = 100;
    Timestamps.Reserve(MaxSamples);
}
```

```cpp
void UActionFrequencyTracker::RecordAction(float Timestamp)
{
    if (Timestamps.Num() >= MaxSamples)
    {
        Timestamps.RemoveAt(0);
    }
    Timestamps.Add(Timestamp);
}

float UActionFrequencyTracker::ComputeActionsPerSecond(float
CurrentTime) const
{
    int32 Count = 0;

    for (float T : Timestamps)
    {
        if (CurrentTime - T <= 1.0f)  // last 1 second
        {
            Count++;
        }
    }

    return static_cast<float>(Count);
}

bool UActionFrequencyTracker::IsFrequencySuspicious(float Threshold) const
{
    if (Timestamps.Num() < 5)
    {
        return false;
    }

    float Rate = ComputeActionsPerSecond(Timestamps.Last());
    return Rate > Threshold;
}
```

This implementation calculates actions per second and flags suspiciously high input rates. When combined with other behavioral detectors, this mechanism helps identify automated systems that repeatedly trigger gameplay actions at machine speed.

Designing Safe and Subtle Countermeasures

Detecting bots, scripts, and macros is only half the battle. The other half is how you respond. Chapters 4 and 5 already taught an important principle: **aggressive security measures reveal themselves to attackers**, and once a cheat developer knows how your system reacts, they will evolve around it.

For macro-detection, you must design countermeasures that

- Do not break legitimate players' progress

- Do not immediately expose your detection logic

- Do not create an opportunity for cheaters to reverse-engineer your rules

- Do not frustrate honest players due to false positives

- Do not produce clear binary signals that an attacker can measure

The goal is to **neutralize automated behavior quietly**.

The following sections show how to use **delayed**, **probabilistic**, and **soft-impact** responses that reduce the benefit of cheating while avoiding direct confrontation.

Delayed Response Strategy

Immediate punishment (such as freezing the game or disconnecting the player) teaches cheat developers exactly when they triggered a detection. Delayed responses remove this feedback loop and force them into uncertainty.

A delayed countermeasure waits for

- Several minutes

- A number of completed encounters

- Or a gameplay milestone

before applying any penalty, because attackers cannot know

- Which detector fired

- Why it fired

- When it fired

- How many times it fired

- Or whether the penalty occurred due to random chance

- Whether the user interface simply behaved normally

This dramatically increases the cost of adapting automation scripts.

Implementing a Delayed Response Manager

The following subsystem stores flagged events and applies countermeasures after randomized delays.

Listing 10-9 introduces the delayed response manager.

- FlagSuspicion() queues a suspicion event.

- ShouldTriggerPenalty() determines whether enough time has passed.

- PenaltyTriggered prevents multiple activations per session.

- SuspicionLevel accumulates multi-system detections.

Listing 10-9. UMacroDelayResponseSubsystem.h

```cpp
#pragma once

#include "CoreMinimal.h"
#include "Subsystems/GameInstanceSubsystem.h"
#include "MacroDelayResponseSubsystem.generated.h"

UCLASS()
class UMacroDelayResponseSubsystem : public UGameInstanceSubsystem
{
    GENERATED_BODY()

private:
    float FirstDetectionTime;
    int32 SuspicionLevel;
    bool bPenaltyTriggered;
```

```
public:
    UMacroDelayResponseSubsystem();

    void FlagSuspicion();
    bool ShouldTriggerPenalty(float CurrentTime) const;
    bool HasTriggeredPenalty() const { return bPenaltyTriggered; }
    void MarkPenaltyTriggered() { bPenaltyTriggered = true; }
};
```

This subsystem introduces a delayed response mechanism for handling suspicious behavior. Instead of reacting immediately, the system accumulates suspicion signals and waits before applying countermeasures.

Listing 10-10 implements delayed activation logic with randomized intervals.

- Constructor resets all fields.

- FlagSuspicion() records the first suspicious event.

- ShouldTriggerPenalty() uses randomized windows to obscure triggers.

- Designed to integrate with attack, movement, and timing detectors.

Listing 10-10. UMacroDelayResponseSubsystem.cpp

```
#include "MacroDelayResponseSubsystem.h"
#include "Math/UnrealMathUtility.h"

UMacroDelayResponseSubsystem::UMacroDelayResponseSubsystem()
{
    FirstDetectionTime = -1.f;
    SuspicionLevel = 0;
    bPenaltyTriggered = false;
}

void UMacroDelayResponseSubsystem::FlagSuspicion()
{
    if (FirstDetectionTime < 0.f)
    {
```

```cpp
        FirstDetectionTime = FPlatformTime::Seconds();
    }
    SuspicionLevel++;
}

bool UMacroDelayResponseSubsystem::ShouldTriggerPenalty(float
CurrentTime) const
{
    if (FirstDetectionTime < 0.f || bPenaltyTriggered == true)
    {
        return false;
    }

    float Delay = FMath::FRandRange(15.f, 45.f);  // random delay window

    if ((CurrentTime - FirstDetectionTime) > Delay && SuspicionLevel >= 3)
    {
        return true;
    }

    return false;
}
```

This implementation introduces randomized response delays that obscure the exact trigger conditions of the detection system. By preventing attackers from linking a specific action to a specific penalty, this approach makes macro adaptation significantly more difficult.

Soft Penalties That Reduce Macro Efficiency

Once a penalty triggers, the goal is not to ban the player instantly. Instead, you quietly reduce macro effectiveness in ways that look like normal gameplay variance or difficulty scaling.

Examples of safe soft penalties:

- Slightly lower damage output

- Slightly lower resource drops

- Slightly slower attack or harvest animations

- Random exhaustion debuffs

- Reduced XP gain

- Reduced movement acceleration

These are not noticeable to new players and look like ordinary gameplay to most users. But for a macro, they break efficiency models.

Soft penalties are

- Untraceable

- Non-catastrophic

- Safe against false detections

- Difficult for cheat developers to update around

Implementing a Soft-Penalty Component

The following component applies a minor debuff when triggered by the delayed response subsystem.

Listing 10-11 introduces a debuff component that reduces efficiency invisibly.

- ApplyPenalty() activates the soft debuff.

- ModifyDamage() or other methods subtly reduce performance.

- PenaltyMultiplier gives developers control over severity.

- Designed to be attached to PlayerState or Character.

Listing 10-11. USoftPenaltyComponent.h

```
#pragma once

#include "CoreMinimal.h"
#include "Components/ActorComponent.h"
#include "SoftPenaltyComponent.generated.h"

UCLASS(ClassGroup=(Security))
class USoftPenaltyComponent : public UActorComponent
```

```
{
    GENERATED_BODY()

private:
    bool bPenaltyActive;
    float PenaltyMultiplier;

public:
    USoftPenaltyComponent();

    void ApplyPenalty(float Multiplier = 0.85f);
    float ModifyDamage(float BaseDamage) const;
    bool IsPenaltyActive() const { return bPenaltyActive; }
};
```

This component defines a lightweight gameplay modifier used to apply subtle penalties to automated players. Rather than blocking the player outright, the system reduces the effectiveness of automated behavior through gradual gameplay adjustments.

Listing 10-12 shows how penalties subtly modify gameplay output.

- Constructor disables the penalty by default.

- ApplyPenalty() switches into a reduced-efficiency mode.

- ModifyDamage() reduces player output invisibly.

- More modifiers can be added (XP gain, stamina regen, etc.).

Listing 10-12. USoftPenaltyComponent.cpp

```
#include "SoftPenaltyComponent.h"

USoftPenaltyComponent::USoftPenaltyComponent()
{
    bPenaltyActive = false;
    PenaltyMultiplier = 1.0f;
}

void USoftPenaltyComponent::ApplyPenalty(float Multiplier)
{
    bPenaltyActive = true;
```

```
    PenaltyMultiplier = Multiplier;
}

float USoftPenaltyComponent::ModifyDamage(float BaseDamage) const
{
    if (!bPenaltyActive)
    {
        return BaseDamage;
    }
    return BaseDamage * PenaltyMultiplier;
}
```

This implementation activates the soft penalty system and modifies gameplay outputs when necessary. Because these adjustments appear to normal gameplay variation, automated users cannot easily determine when the system has been triggered.

Composite Behavior Score

We now introduce the idea of a **Composite Behavior Score (CBS)**, a weighted model that combines multiple detection signals into one normalized score.

Every subsystem contributes

- Timing deviation score

- Movement unpredictability score

- Input entropy score

- Action diversity score

- Context-aware consistency score

The final composite score helps determine whether the behavior resembles a real player or a scripted macro.

Implementing a Composite Behavior Evaluator

This is the central orchestrator that collects results from all macro-detection subsystems you wrote in earlier parts.

It does not directly flag cheaters.

It simply *evaluates* and *scores* behavior.

Listing 10-13 introduces the Composite Behavior Evaluator.

- RecordMetrics() receives subsystem outputs.

- ComputeScore() mixes weighted channels.

- Weighting values allow tuning per game.

- Designed to be fed by movement, attack, rotation, and timing detectors.

- This evaluator does not enforce penalties—it only produces a score.

Listing 10-13. FCompositeBehaviorEvaluator.h

```cpp
#pragma once

struct FCompositeBehaviorEvaluator
{
private:
    float TimingScore;
    float MovementScore;
    float EntropyScore;
    float ActionDiversityScore;
    float ContextScore;

public:
    FCompositeBehaviorEvaluator();

    void RecordMetrics(
        float InTiming,
        float InMovement,
        float InEntropy,
        float InActionDiversity,
        float InContext);

    float ComputeScore() const;
};
```

This evaluator aggregates metrics from multiple behavioral detection systems into a single composite score. By combining signals from timing, movement, and input analysis, the system produces a more reliable estimate of automation likelihood.

Listing 10-14 implements weighted correlation scoring.

- The constructor initializes channels.

- RecordMetrics() receives normalized detector inputs (0 to 1).

- ComputeScore() produces a weighted composite score.

- Developers can easily tune weight values.

Listing 10-14. FCompositeBehaviorEvaluator.cpp

```cpp
#include "CompositeBehaviorEvaluator.h"

FCompositeBehaviorEvaluator::FCompositeBehaviorEvaluator()
{
    TimingScore = 0.f;
    MovementScore = 0.f;
    EntropyScore = 0.f;
    ActionDiversityScore = 0.f;
    ContextScore = 0.f;
}

void FCompositeBehaviorEvaluator::RecordMetrics(
    float InTiming,
    float InMovement,
    float InEntropy,
    float InActionDiversity,
    float InContext)
{
    TimingScore = InTiming;
    MovementScore = InMovement;
    EntropyScore = InEntropy;
    ActionDiversityScore = InActionDiversity;
    ContextScore = InContext;
}
```

```cpp
float FCompositeBehaviorEvaluator::ComputeScore() const
{
    const float TimingWeight = 0.30f;
    const float MovementWeight = 0.25f;
    const float EntropyWeight = 0.20f;
    const float ActionDiversityWeight = 0.15f;
    const float ContextWeight = 0.10f;

    return
        (TimingScore * TimingWeight) +
        (MovementScore * MovementWeight) +
        (EntropyScore * EntropyWeight) +
        (ActionDiversityScore * ActionDiversityWeight) +
        (ContextScore * ContextWeight);
}
```

This implementation calculates a weighted score that reflects the overall probability of automated behavior. Using multiple correlated signals greatly reduces false positives and allows the detection system to operate safely in live gameplay environments.

Behavior Correlation Across Subsystems

Behavior-based macro-detection becomes significantly more reliable when signals are evaluated across multiple subsystems rather than in isolation. Individual signals such as timing irregularities or movement patterns can sometimes appear suspicious on their own, but they may still occur during normal gameplay. By correlating multiple signals together, the detection model can identify patterns that are extremely unlikely to occur during legitimate play.

The composite evaluation model relies on several correlation principles to distinguish automated behavior from human input.

Timing vs. Movement Correlation

Human input tends to vary across both timing and movement. When a player's reaction time changes, their movement patterns typically change as well. Small delays in input often produce slightly different movement paths or positioning adjustments. Macros behave differently. While a macro can introduce timing variation, the movement path it produces usually remains identical across repetitions.

For example, a detection system may observe a situation where

- Timing deviation increases significantly

- Movement paths remain mathematically identical

This mismatch between timing variability and movement consistency is a strong indicator of automated behavior.

Entropy vs. Camera Rotation

Human camera control naturally contains small imperfections. Even experienced players produce slight variations in rotation speed, direction changes, and correction movements. Macros often simulate camera rotation using smooth mathematical interpolation, producing movements that appear unnaturally consistent.

Correlation analysis can therefore detect situations where

- Camera rotation follows overly smooth trajectories

- Rotation adjustments lack micro-corrections

- Rotational entropy remains extremely low

These characteristics often suggest scripted control rather than human input.

Action Diversity vs. Gameplay Context

Human players continuously react to changing gameplay conditions. Their actions vary depending on enemy behavior, environment layout, and moment-to-moment decision making. Macros, however, typically execute pre-scripted action sequences regardless of context.

When analyzing player behavior, the detection system may identify patterns such as

- Rigid rotation patterns

- Identical attack spacing across multiple engagements

- Lack of camera correction after movement

- Identical strafing loops repeated in sequence

When these patterns appear consistently, they strongly suggest automated execution.

Fatigue and Imperfection Modeling

Human performance naturally fluctuates over time. Fatigue, distraction, and reaction delays introduce small imperfections into gameplay behavior. Macros do not experience fatigue. Once activated, they continue to execute actions with consistent timing and precision.

For instance, the system may detect a session containing

- Hundreds of perfectly spaced actions

- Identical timing intervals

- Identical rotation correction patterns

- No degradation in accuracy over long play sessions

When such behavior persists for extended periods, it becomes increasingly unlikely that the actions are being performed manually.

Integrating the Composite Evaluator with Detectors

At this stage, the system includes several behavioral detectors and response mechanisms, including

- Input timing detectors

- Movement pattern detectors

- Action frequency analysis

- Delayed response subsystem

- Soft penalty component

Additional signals such as camera rotation analysis, entropy metrics, and action diversity models can also be integrated into the same evaluation pipeline as the system evolves.

The composite evaluator operates periodically during gameplay. At regular intervals, the behavioral detectors report normalized metrics that describe recent player activity. These values are passed into the composite evaluator, which calculates an aggregated behavior score.

If the computed score exceeds a predefined threshold, the system records suspicion through the delayed response subsystem. Instead of reacting immediately, the delayed penalty system waits a randomized period before applying subtle gameplay adjustments. This delayed strategy prevents attackers from easily identifying which behavior triggered the detection.

This architecture keeps everything modular, extensible, and upgradable.

Gameplay-Integrated Deception Systems

Traditional macro-detection systems operate silently in the background. They observe movement, timing, input entropy, and behavioral irregularities, then raise internal suspicion levels. However, advanced macro authors increasingly mimic human randomness, making pure observational detection insufficient.

To counter this, a modern and highly effective defensive strategy is to **actively shape the gameplay environment itself** to expose automated behavior.

This is known as a **Gameplay-Integrated Deception System (GIDS)**.

A GIDS introduces carefully crafted, optional, and unpredictable in-game stimuli that humans interpret naturally but macros fail to handle correctly. This transforms the battle: rather than only observing behavior, the game *provokes* responses that reveal automation.

The philosophy behind gameplay-integrated deception is straightforward. Automated scripts operate purely on deterministic rules and cannot interpret meaning or context in the same way that human players can. As a result, macros struggle with situations that require interpretation or prioritization.

For example, automated systems cannot reliably

- Interpret the meaning of ambiguous gameplay stimuli

- Prioritize contextual information during decision making

- Ignore bait objects unless explicitly programmed to detect them

- Reason about player intention or long-term strategy

Deception systems exploit this limitation by introducing situations where correct behavior requires interpretation rather than deterministic execution.

Why Deception Works Better Than Observation Alone

When players encounter ambiguous or misleading situations, human behavior tends to exhibit several recognizable characteristics. Players may hesitate, adjust their movement, or make imperfect corrections as they interpret the situation.

Typical human responses include

- Hesitation before committing to an action

- Small random variations in movement or camera control

- Corrective adjustments when the situation is misread

- Contextual reasoning based on nearby threats or objectives

- Inconsistent timing between decisions

Automated scripts behave very differently. Because macros follow deterministic instructions, they typically respond with immediate and perfectly consistent actions. This often results in

- Immediate execution without hesitation

- Perfectly repeated action patterns

- Deterministic input sequences

- Rigid timing intervals

- Complete absence of corrective behavior

These behavioral differences create a measurable gap that deception systems can exploit.

Types of Gameplay Deception Traps

Most deception mechanisms fall into several broad categories that provoke reactions from automation scripts while remaining harmless to human players.

The following categories represent common deception strategies used to expose macro-driven behavior.

Pseudo-interactive Targets (Fake Objects)

One of the simplest deception mechanisms involves objects that appear to be interactable but are intentionally designed to have no real gameplay function. These objects resemble legitimate interaction targets but are positioned in ways that human players quickly recognize as decorative or irrelevant.

Typical characteristics include

- Objects that appear interactable but cannot actually be triggered

- Placement slightly outside standard player routes

- Visibility only under specific camera angles

- Lack of collision logic or interaction responses

- Invisible blocking volumes preventing interaction

Human players typically recognize these elements as background decoration and ignore them. Automated scripts, however, often attempt to move toward them, interact with them, or adjust camera alignment to trigger them. These reactions provide strong indicators of macro-driven behavior.

Timing-Choice Bait (Ambiguous Timing Opportunities)

Another effective deception strategy involves presenting multiple apparent timing opportunities where only one represents the correct interaction moment. Human players naturally hesitate or evaluate the situation before acting.

Examples include

- Two overlapping hit windows

- Two loot pickup flashes occurring in quick succession

- Staggered but visually similar animation cues

- Delayed input windows where the correct timing is ambiguous

Human players typically pause briefly or choose the clearer interaction moment. Macros, however, tend to trigger the first available input opportunity with perfect consistency. This deterministic behavior becomes a reliable detection signal.

Variability Tests (Micro-Decision Chaos Triggers)

Automation scripts depend heavily on deterministic timing and fixed interaction patterns. Introducing small variations into routine tasks can therefore disrupt macro behavior.

These micro-variations may include

- Randomly delayed gather windows

- Slightly shifting interaction hotspots

- Minor offsets in alignment positions

- Subtle variations in input timing requirements

Human players adapt to these changes instinctively, often without noticing them. Macros, on the other hand, struggle to respond to shifting conditions and frequently misalign their actions.

Meaningless Distraction Events

Some deception traps rely on stimuli that appear noticeable but should not trigger any gameplay response. These elements exist purely to observe whether automation scripts react unnecessarily.

Examples include

- A brief flicker on a wall

- A small particle effect or lighting cue

- Ambient sound effects without gameplay meaning

- Dummy UI prompts that do not correspond to actions

- Non-interactive key prompts

Human players generally ignore these stimuli. Automated systems, however, often attempt to respond by clicking, moving the camera, adjusting aim, or attempting interaction. These reactions reveal scripted behavior.

Behavioral Branch Traps

Branching scenarios can also expose automation patterns. When presented with multiple equally plausible choices, human players naturally distribute their decisions across different options.

Examples include

- Two exits with slightly different angles

- Branching paths with similar visual clarity

- Optional pickups placed slightly outside optimal routes

Human players typically choose different paths depending on their perception of the environment. Automation scripts, however, consistently select the same deterministic option based on their programmed logic. Over time, these rigid patterns form highly distinctive behavioral clusters that reveal macro usage.

Design Principles for Successful Deception Systems

To maintain fairness and avoid punishing legitimate players, deception systems must follow several strict design principles.

Zero Negative Impact on Legitimate Play

Deception traps must never cause failure, damage, or frustration for legitimate players. Their purpose is purely observational.

Zero UI Exposure

Traps should never appear as visible user interface elements. Any visible indicator could allow attackers to reverse-engineer the detection system.

Zero Gameplay Requirement

Fake objects or bait mechanics must never be required to complete objectives or progress through the game.

No Failure Penalty for Ignoring Traps

Players must never be punished for ignoring bait objects or deceptive prompts.

Trigger Only Internal Markers

Trap interactions should update internal suspicion counters and feed the delayed response system without revealing any visible feedback.

Cannot Be Saved or Replicated Without Logic

Save systems and replication paths should exclude trap data to prevent detection through data mining.

The following section demonstrates how a lightweight deception component can be implemented in Unreal Engine to integrate these traps into the broader macro-detection pipeline.

Implementing a Simple Deception Trap Component

This section introduces a small deception trap component that

- Spawns periodic fake interaction prompts

- Monitors whether the player attempts to interact

- Records macro-like reactions

- Integrates with the composite evaluator

It is intentionally lightweight so developers can build more complex traps on top of it.

Listing 10-15 introduces a deception trap component.

- SpawnBait() generates bait prompts that humans ignore.

- RecordInteractionAttempt() logs whether the player reacted.

- SuspicionScore accumulates reactions.

- Integrated with the behavior evaluator.

Listing 10-15. UDeceptionTrapComponent.h

```
#pragma once

#include "CoreMinimal.h"
#include "Components/ActorComponent.h"
#include "DeceptionTrapComponent.generated.h"
```

```cpp
UCLASS(ClassGroup=(Security))
class UDeceptionTrapComponent : public UActorComponent
{
    GENERATED_BODY()

private:
    float SuspicionScore;
    float LastSpawnTime;

public:
    UDeceptionTrapComponent();

    void SpawnBait();
    void RecordInteractionAttempt(bool bAttempted);
    float GetSuspicionScore() const;
};
```

This component introduces a gameplay deception mechanism designed to provoke automated reactions. By generating bait events that legitimate players naturally ignore, the system can detect scripted responses that reveal macro behavior.

Listing 10-16 implements a subtle bait-trap system.

- SpawnBait() fires only under controlled random timing.

- bAttempted == true indicates automation.

- Suspicion grows slowly to avoid false positives.

- The score is later correlated with timing and movement evaluators.

Listing 10-16. UDeceptionTrapComponent.cpp

```cpp
#include "DeceptionTrapComponent.h"
#include "Math/UnrealMathUtility.h"
#include "Engine/World.h"

UDeceptionTrapComponent::UDeceptionTrapComponent()
{
    SuspicionScore = 0.f;
    LastSpawnTime = 0.f;
}
```

```cpp
void UDeceptionTrapComponent::SpawnBait()
{
    float CurrentTime = GetWorld()->GetTimeSeconds();

    if ((CurrentTime - LastSpawnTime) > FMath::FRandRange(5.f, 15.f))
    {
        LastSpawnTime = CurrentTime;
        // Spawn a fake prompt, invisible to gameplay logic
    }
}

void UDeceptionTrapComponent::RecordInteractionAttempt(bool bAttempted)
{
    if (bAttempted)
    {
        SuspicionScore += 1.f;
    }
}

float UDeceptionTrapComponent::GetSuspicionScore() const
{
    return SuspicionScore;
}
```

This implementation spawns bait interactions and records whether the player attempts to react to them. Repeated interaction attempts with these traps strongly suggest automated scripts rather than genuine player behavior.

Using Deception Outputs in the Macro-Detection Pipeline

The signals generated by deception traps do not operate in isolation. Instead, they feed into the broader macro-detection pipeline and strengthen the reliability of other behavioral detectors. When a player interacts with bait elements in ways that legitimate players rarely would, the system records these events as behavioral signals that contribute to the overall suspicion model.

These signals can be integrated into several systems within the detection architecture, including

- The Composite Behavior Evaluator, where deception events contribute to the overall behavior score

- The delayed response system, which accumulates suspicion before triggering countermeasures

- Gameplay analytics systems, which record abnormal interaction patterns for later analysis

- Hidden progression or achievement gating systems, which can quietly halt progression under suspicious conditions

- Soft-penalty logic, which subtly reduces the effectiveness of automated behavior

In practice, even a single bait interaction occurring within an already suspicious context can contribute to a measurable increase to the suspicion score.

Soft-Penalty Systems and Graduated Response Strategies

The soft-penalty concepts introduced earlier can be extended into a broader graduated response strategy. Direct punishment of macro users is often counterproductive. It helps attackers identify exactly which behavior triggered detection. Once they know the rules, they rewrite the macro to avoid them. This is why professional-grade anti-cheat systems rarely apply immediate or explicit penalties.

Instead, modern single-player defense relies on **soft-penalty systems** that

- Avoid revealing detection logic

- Degrade the impact of automated play

- Maintain the integrity of progression without punishing innocent players

- Create a gradual divergence between legitimate and automated users

- Encourage attackers to abandon automated strategies

These systems work silently in the background and ensure that game balance remains intact even in the presence of macros.

Soft penalties pair perfectly with the earlier **Composite Behavior Evaluator** and **Gameplay Deception Systems**, forming a cohesive security posture that does not compromise the player experience.

Why Soft Penalties Are More Effective Than Hard Blocks

Traditional anti-cheat systems often rely on hard enforcement mechanisms. When suspicious behavior is detected, the system may immediately disable progression, block actions, or present a warning message to the player. Although this approach may seem effective at first glance, it introduces several important drawbacks that can weaken the overall security model.

Hard blocks typically create three major problems for developers:

- They reveal the existence and timing of the detection system.

- They transform detection into a puzzle that attackers can analyze and bypass.

- They generate support requests and false-positive complaints from legitimate players.

Because of these limitations, modern behavioral detection systems increasingly rely on soft penalties rather than immediate enforcement.

Soft-penalty systems operate by subtly altering gameplay conditions when suspicious automation is detected. These changes are designed to remain invisible to legitimate players while gradually reducing the effectiveness of automated scripts.

Categories of Soft Penalties

Soft penalties can take several forms depending on the design goals of the game. Rather than applying a single punishment, most systems gradually introduce small changes that accumulate over time.

The following categories represent common soft-penalty mechanisms used in behavior-based macro-detection systems.

Reward Degradation Systems

Reward degradation systems quietly reduce the efficiency of actions that appear to be automated. The goal is not to block progress entirely but to make macro-driven gameplay less productive over time.

Examples of reward degradation mechanisms include

- Lowering experience gains

- Reducing currency drops

- Decreasing resource yield

- Slightly slowing progress on incremental tasks

For legitimate players, a small reduction in rewards across several sessions is rarely noticeable. Automation scripts, however, depend heavily on maximizing efficiency. Even a modest reduction in reward output can significantly reduce the profitability of macro-driven play.

Soft Locks on Progression Gates

Macros frequently target progression systems that involve repeated interaction loops. These may include skill unlock trees, crafting chains, or resource conversion mechanics. Soft locks introduce small delays or additional conditions that slow automated progression without blocking legitimate players.

Common implementations include

- Postponing certain unlock triggers

- Adding additional prerequisites to progression milestones

- Delaying tier advancement by short intervals

Human players typically adapt naturally to these delays and continue progressing without difficulty. Automation scripts, however, often fail to interpret the delay correctly and may become trapped in inefficient loops.

Invisible Cooldown Inflation

Another effective approach involves dynamically adjusting interaction cooldowns when behavior exceeds normal human limits.

If the system detects interactions occurring faster than a typical player could perform them, the game may quietly modify timing constraints.

Examples include

- Increasing interaction cooldown durations

- Slightly extending ability recast timers

- Lengthening crafting completion times

- Slowing down high-frequency gathering loops

Because these adjustments remain subtle, they do not disrupt legitimate gameplay. However, they directly undermine the high-frequency execution patterns used by automation scripts.

Micro-Friction Systems

Micro-friction systems introduce very small variations into gameplay interactions. These variations are designed to be imperceptible to human players but disruptive to deterministic automation routines.

Examples include

- Slight variation in interaction radius

- Small camera offset adjustments

- Randomized response timing windows

- Minor shifts in prompt appearance timing

Human players naturally compensate for these variations without conscious effort. Macros, however, rely on precise input timing and positioning, which causes them to misalign actions or trigger inputs incorrectly.

Quiet Achievement Freezes and Unlock Gating

Another subtle penalty mechanism involves temporarily halting progression within long-term achievement or mastery systems. If a player is repeatedly detected performing suspicious automated loops, the system may quietly suspend progression tracking.

Typical implementations include

- Pausing achievement tracking

- Preventing long-term goals from progressing

- Suspending mastery milestone updates

The player does not receive any visible errors or warning messages. Progress simply appears to stall until the suspicion score drops below the enforcement threshold.

The Suspicion-to-Penalty Curve

Soft-penalty systems operate most effectively when penalties are introduced gradually rather than applied abruptly. Instead of triggering immediate punishments, the system maps the player's accumulated suspicion score onto a scaling curve that determines how strongly the game begins to interfere with automated behavior.

This scaling model allows the detection system to respond proportionally to suspicious activity while avoiding sudden gameplay disruptions for legitimate players.

A typical suspicion-to-penalty progression may follow a structure similar to the following:

- *Low Suspicion*: No penalties are applied and gameplay proceeds normally.

- *Moderate Suspicion*: Small amounts of gameplay friction begin to appear.

- *High Suspicion*: Delays and reward reductions become noticeable to automated systems.

- *Critical Suspicion*: Stronger reward degradation and progression restrictions are activated.

By mapping suspicion levels onto a controlled penalty curve, the system can continuously adjust enforcement strength without ever exposing the exact moment at which automation has been detected.

Integrating Soft Penalties into the Detection Pipeline

Soft penalties should not be implemented directly inside gameplay systems. Instead, they should be managed through a dedicated evaluation component that receives suspicion scores and determines the appropriate penalty level.

Separating this logic from gameplay code improves maintainability and allows designers to tune enforcement behavior without modifying core systems.

Listing 10-17 introduces a Soft Penalty Evaluator Subsystem.

- SuspicionScore is aggregated from previous evaluators.

- PenaltyLevel represents the current severity.

- UpdatePenaltyLevel() maps suspicion → penalty.

- Used across gameplay systems to dynamically adjust behavior.

Listing 10-17. USoftPenaltySubsystem.h

```cpp
#pragma once

#include "CoreMinimal.h"
#include "Subsystems/GameInstanceSubsystem.h"
#include "SoftPenaltySubsystem.generated.h"

UCLASS()
class USoftPenaltySubsystem : public UGameInstanceSubsystem
{
    GENERATED_BODY()

private:
    float SuspicionScore;
    int32 PenaltyLevel;
```

```
public:
    USoftPenaltySubsystem();

    void AddSuspicion(float Amount);
    void UpdatePenaltyLevel();
    int32 GetPenaltyLevel() const;
    float GetSuspicionScore() const;
};
```

This subsystem centralizes the management of behavioral suspicion levels and penalty scaling. By separating detection logic from gameplay adjustments, the system remains modular and easier to tune during development.

Listing 10-18 implements the penalty escalation logic.

- Suspicion score is cumulative.

- Penalty level is derived from configurable thresholds.

- Other systems can query PenaltyLevel.

- This subsystem never applies penalties directly.

Listing 10-18. USoftPenaltySubsystem.cpp

```
#include "SoftPenaltySubsystem.h"

USoftPenaltySubsystem::USoftPenaltySubsystem()
{
    SuspicionScore = 0.f;
    PenaltyLevel = 0;
}

void USoftPenaltySubsystem::AddSuspicion(float Amount)
{
    SuspicionScore += Amount;
    UpdatePenaltyLevel();
}
```

```cpp
void USoftPenaltySubsystem::UpdatePenaltyLevel()
{
    if (SuspicionScore < 10.f)
    {
        PenaltyLevel = 0;   // No penalties
    }
    else if (SuspicionScore < 25.f)
    {
        PenaltyLevel = 1;   // Mild penalties
    }
    else if (SuspicionScore < 50.f)
    {
        PenaltyLevel = 2;   // Moderate penalties
    }
    else
    {
        PenaltyLevel = 3;   // Heavy penalties
    }
}

int32 USoftPenaltySubsystem::GetPenaltyLevel() const
{
    return PenaltyLevel;
}

float USoftPenaltySubsystem::GetSuspicionScore() const
{
    return SuspicionScore;
}
```

This implementation converts accumulated suspicion values into graduate penalty levels. Gameplay systems can query this subsystem to apply subtle balancing adjustments without exposing the underlying detection logic.

Using Penalty Levels in Gameplay Systems

Once the suspicion-to-penalty curve has been established, gameplay systems must be able to consume the resulting penalty levels without needing to understand how those levels were produced. This separation is important because it prevents gameplay code from exposing the internal logic of the detection system.

Instead of querying suspicion scores directly, gameplay subsystems simply read the current penalty level and adjust behavior accordingly. By isolating enforcement from detection, the system preserves stealth and prevents attackers from identifying the precise conditions that triggered the penalty.

Typical gameplay effects tied to penalty levels may include

- *Penalty Level 1*: Small delays in gathering or interaction mechanics

- *Penalty Level 2*: Slightly reduced resource yields or reward efficiency

- *Penalty Level 3*: Temporary suspension of achievement progression or mastery tracking

In practice, macro users often fail to notice the early stages of these penalties. Minor delays or small reward reductions are easily interpreted as normal gameplay variance. As suspicion continues to accumulate, however, higher penalty levels gradually introduce enough inefficiency that automated play becomes significantly less effective.

Because the gameplay systems only react to penalty levels and never access the underlying suspicion model, the detection pipeline remains hidden from observation.

Fusing Soft Penalties with Deception and Timing Detection

Soft penalties become significantly more effective when combined with the behavioral detection systems introduced earlier in this chapter. Rather than relying on a single signal, the macro-detection pipeline aggregates multiple independent indicators of suspicious behavior.

Each detection subsystem contributes signals that increase the overall suspicion score:

- Deception traps generate signals when players interact with bait objects or deceptive stimuli.

- Timing detectors identify reaction delays or action intervals that are statistically improbable for human input.

- Entropy-based evaluators detect low randomness patterns that indicate scripted behavior.

- Soft penalty systems apply gradual gameplay pressure without revealing the presence of detection logic.

Together, these systems form a layered defensive architecture. No single detector determines the outcome, and enforcement decisions are based on the combined evidence from multiple behavioral signals.

Conclusion

In this chapter, we shifted from protecting memory and runtime variables to protecting the behavioral patterns of player interaction. Macro tools do not manipulate memory directly. Instead, they automate inputs with perfect timing, repetition, and precision.

By analyzing input timing, movement patterns, action frequency, and contextual behavior, developers can detect automation without intrusive anti-cheat systems. When combined with deception systems, delayed responses, and soft penalties, these techniques allow single-player games to discourage automation while preserving the experience for legitimate players.

The next chapter moves from behavioral defenses to build-level security. We will examine how Unreal Engine packaging, configuration files, and build settings can expose new vulnerabilities if not carefully controlled.

CHAPTER 11

Securing Unreal Build Configurations

Modern single-player security does not end with runtime protections and save file hardening. Even if your in-game systems are carefully defended, an insecure build configuration can quietly undermine everything. A single forgotten setting such as shipping a development build, including full debug symbols, or leaving a developer module enabled can expose console commands, stack traces, internal structure layouts, and runtime hooks that attackers may use for reverse engineering.

This chapter focuses on build-time security for Unreal Engine projects. Earlier chapters concentrated on protecting runtime variables, save systems, Blueprint exposure, and automation detection. In contrast, this chapter examines how the executable itself is produced and which build and packaging settings influence security.

Several build mistakes significantly simplify reverse engineering and runtime exploitation. Common examples include the following situations:

- Shipping a development or test build by mistake

- Leaving verbose logs, asserts, or check macros enabled

- Distributing unstripped PDB or symbol data that reveal function names and structures

- Including editor or developer modules inside shipping builds

- Allowing configuration flags to be overridden through command line arguments or INI files

© Sheikh Sohel Moon 2026

S. S. Moon, *Securing Single-Player Games in Unreal Engine*, https://doi.org/10.1007/979-8-8688-2833-1_11

By the end of this chapter, you will understand several practical techniques for hardening Unreal Engine build configurations. In particular, you will learn how to

- Differentiate the security implications of development, test, and shipping builds

- Harden your Target.cs configuration for safe shipping binaries

- Control symbol and PDB handling so debug information is never shipped accidentally

- Trim developer modules and plugins from your shipping build

- Implement automated configuration validation inside the build pipeline

The goal is not to make the build system complicated. Instead, the goal is to make the process deliberate. Each build option that might expose internal information should be evaluated and either disabled, restricted, or handled through a controlled build pipeline.

Why Build Configuration Is a Security Surface

Build configuration is often treated as a deployment concern rather than a security concern. Teams typically focus on optimization levels, packaging size, and platform compatibility. In practice, however, build settings strongly influence how easily a game can be reverse engineered and how much internal information becomes visible to attackers.

For example, shipping a development build unintentionally exposes several debugging features that were never intended for players. In such cases, the release build may still include

- Active assert and check macros

- Detailed logs and stack traces

- Developer commands and debugging tools

- Modules used only during internal development

A similar risk appears when debug symbol files are distributed alongside the executable. These symbols provide critical diagnostic information during development, but they also expose valuable insight into the internal architecture of the game. When symbol files are available, attackers gain the ability to

- Map memory addresses directly to function names

- Identify gameplay systems and internal classes

- Accelerate debugging and reverse engineering workflows

Plugins and modules can introduce additional exposure. A leftover debugging plugin or profiling tool may provide hooks, developer commands, or network features that were never designed for hostile environments.

Recognizing build configuration as a security surface changes how teams approach release builds. Instead of relying on default presets, developers should define a hardened shipping configuration and treat deviations from that configuration as potential vulnerabilities.

Understanding Development, Test, and Shipping from a Security Perspective

Unreal Engine supports several build configurations that control optimization level, debugging behavior, and runtime diagnostics. The most commonly used configurations include the following:

- Development

- DebugGame

- Test

- Shipping

From a security perspective, these configurations differ in several important areas:

- How much internal information they expose

- Which checks and asserts remain active

- Which modules and subsystems remain compiled into the executable

Development and DebugGame builds are designed for internal testing and debugging. These configurations typically include

- Verbose logging

- Extended diagnostics and crash reports

- Lower optimization levels

- Development-only modules and tools

Test builds occupy a middle ground between development and shipping. They may still contain diagnostics or debugging features that are acceptable for internal QA but not appropriate for a public release.

Shipping builds are intended for distribution to players. They prioritize optimization and remove most debugging features. Typical characteristics of shipping builds include

- Aggressive compiler optimizations

- Reduced runtime diagnostics

- Streamlined module dependencies

However, simply selecting "Shipping" in the editor does not guarantee a secure release. Developers must still ensure that build targets, packaging scripts, and configuration files are aligned with a hardened shipping configuration.

The following sections demonstrate how to implement those safeguards.

Hardening Target Rules for Shipping Builds

The primary control point for Unreal build configuration is the Target Rules file, typically named something like *MyGame.Target.cs*. This file defines how builds are produced for specific targets such as the runtime game, editor, or dedicated server.

When preparing a shipping build, the target configuration should enforce a number of restrictions. In particular, the build should ensure that

- Editor modules are never compiled into the runtime game

- Development-only features are disabled

- Verbose logging and check macros are minimized

- Packaged builds consistently use shipping settings

These safeguards are typically implemented through explicit properties defined in the Target Rules class.

Listing 11-1 demonstrates a hardened target configuration that helps enforce these constraints.

- Type = TargetType.Game; ensures this target is a runtime game, not an editor or tool.

- bBuildEditor = false; prevents editor modules from being accidentally linked into the shipping build.

- bUseChecksInShipping = false; disables expensive check macros that leak internal logic and function paths.

- bUseLoggingInShipping = false; reduces log verbosity to limit information leakage.

- DefaultBuildSettings is set to a modern standard for consistent and secure defaults.

Listing 11-1. SecureGameTarget.cs

```
using UnrealBuildTool;
using System.Collections.Generic;

public class SecureGameTarget : TargetRules
{
    public SecureGameTarget(TargetInfo Target) : base(Target)
    {
        Type = TargetType.Game;

        bBuildEditor = false;

        // Ensure modern, consistent defaults
        DefaultBuildSettings = BuildSettingsVersion.V2;

        // Security-focused flags
        bUseChecksInShipping = false;
        bUseLoggingInShipping = false;
```

```
        ExtraModuleNames.AddRange(new string[] { "MyGame" });
    }
}
```

This target configuration does not by itself enforce shipping builds, but it ensures that when you **do** build for shipping, you are not unintentionally carrying developer checks and verbose logging into your public binaries.

Controlling Symbol Files and PDB Handling

Debug symbols and PDB files are essential during development. They allow developers to interpret call stacks, inspect memory layouts, and trace execution through specific functions. During internal debugging, this information significantly accelerates problem diagnosis.

The same information becomes extremely valuable to reverse engineers. When PDB files are distributed alongside the executable, attackers can use them to reconstruct the internal structure of the game. With access to these symbols, a reverse engineer can

- Map addresses directly to class and function names

- Locate gameplay systems such as inventory, health, or save management

- Identify security-related functions through symbolic names

Earlier chapters introduced systems such as *FSecureFloat* and *FCompositeBehaviorEvaluator*. Without debug symbols, locating these systems requires deeper reverse engineering. When PDB files are present, those names become immediately visible in debugging tools.

For this reason, PDB files should be treated as sensitive build artifacts. A secure workflow typically follows several practices:

- Generate debug symbols for internal development builds.

- Archive symbol files securely on a symbol server or internal storage.

- Exclude all debug artifacts from packaged builds.

Many teams enforce this policy through build scripts integrated into their continuous integration pipeline.

Listing 11-2 outlines a simple Windows packaging script fragment that removes PDB and related debug files from the final distribution folder.

- BuildOutput points to the directory where Unreal writes built binaries.

- DistributionOutput points to the folder used for packaging the final game.

- Copy-Item transfers only the required runtime files.

- Remove-Item deletes .pdb, .exp, and .ilk files so they are not shipped.

Listing 11-2. PackageAndStripSymbols.ps1

```
param(
    [string]$BuildOutput = "C:\MyGame\Binaries\Win64",
    [string]$DistributionOutput = "C:\MyGame\Builds\Shipping"
)
New-Item -ItemType Directory -Force -Path $DistributionOutput | Out-Null

Copy-Item "$BuildOutput\MyGame-Win64-Shipping.exe"
$DistributionOutput -Force
Copy-Item "$BuildOutput\Content" $DistributionOutput -Recurse -Force

Get-ChildItem -Path $DistributionOutput -Include *.pdb, *.exp,
*.ilk -Recurse |
    Remove-Item -Force
```

This script is intentionally minimal. In a real production environment, you would integrate this step into your CI pipeline and add logging, error handling, and symbol archival to a secure server. The security goal remains the same: keep debug symbols available to your team, but never to your players.

Trimming Dangerous Developer Modules and Plugins

Unreal projects often accumulate a wide range of plugins and modules during development. Over time, teams may add tools such as

- Profiling utilities

- Developer debugging tools

- Editor extensions

- Visualization helpers

- Experimental subsystems

While these components are extremely useful during development, they may introduce unnecessary risk if included in a shipping build. Certain modules may expose functionality such as

- Debug menus

- Developer console commands

- HTTP endpoints used for testing

- Experimental networking features

- Verbose diagnostics and logging

To reduce this attack surface, the shipping build should contain only the modules required to run the game. Achieving this separation typically involves several practices:

- Isolating editor-only modules from runtime modules

- Restricting shipping builds to essential runtime dependencies

- Ensuring developer or editor modules cannot compile into the shipping binary

These controls are usually implemented within *.Build.cs* files.

Listing 11-3 shows a secure game module configuration that isolates editor dependencies and restricts developer modules.

- PublicDependencyModuleNames includes only essential runtime modules.

- PrivateDependencyModuleNames contains internal modules needed at runtime.

- if (Target.bBuildEditor) gates editor-only dependencies to prevent shipping from linking them.

- Developer and test utilities are wrapped in #if WITH_EDITOR or Target.bBuildEditor to keep them out of shipping.

Listing 11-3. MyGame.Build.cs

```
using UnrealBuildTool;

public class MyGame : ModuleRules
{
    public MyGame(ReadOnlyTargetRules Target) : base(Target)
    {
        PCHUsage = PCHUsageMode.UseExplicitOrSharedPCHs;

        PublicDependencyModuleNames.AddRange(
            new string[]
            {
                "Core",
                "CoreUObject",
                "Engine",
                "InputCore"
            });

        PrivateDependencyModuleNames.AddRange(
            new string[]
            {
                "Slate",
                "SlateCore"
            });
```

```
    if (Target.bBuildEditor)
    {
        PrivateDependencyModuleNames.AddRange(
            new string[]
            {
                "UnrealEd",
                "EditorSubsystem",
                "Kismet"
            });
    }
  }
}
```

This pattern ensures that editor-related modules never appear in your shipping game, even if someone accidentally builds the wrong target. By constraining module dependencies, you reduce potential attack surfaces and avoid shipping developer-only systems that were never designed for hostile environments.

Guarding Build Flags That Affect Security

Build flags influence subtle aspects of runtime behavior, including logging verbosity, error handling, and diagnostic output. Some flags primarily affect performance, while others determine how much internal information becomes visible to users.

From a security standpoint, developers should review build flags carefully and decide which settings are acceptable for shipping builds. In particular, teams should evaluate options related to

- Runtime checks and assertions

- Logging verbosity in shipping builds

- Crash reporting and analytics configuration

- Command-line arguments permitted during packaging

These settings may be controlled through Target.cs files, configuration files, and packaging scripts. Rather than relying on manual review, many teams add automated validation to their build pipeline.

Automated Configuration Validation in the Build Pipeline

Configuration files such as *DefaultEngine.ini*, *DefaultGame.ini*, and *DefaultEditor.ini* gradually accumulate settings throughout development. Even if console access and CVar restrictions were addressed in earlier chapters, new configuration values may still introduce unintended exposure.

To prevent these issues from reaching release builds, the build pipeline can include a validation step that scans configuration files for risky settings. This validation process typically checks for patterns such as

- Dangerous CVar overrides

- Debug or cheat features enabled by default

- Overly verbose logging settings

- Developer maps or test profiles included in shipping builds

A well-designed validator performs several tasks during the build process:

- Automatically runs during CI for shipping builds

- Fails the build when high-risk patterns are detected

- Reports clear messages so developers can resolve
  configuration issues

The validator itself does not modify game behavior. Its role is simply to prevent insecure configurations from reaching players.

Listing 11-4 defines a simple configuration validator in C#, designed to be run as part of your packaging pipeline.

- ConfigPaths holds the INI files of interest.

- ForbiddenPatterns contains strings associated with dangerous
  settings.

- ScanFile() checks each configuration file for any forbidden pattern.

- Main() aggregates results and fails the process if violations are found.

Listing 11-4. ConfigValidator.cs

```csharp
using System;
using System.IO;
using System.Collections.Generic;

class ConfigValidator
{
    static readonly string[] ConfigPaths =
    {
        @"Config\DefaultEngine.ini",
        @"Config\DefaultGame.ini"
    };

    static readonly string[] ForbiddenPatterns =
    {
        "bEnableCheats=True",
        "DebugExec",
        "r.DebugRender",
        "net.AllowCheats=True"
    };

    static bool ScanFile(string FullPath)
    {
        if (!File.Exists(FullPath))
        {
            return true;
        }

        string[] Lines = File.ReadAllLines(FullPath);
        bool bOk = true;

        foreach (string Line in Lines)
        {
            foreach (string Pattern in ForbiddenPatterns)
            {
                if (Line.Contains(Pattern, StringComparison.
                OrdinalIgnoreCase))
```

```
                {
                    Console.WriteLine($"[SECURITY] Forbidden pattern
                    '{Pattern}' found in {FullPath}: {Line}");
                    bOk = false;
                }
            }
        }

        return bOk;
    }

    static int Main(string[] args)
    {
        bool bAllOk = true;

        foreach (string RelativePath in ConfigPaths)
        {
            string FullPath = Path.Combine(Directory.GetCurrentDirectory(),
            RelativePath);
            bAllOk &= ScanFile(FullPath);
        }

        if (!bAllOk)
        {
            Console.WriteLine("[SECURITY] Configuration validation
            failed.");
            return 1;
        }

        Console.WriteLine("[SECURITY] Configuration validation passed.");
        return 0;
    }
}
```

In practice, you would refine the ForbiddenPatterns list and integrate this tool into your CI system. The important concept is that build validation becomes automated instead of relying on someone remembering to review configuration files before release.

Build Pipeline Hardening and Reproducible Security

Hardening individual files is useful, but modern game development relies on automated build systems. It is not enough to configure one development machine correctly. You must ensure that any build produced by your pipeline follows the same security rules.

Build pipeline hardening includes

- Creating dedicated targets for shipping builds with hardened settings

- Centralizing scripts for packaging, symbol stripping, and configuration validation

- Disallowing ad hoc local builds as release candidates

- Documenting security expectations for build and release engineers

You should aim for a pipeline where

- The release build is always produced by a controlled machine or CI environment

- The process always runs configuration and symbol validators

- Failing validations block releases automatically

- Build artifacts such as PDBs and logs are archived securely but never shipped

This mindset mirrors secure software development practices in other industries. You are not just building a game; you are building a reproducible and verifiable process for producing safe binaries.

Case Study 1: Shipping a Development Build by Accident

An indie team working on a narrative-driven action game shipped what they believed was a shipping build. Their testers had been using a development configuration to debug AI behavior. On release day, one of those builds was packaged and uploaded instead of the intended shipping binary.

Players quickly discovered

- An unlocked developer console

- An internal debug camera

- Verbose log output written to disk

- Stack traces containing internal function names

- Cheat-like commands used during development

Within days, a community tool emerged that

- Exploited console commands to skip levels

- Toggled AI behavior directly

- Modified CVar values to disable core mechanics

Despite efforts to patch the game, community expectations were set. Many players now saw the "exposed" version as the default, and the patched shipping builds felt restrictive.

The key lesson is straightforward:

- Never trust a manual selection of build configuration.

- Always automate verification of build types and targets.

- Avoid shipping development builds under any circumstance.

By hardening target settings and using build validation, the team could have caught the mistake before release.

Case Study 2: Debug Symbols and Rapid Reverse Engineering

Another studio released a single-player tactics game with a strong resource economy and sophisticated AI. The game shipped without any overt developer tools, and save files were partially encrypted. However, the team unknowingly packaged full PDB symbol files alongside the main executable on PC.

Reverse engineers quickly used the PDBs to

- Map every function address to a readable name

- Locate key systems such as ApplyDamageToUnit, ComputeLootDrop, and ApplyDifficultyModifiers

- Find internal balancing constants and damage curves

- Identify the encryption and decryption functions used for save files

Within weeks, several trainers appeared that

- Bypassed difficulty scaling

- Forced maximum loot drops

- Disabled AI behavioral modifiers

The developers had implemented meaningful runtime defenses, but the presence of PDBs gave attackers a detailed map of the game's internals. The long-term result was a proliferation of cheat tools that were far more powerful than they would have been without debug symbols.

The core lesson is that build artifacts are part of your attack surface. Symbol data is not harmless metadata. It is a detailed blueprint of your code.

Conclusion

Protecting a game involves more than defending runtime variables or encrypting save files. The security of the final executable also depends on how the build process is configured and which artifacts are included in the distributed package. Symbol files, debug modules, and configuration settings can all influence how easily attackers analyze and manipulate a game.

This chapter examined how Unreal build configurations affect the security of the final binary. You explored techniques for hardening Target Rules, controlling debug symbol distribution, isolating developer modules, and validating configuration files during the build process.

In the next chapter, attention shifts from binaries to assets. Chapter 12 examines methods for protecting *.pak* files and game data against extraction and tampering. You will explore Unreal's packaging system along with encryption and obfuscation strategies that make it significantly more difficult to unpack or modify game content.

CHAPTER 12

Protecting Assets and Game Data

Assets are the heart of any Unreal Engine game. They define the visual style, shape the world, support the audio atmosphere, and contribute directly to gameplay systems. When a project is packaged for release, these assets are typically stored inside PAK files that are distributed with the final build.

Although packaging simplifies distribution, it also introduces a potential attack surface. Many publicly available tools can extract or modify PAK archives if the build has not been configured securely. Once extracted, assets can reveal gameplay logic, balance parameters, or proprietary content.

This chapter explains the principles and practical techniques for protecting packaged assets and game data from extraction or modification. The objective is not to hide every asset completely, which is rarely feasible, but to increase the effort required for tampering so that casual modification becomes impractical.

Figure 12-1 illustrates a layered asset protection pipeline combining PAK encryption, runtime asset validation, data obfuscation, and external file encryption.

© Sheikh Sohel Moon 2026

S. S. Moon, *Securing Single-Player Games in Unreal Engine*, https://doi.org/10.1007/979-8-8688-2833-1_12

Figure 12-1. *Layered asset protection model combining secure PAK packaging, runtime asset integrity validation, and external data encryption*

Understanding Asset Threats in Single-Player Games

Asset tampering affects more than visual presentation. Attackers may modify assets to bypass gameplay restrictions, remove obstacles, increase visibility, or disrupt the intended balance of the game.

When assets are extracted, they can also reveal valuable information about the internal structure of the game. By analyzing asset data, attackers may learn details about enemy behaviors, gameplay timing systems, or internal configuration parameters that can later support more sophisticated exploits.

Several common asset tampering strategies appear in single-player games. These include actions such as

- Extracting Blueprint bytecode or material graphs to study internal logic

- Editing data tables that define weapon damage, spawn rates, or AI behavior

- Replacing animation montages to cancel recovery frames or stun windows

- Modifying maps to remove obstacles or open closed routes

- Editing skeletal meshes or collision data to gain unfair hitbox advantages

- Extracting audio, textures, or cinematic content for redistribution

- Analyzing game structure so that future cheats are easier to develop

This chapter focuses primarily on protecting packaged data at rest. Earlier chapters addressed runtime tampering and automation abuse, while later chapters examine monitoring techniques used after release.

Securing PAK Files Using Unreal Build Settings

Unreal Engine already provides several mechanisms for protecting packaged content. Encryption and signing features within the packaging system help prevent unauthorized tools from opening or modifying PAK archives.

When these protections are enabled, the game verifies the integrity of packaged assets before loading them. Any tampered archive fails validation and cannot be used by the game.

A secure packaging configuration typically enables multiple layers of protection. Important settings include the following options:

- bEncryptPak enables AES encryption for packaged PAK archives.

- bSignPak enables signature checks so modified PAK files fail validation.

- bEncryptUAssetFiles applies encryption to individual asset files inside the PAK.

- bEncryptIniFiles protects configuration files that may expose gameplay flags.

Listing 12-1 demonstrates a minimal packaging configuration that activates these protections.

- bEncryptPak enables AES encryption for packaged PAK archives.

- bSignPak enables signature validation so modified PAK files fail to load.

- bEncryptUAssetFiles encrypts individual asset files inside the PAK archive.

- bEncryptIniFiles encrypts configuration files that may expose gameplay flags or developer settings.

Listing 12-1. DefaultGame.ini (PAK Encryption Settings)

```
[/Script/UnrealEd.ProjectPackagingSettings]
bEncryptPak=true
bSignPak=true
bEncryptUAssetFiles=true
bEncryptIniFiles=true
```

These settings strengthen the packaging process by preventing straightforward asset extraction or modification. When combined with runtime validation systems, they form the foundation of asset protection.

Introducing an Asset Integrity Manager

Although PAK encryption provides a strong first layer of protection, additional runtime validation can strengthen the security model. A dedicated asset integrity system allows the game to verify that critical files have not changed since the build was shipped.

The idea is straightforward. During development, a trusted hash is generated for important assets. At runtime, the game recomputes the hash of the asset currently on disk and compares it with the expected value. If the values differ, the system can assume the asset has been modified.

An integrity manager typically maintains a registry of protected assets along with their expected hash values. Its responsibilities generally include the following operations:

- Storing known reference hashes for protected assets

- Registering assets that require validation

- Computing hashes for files during runtime verification

- Scanning all registered assets during integrity checks

Listing 12-2 declares the UAssetIntegrityManager class, which tracks known hashes for important assets and exposes simple validation functions.

- UAssetIntegrityManager is a UObject-based manager responsible for validating asset files.

- KnownHashes stores a mapping between asset paths and their expected reference hashes.

- RegisterAsset() associates an asset path with its expected hash value.

- ValidateAsset() calculates the current hash of a specific asset and compares it with the stored reference.

- ValidateAll() iterates through every registered asset and verifies their integrity.

Listing 12-2. UAssetIntegrityManager.h

```
#pragma once

#include "CoreMinimal.h"
#include "UObject/Object.h"
#include "AssetIntegrityManager.generated.h"

UCLASS()
class UAssetIntegrityManager : public UObject
{
    GENERATED_BODY()

private:
    TMap<FString, FString> KnownHashes;

public:
    void RegisterAsset(const FString& AssetPath, const FString& Hash);
```

```
    bool ValidateAsset(const FString& AssetPath) const;
    bool ValidateAll() const;
};
```

This class defines the central interface for asset integrity validation. It allows gameplay systems to register important files and verify that those files remain unchanged during runtime.

Listing 12-3 implements the functionality declared in the UAssetIntegrityManager header. The implementation loads asset data from disk, computes a hash value, and compares it against the reference stored in the manager.

- RegisterAsset() inserts or updates a hash entry for a given asset path.

- ValidateAsset() loads the file data and calculates an MD5 checksum.

- KnownHashes.Find() retrieves the expected reference hash associated with the asset.

- ValidateAll() loops through every registered asset and stops when any validation fails.

Listing 12-3. UAssetIntegrityManager.cpp

```
#include "AssetIntegrityManager.h"
#include "Misc/FileHelper.h"
#include "Misc/Paths.h"
#include "Misc/SecureHash.h"

void UAssetIntegrityManager::RegisterAsset(const FString& AssetPath, const
FString& Hash)
{
    KnownHashes.Add(AssetPath, Hash);
}

bool UAssetIntegrityManager::ValidateAsset(const FString& AssetPath) const
{
    FString FullPath = FPaths::ProjectContentDir() + AssetPath;
    TArray<uint8> Data;
```

```cpp
    if (!FFileHelper::LoadFileToArray(Data, *FullPath))
    {
        return false;
    }

    FString CurrentHash = FMD5::HashBytes(Data.GetData(), Data.Num());
    const FString* Known = KnownHashes.Find(AssetPath);

    return Known && *Known == CurrentHash;
}

bool UAssetIntegrityManager::ValidateAll() const
{
    for (const auto& Pair : KnownHashes)
    {
        if (!ValidateAsset(Pair.Key))
        {
            return false;
        }
    }
    return true;
}
```

This implementation allows the game to quietly detect modified assets before they are used. If an asset fails validation, the game can log the event or prevent further processing.

Obfuscating Critical Game Data

Even when PAK encryption is enabled, some projects still ship small data files outside the cooked asset pipeline. These files might include configuration fragments, tuning parameters, or lightweight gameplay data stored in formats such as JSON or CSV.

Because these formats are easy to read and edit, they are attractive targets for tampering. One simple defensive technique is obfuscation. Obfuscation does not aim to provide strong cryptographic protection; instead, it makes the raw data difficult to interpret without understanding the decoding method.

A lightweight obfuscation system typically performs a simple transformation on the file's bytes. In many cases, a reversible operation such as XOR scrambling is sufficient to discourage casual editing.

Listing 12-4 introduces a lightweight XOR obfuscator. It is not a full cryptographic system. Its role is to provide a simple and fast way to scramble small but sensitive configuration or balance files.

- FSimpleXORObfuscator is a stateless utility struct used for lightweight data scrambling.

- Obfuscate() applies a bitwise XOR operation to every byte using a provided key.

- Deobfuscate() reverses the process using the same key.

- Key is a single byte used as the scrambling value during both operations.

Listing 12-4. FSimpleXORObfuscator.h

```cpp
#pragma once

#include "CoreMinimal.h"

struct FSimpleXORObfuscator
{
    static void Obfuscate(TArray<uint8>& Data, uint8 Key);
    static void Deobfuscate(TArray<uint8>& Data, uint8 Key);
};
```

This helper provides a lightweight way to obscure small configuration values or tuning parameters so that they are not immediately readable in packaged files.

Listing 12-5 provides the implementation of the XOR obfuscator introduced earlier. The functions iterate through each byte of the data buffer and apply the XOR operation.

- Byte iteration loop visits every byte stored in the array.

- Byte ^= Key applies the XOR transformation to scramble the data.

- Obfuscate() transforms the plaintext buffer into obfuscated data.

- Deobfuscate() applies the same transformation again to restore the original bytes.

Listing 12-5. FSimpleXORObfuscator.cpp

```cpp
#include "SimpleXORObfuscator.h"

void FSimpleXORObfuscator::Obfuscate(TArray<uint8>& Data, uint8 Key)
{
    for (uint8& Byte : Data)
    {
        Byte ^= Key;
    }
}

void FSimpleXORObfuscator::Deobfuscate(TArray<uint8>& Data, uint8 Key)
{
    for (uint8& Byte : Data)
    {
        Byte ^= Key;
    }
}
```

Because XOR is symmetric, the same operation both obfuscates and restores the data. This makes the helper simple to integrate into asset loading or configuration parsing routines.

Runtime Verification of Game Data Tables

Gameplay balance in many games is controlled through data tables. These tables often define damage curves, spawn probabilities, AI parameters, or progression thresholds. Because of their influence on gameplay, they are natural targets for attackers who want to alter game mechanics.

Runtime verification helps ensure that data tables have not been modified. By computing a hash of the table's contents and comparing it to a known reference value, the game can detect unauthorized edits before trusting the data.

A verification component typically performs several tasks:

- Receiving a reference to a target data table

- Converting the table contents into a serialized string representation

- Computing a hash of the serialized data

- Comparing the computed value with the expected reference hash

Listing 12-6 declares a component used to verify the integrity of Unreal Engine data tables during runtime. This component can be attached to gameplay systems that rely heavily on table-driven configuration.

- UDataTableVerifierComponent is an ActorComponent responsible for validating data tables.

- VerifyTableIntegrity() computes a hash of the table contents and compares it with a known reference value.

- UDataTable pointer identifies the table that should be verified.

- ExpectedHash represents the trusted hash generated during development.

Listing 12-6. UDataTableVerifierComponent.h

```
#pragma once

#include "CoreMinimal.h"
#include "Components/ActorComponent.h"
#include "Engine/DataTable.h"
#include "DataTableVerifierComponent.generated.h"

UCLASS(ClassGroup=(Security))
class UDataTableVerifierComponent : public UActorComponent
{
    GENERATED_BODY()

public:
    bool VerifyTableIntegrity(UDataTable* Table, const FString&
ExpectedHash) const;
};
```

This component allows the game to verify that gameplay balance data has not been modified before the system relies on it.

Listing 12-7 implements the data table verification logic by converting table data into a string representation and hashing the resulting byte buffer.

- GetTableAsString() serializes the entire table into a textual format.

- FTCHARToUTF8 converts the serialized string into a UTF-8 byte buffer.

- FMD5::HashBytes() computes the checksum used to verify integrity.

- ExpectedHash comparison determines whether the data has been altered.

Listing 12-7. UDataTableVerifierComponent.cpp

```cpp
#include "DataTableVerifierComponent.h"
#include "Misc/SecureHash.h"

bool UDataTableVerifierComponent::VerifyTableIntegrity(UDataTable* Table,
const FString& ExpectedHash) const
{
    if (!Table)
    {
        return false;
    }

    FString TableString = Table->GetTableAsString();
    FTCHARToUTF8 Converter(*TableString);
    FString CurrentHash = FMD5::HashBytes(
        reinterpret_cast<const uint8*>(Converter.Get()),
        Converter.Length()
    );

    return CurrentHash == ExpectedHash;
}
```

This verification step ensures that changes to data tables cannot silently alter gameplay systems without detection.

Map Integrity Validation

Map assets deserve special attention because they define spatial layout, navigation routes, camera behavior, and encounter pacing. A modified map can fundamentally alter gameplay by removing obstacles, exposing shortcuts, or bypassing scripted encounters.

While the Asset Integrity Manager can validate any file type, registering maps explicitly provides a useful illustration of how asset monitoring works in practice.

During initialization, the game registers important maps with the integrity manager. Each registration associates the logical path of the map with its expected reference hash. If the map file is modified after shipping, the validation system detects the mismatch.

A typical map registration process includes the following elements:

- Specifying the logical asset path under the content directory

- Storing the expected hash generated during the build process

- Validating the asset early during the game startup sequence

Listing 12-8 demonstrates how a map asset can be registered with the integrity manager so that the game monitors it for unexpected changes.

- RegisterAsset() registers a map asset path with the integrity manager.

- TEXT("Maps/MainMap.umap") identifies the logical location of the map asset.

- EXPECTED_HASH_VALUE_HERE represents the trusted reference hash generated during development.

- The integrity manager later validates the file during runtime checks.

Listing 12-8. Registering a Map in UAssetIntegrityManager

```
AssetIntegrityManager->RegisterAsset(
    TEXT("Maps/MainMap.umap"),
    TEXT("EXPECTED_HASH_VALUE_HERE")
);
```

Registering maps in this way allows the game to detect unauthorized changes to level geometry or navigation data.

Lightweight Encryption for Custom Data Files

Some projects store additional gameplay data outside Unreal's cooked asset pipeline. Examples include difficulty tuning profiles, AI behavior definitions, or narrative branching configurations.

These files are often small binary blobs or serialized structures that remain accessible on the filesystem. Encrypting them before packaging provides an additional layer of protection, even if an attacker gains direct file access.

A simple encryption utility typically provides functions for both encryption and decryption operations. The helper shown in Listing 12-9 exposes two primary capabilities:

- Encrypting plaintext byte arrays using an AES key

- Decrypting encrypted byte arrays back into plaintext

The interface accepts a key provided by the game and returns a success flag to indicate whether the operation completed correctly.

Listing 12-9 declares the `FAESUtility` helper struct used for encrypting and decrypting custom data files using Unreal Engine's AES functions.

- FAESUtility provides a lightweight wrapper around Unreal's AES functionality.

- EncryptData() encrypts plaintext data using a provided AES key.

- DecryptData() restores encrypted data back to plaintext.

- Key is the byte array containing the encryption key.

Listing 12-9. FAESUtility.h

```cpp
#pragma once

#include "CoreMinimal.h"

struct FAESUtility
{
    static bool EncryptData(const TArray<uint8>& InData, TArray<uint8>&
    OutData, const TArray<uint8>& Key);
    static bool DecryptData(const TArray<uint8>& InData, TArray<uint8>&
    OutData, const TArray<uint8>& Key);
};
```

This helper allows developers to protect small external data files without building a full encryption subsystem.

Listing 12-10 implements the encryption helper by calling Unreal's built-in AES utilities directly on byte buffers.

- OutData initialization copies the input buffer before encryption or decryption.

- FAES::EncryptData() performs in-place AES encryption on the data buffer.

- FAES::DecryptData() restores encrypted data to its original form.

- Key buffer provides the AES key used during both operations.

Listing 12-10. FAESUtility.cpp

```cpp
#include "AESUtility.h"
#include "Misc/AES.h"

bool FAESUtility::EncryptData(const TArray<uint8>& InData, TArray<uint8>&
OutData, const TArray<uint8>& Key)
{
    OutData = InData;
    FAES::EncryptData(OutData.GetData(), OutData.Num(), Key.GetData());
    return true;
}

bool FAESUtility::DecryptData(const TArray<uint8>& InData, TArray<uint8>&
OutData, const TArray<uint8>& Key)
{
    OutData = InData;
    FAES::DecryptData(OutData.GetData(), OutData.Num(), Key.GetData());
    return true;
}
```

This implementation allows small configuration files or binary data blobs to be encrypted before packaging, preventing straightforward inspection or modification.

Conclusion

Assets represent a substantial portion of a game's intellectual property as well as many of its gameplay systems. Protecting these assets helps preserve balance, prevents unauthorized modification, and safeguards proprietary content.

This chapter introduced several techniques that strengthen asset protection in Unreal Engine projects. Packaging encryption and signing help secure PAK archives. Runtime validation systems such as the Asset Integrity Manager and data table verification components allow the game to detect modified files during execution. Lightweight obfuscation and AES-based encryption protect smaller data files that might otherwise remain exposed.

The next chapter shifts focus toward monitoring tampering after release. It explores telemetry strategies and techniques for identifying suspicious behavior in the wild while maintaining player privacy and system stability.

CHAPTER 13

Monitoring Tampering in the Wild

Tampering does not end when the game ships. Once players begin interacting with your systems under real conditions, new attack patterns emerge, unexpected exploits appear, and previously unseen combinations of tools and cheats begin to surface. Even if every security measure from Chapters 4 through 12 is implemented correctly, attackers will continue testing your systems, intentionally or unintentionally, in ways no internal testing environment can predict.

This chapter covers how to detect those actions *after* the game has been released, how to record meaningful security events, and how to correlate information across multiple systems without harming performance or overwhelming your players with invasive checks. The goal is to create a silent, low-impact monitoring layer that helps you understand attacker behavior in the wild and improve your game's resilience over time.

Monitoring is not about punishment. It is about learning. By collecting the right signals safely and unobtrusively, you can improve stability, fix vulnerabilities, and harden your systems for future patches. This chapter provides pragmatic tools for doing exactly that.

Why Post-Launch Monitoring Matters

Once your game is released to a real player population, it begins operating under conditions that internal testing cannot fully reproduce. Players experiment with mechanics in unexpected ways, combine tools creatively, and sometimes attempt to manipulate systems intentionally. Monitoring helps developers understand how real-world player behavior interacts with security systems after release.

S. S. Moon, *Securing Single-Player Games in Unreal Engine,* https://doi.org/10.1007/979-8-8688-2833-1_13

Post-launch monitoring offers several important advantages. In particular, it provides

- The ability to detect exploit paths that were not discovered during development

- Insight into how players interact with defensive systems

- Data on abnormal gameplay patterns that may indicate tampering

- Crash signatures caused by injected modules or runtime manipulation

- Real-world validation of assumptions made earlier during development

Effective monitoring systems also share several practical characteristics that help them operate reliably in production environments. A well-designed monitoring layer should remain

- Lightweight

- Invisible to players

- Non-invasive

- Reliable

- Easy to aggregate across sessions

- Inexpensive to compute during gameplay

Figure 13-1 illustrates the telemetry architecture used for post-launch tamper monitoring. Security signals generated by runtime protection systems are captured by a centralized logging layer, stored in a telemetry buffer, and analyzed by a behavioral correlation system that helps developers identify exploit patterns and improve future patches.

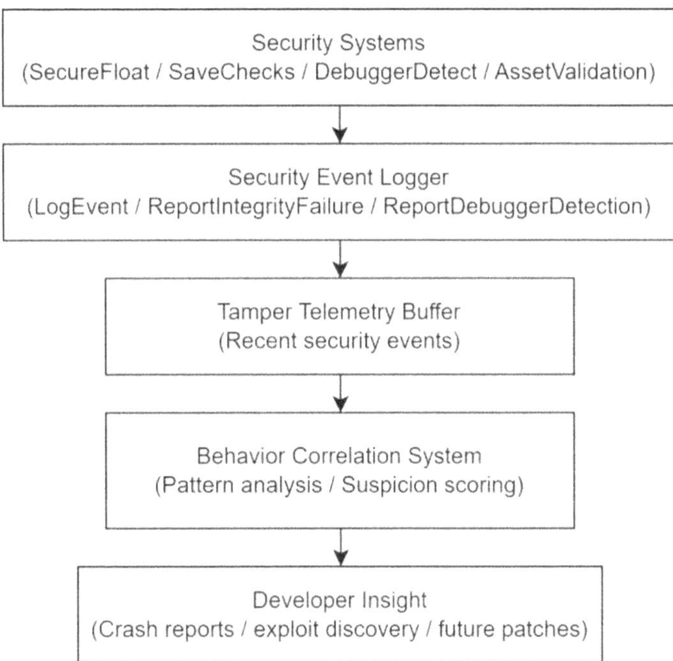

Figure 13-1. *Runtime tamper monitoring pipeline combining security event logging, telemetry buffering, behavioral correlation, and post-release exploit analysis*

Collecting Signals Without Hurting Performance

Security telemetry must never compromise performance, introduce frame-rate drops, or create visible side effects. If players notice logging spikes or frame hitches, they may interpret the game as unstable rather than secure.

A practical approach is event-driven logging. Instead of collecting information in every frame, the engine records only meaningful events when they occur. Typical examples of these security-relevant events include

- Integrity failures from secure variable wrappers

- Debugger or injection detection signals

- Abnormal save validation results

- Suspicious CVar or console command usage

- Repeated crashes from the same module or memory region

- Abnormal input timing patterns discussed in Chapter 10

To support this pattern, the chapter introduces a small reusable logging utility.

Listing 13-1 introduces a lightweight logging utility used to record security-relevant events. The goal is to provide a single interface that every security subsystem can use when reporting tampering activity.

- LogEvent() writes a security-relevant event to disk.

- Category allows grouping by subsystem.

- Message stores the human-readable detail.

- Everything writes through UE_LOG for optional external output.

Listing 13-1. SecurityLog.h

```
#pragma once

#include "CoreMinimal.h"

class FSecurityLog
{
public:
    static void LogEvent(const FString& Category, const FString& Message);
};
```

This interface establishes a centralized logging mechanism that can be reused across the entire security monitoring layer.

Listing 13-2 implements the security log writer by generating a timestamped message and writing it to both the Unreal logging system and a dedicated security log file.

- Timestamp generation records when the security event occurred.

- UE_LOG forwards the message to Unreal's standard logging output.

- Security.log file stores a persistent record of tamper-related events.

- FILEWRITE_Append ensures new entries are added without overwriting existing data.

Listing 13-2. SecurityLog.cpp

```cpp
#include "SecurityLog.h"
#include "Misc/FileHelper.h"
#include "Misc/Paths.h"
#include "HAL/FileManager.h"

void FSecurityLog::LogEvent(const FString& Category, const FString&
Message)
{
    FString Timestamp = FDateTime::Now().ToString();
    FString Output = FString::Printf(TEXT("[%s] [%s] %s\n"), *Timestamp,
    *Category, *Message);

    UE_LOG(LogTemp, Warning, TEXT("%s"), *Output);

    FString Path = FPaths::ProjectSavedDir() / TEXT("Security.log");
    FFileHelper::SaveStringToFile(Output, *Path, FFileHelper::EEncoding
    Options::AutoDetect, &IFileManager::Get(), FILEWRITE_Append);
}
```

This implementation allows the game to quietly record tampering signals while maintaining extremely low runtime overhead.

Event-Driven Security Logging

Event-driven logging works by recording meaningful actions only when they occur. For example, if the integrity system flags a mismatch, if a debugger is detected, or if a tampered map hash is found, the system fires a logging event.

This section introduces a subsystem that acts as a central dispatcher for security-related events.

Listing 13-3 introduces a subsystem responsible for forwarding security events to the central logging system. By routing events through a subsystem, multiple security features can report activity through a single interface.

- USecurityEventLogger is a GameInstance subsystem that manages security reporting.

- ReportEvent() forwards a generic event category and message to the logger.

- ReportIntegrityFailure() records asset integrity violations.

- ReportDebuggerDetection() logs the presence of a runtime debugger.

Listing 13-3. USecurityEventLogger.h

```
#pragma once

#include "CoreMinimal.h"
#include "Subsystems/GameInstanceSubsystem.h"
#include "SecurityEventLogger.generated.h"

UCLASS()
class USecurityEventLogger : public UGameInstanceSubsystem
{
    GENERATED_BODY()

public:
    void ReportEvent(const FString& Category, const FString& Message);
    void ReportIntegrityFailure(const FString& AssetName);
    void ReportDebuggerDetection();
};
```

This subsystem provides a consistent entry point for security-related telemetry generated throughout the game.

Listing 13-4 implements the event forwarding subsystem by passing all messages to the shared logging utility.

- ReportEvent() forwards the event directly to the FSecurityLog system.

- ReportIntegrityFailure() constructs a descriptive message when asset hashes fail validation.

- ReportDebuggerDetection() logs a runtime debugger detection event.

- The subsystem centralizes event routing for future telemetry extensions.

Listing 13-4. USecurityEventLogger.cpp

```cpp
#include "SecurityEventLogger.h"
#include "SecurityLog.h"

void USecurityEventLogger::ReportEvent(const FString& Category, const
FString& Message)
{
    FSecurityLog::LogEvent(Category, Message);
}

void USecurityEventLogger::ReportIntegrityFailure(const FString& AssetName)
{
    ReportEvent(TEXT("IntegrityFailure"), FString::Printf(TEXT("Asset
    modified: %s"), *AssetName));
}

void USecurityEventLogger::ReportDebuggerDetection()
{
    ReportEvent(TEXT("Debugger"), TEXT("Debugger detected at runtime."));
}
```

By routing events through this subsystem, all security systems produce standardized log entries that can be analyzed consistently.

Monitoring Integrity Failures Across Systems

Earlier chapters introduced multiple defensive mechanisms that generate security-related signals during gameplay. Each of these systems produces useful information that can help identify tampering attempts.

Examples of these signal sources include

- Secure variable wrappers (Chapter 4)

- Debugger detection (Chapter 5)

- Save data integrity checks (Chapters 6 and 7)

- Blueprint logic exposure (Chapter 8)

- Console and CVar misuse (Chapter 9)

- Macro-detection heuristics (Chapter 10)

- Build-config hardening (Chapter 11)

- Asset protection (Chapter 12)

Monitoring unifies signals from all these sources into a consistent event stream that developers can analyze after release.

Listing 13-5 defines a small structure used to represent integrity-related events generated by various security systems.

- FIntegrityEvent stores structured tamper event information.

- Type identifies the type of security event that occurred.

- Target identifies the asset or subsystem affected.

- Detail stores additional context describing the event.

- Constructor initializes the event fields during creation.

Listing 13-5. FIntegrityEvent.h

```cpp
#pragma once

#include "CoreMinimal.h"

struct FIntegrityEvent
{
    FString Type;
    FString Target;
    FString Detail;
```

```
FIntegrityEvent(const FString& InType, const FString& InTarget, const
FString& InDetail)
    : Type(InType), Target(InTarget), Detail(InDetail) {}
};
```

This structure provides a simple and consistent representation of tampering events across multiple security systems.

Listing 13-6 demonstrates how integrity events are reported using the previously defined event structure and logging subsystem.

- ReportIntegrityEvent() is a helper function that forwards events to the logger.

- WorldContext provides access to the active game world.

- GetSubsystem() retrieves the USecurityEventLogger instance.

- Logger->ReportEvent() records the event through the central logging system.

Listing 13-6. FIntegrityEvent.cpp

```
#include "IntegrityEvent.h"
#include "SecurityEventLogger.h"
#include "Engine/Engine.h"

void ReportIntegrityEvent(UObject* WorldContext, const
FIntegrityEvent& Event)
{
    if (UWorld* World = WorldContext->GetWorld())
    {
        if (USecurityEventLogger* Logger = World->GetGameInstance()->GetSub
        system<USecurityEventLogger>())
        {
            Logger->ReportEvent(Event.Type, Event.Detail);
        }
    }
}
```

This helper function allows any subsystem to report integrity failures without directly interacting with the logging implementation.

Building a Tamper Telemetry Buffer

When a large number of events occur in a short time, for example, repeated save-tamper attempts, the logging system needs a way to capture information without flooding the log output.

A telemetry buffer solves this problem by storing a limited number of recent events while discarding older entries as the buffer fills. A well-designed telemetry buffer typically performs several functions.

A telemetry buffer should

- Store a fixed number of recent events

- Avoid dynamic memory churn

- Provide quick insertion

- Allow aggregation for pattern analysis

Listing 13-7 introduces a telemetry buffer designed to store recent tampering events without overwhelming the logging system.

- FTamperTelemetryBuffer stores a rolling set of security events.

- Events maintains the internal array of recorded entries.

- MaxEntries defines the maximum buffer capacity.

- AddEvent() inserts a new entry into the telemetry buffer.

- GetEvents() returns the current contents of the buffer.

Listing 13-7. FTamperTelemetryBuffer.h

```cpp
#pragma once

#include "CoreMinimal.h"

struct FTamperTelemetryBuffer
{
private:
    TArray<FString> Events;
    int32 MaxEntries;
```

```
public:
    FTamperTelemetryBuffer(int32 InMaxEntries = 50);

    void AddEvent(const FString& Entry);
    TArray<FString> GetEvents() const;
};
```

This structure provides a lightweight mechanism for retaining recent tampering signals for analysis.

Listing 13-8 implements the telemetry buffer mechanics used to maintain a fixed number of recent events.

- Constructor initializes the maximum buffer size.

- AddEvent() inserts new entries while removing the oldest event when capacity is exceeded.

- Events.RemoveAt() maintains the fixed-size circular behavior.

- GetEvents() returns the stored event list for analysis.

Listing 13-8. FTamperTelemetryBuffer.cpp

```
#include "TamperTelemetryBuffer.h"

FTamperTelemetryBuffer::FTamperTelemetryBuffer(int32 InMaxEntries)
{
    MaxEntries = InMaxEntries;
}

void FTamperTelemetryBuffer::AddEvent(const FString& Entry)
{
    if (Events.Num() >= MaxEntries)
    {
        Events.RemoveAt(0);
    }
    Events.Add(Entry);
}
```

```
TArray<FString> FTamperTelemetryBuffer::GetEvents() const
{
    return Events;
}
```

This buffer prevents excessive log output while still preserving enough information to analyze recent tampering behavior.

Detecting Patterns Over Time

A single integrity failure rarely provides enough information to determine whether tampering is occurring. In practice, attackers often experiment with multiple techniques during the same session.

Over time, several types of suspicious activity may appear, such as

- Repeated save rollbacks

- Continuous CVar tampering

- Debugger attach attempts

- Missing map hashes

- Macro-like movement or timing patterns

Correlating these events over time provides a clearer picture of player behavior and helps distinguish experimentation from deliberate tampering.

Listing 13-9 introduces a subsystem responsible for correlating security events and computing a behavioral suspicion score.

- UBehaviorCorrelationSubsystem aggregates security telemetry events.

- RecentEvents stores the history of recorded event messages.

- AddEvent() records new event data into the subsystem.

- ComputeSuspicionScore() calculates a score based on detected patterns.

Listing 13-9. UBehaviorCorrelationSubsystem.h

```cpp
#pragma once

#include "CoreMinimal.h"
#include "Subsystems/GameInstanceSubsystem.h"
#include "BehaviorCorrelationSubsystem.generated.h"

UCLASS()
class UBehaviorCorrelationSubsystem : public UGameInstanceSubsystem
{
    GENERATED_BODY()

private:
    TArray<FString> RecentEvents;

public:
    void AddEvent(const FString& Event);
    float ComputeSuspicionScore() const;
};
```

This subsystem allows multiple tampering signals to be analyzed together instead of evaluating each event in isolation.

Listing 13-10 implements the behavior correlation logic used to evaluate suspicious activity patterns over time.

- AddEvent() stores events while maintaining a bounded event history.

- RecentEvents.RemoveAt() removes the oldest event when the buffer exceeds its limit.

- ComputeSuspicionScore() evaluates events and applies weighted scoring.

- Event string checks identify patterns such as debugger detection or integrity failures.

Listing 13-10. UBehaviorCorrelationSubsystem.cpp

```cpp
#include "BehaviorCorrelationSubsystem.h"

void UBehaviorCorrelationSubsystem::AddEvent(const FString& Event)
{
    RecentEvents.Add(Event);
    if (RecentEvents.Num() > 100)
    {
        RecentEvents.RemoveAt(0);
    }
}

float UBehaviorCorrelationSubsystem::ComputeSuspicionScore() const
{
    float Score = 0.f;

    for (const FString& E : RecentEvents)
    {
        if (E.Contains(TEXT("Debugger"))) Score += 2.f;
        if (E.Contains(TEXT("IntegrityFailure"))) Score += 1.5f;
        if (E.Contains(TEXT("SaveTamper"))) Score += 1.f;
    }

    return Score;
}
```

This scoring mechanism provides a lightweight method for identifying suspicious behavior trends without introducing gameplay penalties.

Using Crash Reports As Security Signals

Crash logs are often the most overlooked security asset in a single-player title. Many forms of tampering produce crashes that follow identifiable patterns:

- Crashes involving injected DLLs

- Crashes caused by breakpoint manipulation

- Invalid memory after trainer detachment

- Corruption of encrypted save buffers

- Broken Blueprint flow caused by modified assets

When a crash report shows

- Suspicious module names

- Missing engine modules

- Pointers redirected to non-UE regions

- Deleted or overwritten .pak file signatures

It often indicates tampering rather than a random bug.

This chapter encourages you to analyze crash data for

- Injection artifacts

- Modified call paths

- Suspect library loading

- Unreal function pointer inconsistencies

Crash-driven anomaly detection is one of the most effective long-term monitoring strategies.

Case Study 1: Repeated Save File Rollback Attempts

A story-driven RPG observed players repeatedly loading older save files to exploit resource regeneration. The tamper telemetry buffer recorded

- Dozens of "SaveTamper: rollback detected" entries

- Exact timing of repeated rollbacks

- Persistent rollback loops over long sessions

The correlation subsystem classified these as a high-risk pattern. Although the game did not penalize players directly, the developer used this data to patch the exploit by marking certain resources as non-regenerative on reload.

Monitoring provided insight into real-world abuse, enabling a targeted gameplay fix.

Case Study 2: Map Integrity Failures Exposing Hidden Shortcuts

A first-person adventure title observed repeated integrity failures on one particular map file. The asset integrity manager reported

- "IntegrityFailure: Maps/Undercity.umap"

- Mismatched hash values

- Repeated failures from the same user sessions

Analysis later revealed that players were unpacking .pak files and modifying level geometry to open unintended paths. Monitoring made this visible—even without intrusive scanning—leading the developer to implement stronger asset encryption and prevent map modification in future updates.

Conclusion

Monitoring gameplay behavior after release plays an important role in maintaining the security of a single-player game. Even well-designed defensive systems cannot anticipate every exploit path or player interaction pattern. Observing how systems behave under real-world conditions helps developers refine protections and close vulnerabilities.

This chapter explores how lightweight monitoring systems can capture meaningful tampering signals without affecting performance. By correlating these signals, analyzing crash patterns, and tracking behavior over time, developers gain valuable insight into how their security systems perform in the wild.

With monitoring and detection mechanisms in place, the defensive architecture described throughout the book becomes more complete. The next chapter turns into a related challenge: supporting ethical modding communities while preserving the boundaries of your security systems. Chapter 14 explores how to encourage creative player modifications without exposing core gameplay mechanics to abuse.

CHAPTER 14

The Line Between Cheating and Modding

Modding is one of the most powerful ways to extend the life of a single-player game. Some of the most beloved games in history owe their longevity to mods. But when modding is implemented without boundaries, it becomes a direct path for tampering. Cheat tables, unofficial patches, difficulty removers, and progression unlockers often start from the same vectors that modding uses.

This chapter explains how to separate modding from cheating and how to build internal layers that allow creativity without compromising core integrity.

What Makes Modding Different from Cheating

Before supporting mods in a game, developers must define clear boundaries between acceptable customization and behavior that undermines the game's design. Players often modify games for creative purposes, but some modifications aim to bypass progression systems or remove intended challenges.

Modding is usually motivated by creative and community-driven goals. Common motivations include

- Creative expression

- Extending replayability

- Community engagement

- Personalization of the gameplay experience

Cheating, in contrast, typically focuses on bypassing game systems that define progression or difficulty. Common motivations include

- Skipping progression systems

- Unlocking content without completing requirements

- Bypassing gameplay challenges

- Tampering with protected game systems

A well-designed system acknowledges that both behaviors can originate from similar technical entry points. The goal of a secure modding framework is to clearly separate permitted creativity from actions that compromise game integrity.

The Security Boundary: What Must Never Be Moddable

Not every system in a game can safely support modding. Certain gameplay mechanisms must remain protected because they influence progression, difficulty, or system integrity.

The protected portion of the game typically includes systems such as the following:

- Currency, XP, and level progression

- Quest states and completion flags

- Unlockables, upgrades, and branching story outcomes

- Enemy stats and AI behaviors that affect challenge

- Save file integrity, checksums, and anti-rollback systems

- Internal security systems such as wrappers or detectors

- Telemetry and analytics behavior

These components form the secure core of the game. While mods may interact with the surrounding systems, direct modification of these protected elements should not be possible.

Structuring Unreal Projects for Safe Modding

Mods should interact with the game only through carefully controlled entry points. Unreal Engine's modular architecture makes this possible when the project structure is designed with security boundaries in mind.

Several architectural practices help establish safe modding boundaries within an Unreal project. These practices include

- Exposing a limited API through BlueprintCallable functions

- Using plugin architectures for mod loading

- Keeping protected logic inside C++ and internal classes

- Creating "read-only" data surfaces for modders

- Allowing cosmetic or non-critical tweaks only

- Restricting access to GameState, GameInstance, or SaveGame objects

This separation ensures that modding functionality remains isolated from the systems responsible for gameplay balance or player progression.

Safe Modding Categories

The safest types of mods are those that do not modify the rules governing gameplay. Instead, they focus on presentation, accessibility, or personalization features.

Examples of mod categories that are generally safe to support include

- Visual mods (textures, colors, UI rearrangements)

- Audio mods (new sound effects, music packs)

- Cosmetic weapon skins

- Lighting or post-processing adjustments

- Photo mode enhancements

- UI add-ons that read exposed data but cannot write to it

- Accessibility improvements

These types of modifications encourage creativity while avoiding direct manipulation of gameplay systems.

What Should Never Be Exposed to Modders

Some engine systems and gameplay components should never be exposed through modding APIs. Providing access to these systems can allow players to build tools that function as cheats rather than creative modifications.

Developers should avoid exposing modding access to systems such as

- PlayerController logic

- Character stats, weapon damage, health systems

- AI decision trees or BT nodes

- GameState authoritative data

- Internal anti-tamper components

- SaveGame validation logic

- Replication rules (even for single player)

Even in single-player games, exposing these systems can allow modifications that undermine progression, balance, or system integrity.

Building a Safe Modding API

A controlled API is one of the most effective ways to support modding while maintaining strong security boundaries. Instead of exposing entire systems, developers can provide carefully designed functions that allow customization without revealing gameplay-critical internals.

These APIs typically expose limited functionality intended for safe modifications. For example, a modding interface may allow cosmetic adjustments or read-only access to certain values while preventing any modification of gameplay systems.

Listing 14-1 introduces a minimal modding interface designed to support cosmetic and non-gameplay customization. The goal of this interface is to allow modders to interact with the game through clearly defined functions without exposing internal gameplay systems or sensitive engine objects.

- UModdingAPI is a lightweight UObject-based interface used to expose safe modding functions.

- ApplyColorScheme() provides a cosmetic customization hook for modifying visual themes.

- ReplaceMusicTrack() allows modders to swap audio assets without touching gameplay logic.

- GetPlayerSpeedReadOnly() exposes a gameplay value in read-only form so that modders can reference information without modifying internal data.

- The class intentionally inherits from UObject instead of gameplay classes to avoid exposing direct access to gameplay systems.

Listing 14-1. UModdingAPI.h

```
#pragma once

#include "CoreMinimal.h"
#include "UObject/NoExportTypes.h"
#include "ModdingAPI.generated.h"

UCLASS()
class UModdingAPI : public UObject
{
    GENERATED_BODY()

public:

    UFUNCTION(BlueprintCallable, Category="Modding|Cosmetics")
    void ApplyColorScheme(FLinearColor NewColor);

    UFUNCTION(BlueprintCallable, Category="Modding|Audio")
    void ReplaceMusicTrack(const FString& TrackPath);

    UFUNCTION(BlueprintPure, Category="Modding|ReadOnly")
    float GetPlayerSpeedReadOnly() const;
};
```

This interface establishes a controlled entry point for modding features. By restricting access to cosmetic functions and read-only values, the system prevents modders from interacting with gameplay-critical mechanics.

Listing 14-2 provides the implementation of the modding API functions introduced in the previous listing. The implementation ensures that modding functionality remains limited to presentation-level changes while preventing modifications to gameplay logic.

- ApplyColorScheme() applies visual changes only and does not interact with gameplay state.

- ReplaceMusicTrack() replaces background music through asset references without modifying gameplay systems.

- GetPlayerSpeedReadOnly() returns a copied value rather than exposing the internal movement component.

- The implementation deliberately avoids returning pointers to gameplay objects or engine subsystems.

- Each function is designed so that modders can customize presentation without affecting balance or progression.

Listing 14-2. UModdingAPI.cpp

```cpp
#include "ModdingAPI.h"
#include "Kismet/GameplayStatics.h"

void UModdingAPI::ApplyColorScheme(FLinearColor NewColor)
{
    // Cosmetic only
}

void UModdingAPI::ReplaceMusicTrack(const FString& TrackPath)
{
    // Cosmetic only
}
```

```
float UModdingAPI::GetPlayerSpeedReadOnly() const
{
    // Return a copy so modders cannot modify internal objects
    return 600.f;
}
```

This implementation demonstrates how a modding API can safely expose customization features while preserving strict boundaries around gameplay systems.

Case Study 1: Safe UI Modding Without Gameplay Access

A developer allowed UI mods through a limited Blueprint API that exposed menu widgets and HUD elements. Players created custom UI layouts and mini-maps, which increased the game's popularity.

Because gameplay values were never exposed

- No XP modifiers were possible.

- No stat changes or difficulty alterations occurred.

- Mods did not break progression or save data.

This demonstrates how safe modding increases player happiness without weakening security.

Case Study 2: A Gameplay "Mod" That Turned into Cheating

Another game allowed BlueprintCallable access to CharacterMovementComponent for "experimental modding." Within days, players released mods that

- Tripled sprint speed

- Disabled stamina drain

- Removed incoming damage

- Unlocked boss rooms prematurely

Those mods were popular but they were cheats, not mods. After tightening the API and removing gameplay-critical functions, the issue was resolved. This highlights the importance of establishing security boundaries early.

Conclusion

Modding and cheating often originate from similar technical entry points, which makes clear boundaries essential. Supporting creative player modifications while maintaining gameplay integrity requires careful design.

This chapter demonstrated how developers can provide modding capabilities without exposing gameplay-critical systems. By defining protected subsystems, designing controlled APIs, and limiting modding access to cosmetic or non-progression features, developers can encourage community creativity while preserving the intended gameplay experience.

Appendixes

The appendixes in this book are designed as practical tools that support the ideas explored in the main chapters. While the chapters explain concepts, architecture, attack models, and defensive strategies in depth, the appendixes gather the most important information into concise references. These sections are organized so that readers can revisit them throughout development, testing, and release. The goal is to provide developers with clear guidance they can use during rapid problem-solving or final verification. Each appendix focuses on an area where a structured checklist, a consolidated set of notes, or a curated list of tools can significantly improve daily security decisions. By keeping these references together in one place, readers can ensure that the principles of the book remain actionable long after the first read.

Appendix A

Unreal Engine Security Checklist
Security in a single-player game is strongest when applied consistently across the entire development process. This appendix provides a complete checklist to verify that your project maintains the protections described throughout the book. It can be used during early development, internal reviews, optimization stages, and pre-release evaluations.

Architectural Security Checklist

- Confirm that no critical values exist as plain floats, integers, or Booleans.

- Ensure there are no single points of failure in gameplay systems.

© Sheikh Sohel Moon 2026
S. S. Moon, *Securing Single-Player Games in Unreal Engine,* https://doi.org/10.1007/979-8-8688-2833-1

- Distribute player state across components rather than storing everything in one struct.

- Remove unnecessary systems that increase the attack surface.

- Use encapsulation to avoid direct value access.

- Limit reliance on global singletons.

Memory Layout and Predictability

- Avoid sequential storage of related values.

- Prevent predictable ordering of sensitive variables.

- Ensure no debug variables remain in the final build.

- Remove development shortcuts that follow consistent memory patterns.

Blueprint and Reflection Exposure

- Limit BlueprintReadWrite exposure for sensitive values.

- Remove reflection visibility when not required.

- Confirm UI widgets do not read gameplay state directly.

- Ensure editing categories do not reveal internal logic.

Runtime Variable Protection Checklist

- Use secure wrappers for critical values.

- Maintain redundancy for important variables.

- Validate shadow values or secondary representations regularly.

- Introduce unpredictable transformations to reduce scanning reliability.

Behavioral Monitoring

- Enable freeze detection on sensitive values.
- Record suspicious changes for internal review.
- Maintain rolling history for frequently updated values.

Noise and Obfuscation

- Surround protected variables with memory noise pools.
- Ensure noise values change realistically.
- Prevent noise values from influencing gameplay.

Debugging and Injection Detection Checklist

- Use multiple debugger detection techniques.
- Trigger detection during startup and gameplay.
- Monitor loaded modules for unexpected entries.
- Watch for abnormal thread activity.
- Detect suspicious changes in execution flow.
- Validate that key logic paths cannot be bypassed easily.

Save System Security Checklist

- Validate every field on load.
- Reject impossible or inconsistent values.
- Use integrity checks to detect edited or duplicated saves.
- Maintain versioning for forward compatibility.
- Remove test fields and unnecessary SaveGame properties.
- Avoid exposing sensitive internal structures through save metadata.

Blueprint Security Checklist

- Remove unnecessary BlueprintCallable functions.
- Ensure exec functions do not ship in final builds.
- Prevent Blueprint graphs from exposing sensitive internal data.
- Remove or hide debug variables and development categories.

Console and Config Security Checklist

- Disable the console in shipping builds.
- Remove test commands.
- Ensure sensitive CVars do not appear in config files.
- Remove debugging and profiling options.
- Confirm no development flags remain in the final package.

Packaging and Build Security Checklist

- Strip debugging symbols from the shipping build.
- Never release development or test builds.
- Encrypt PAK files.
- Confirm PAK indices do not expose internal work.
- Remove DataTables that contain raw sensitive data.
- Ensure no test DLLs or unused modules remain.

Post-Release Monitoring Checklist

- Track suspicious events across players.
- Detect impossible value patterns.

- Validate new patches against all security measures.

- Monitor cheat forums and trainer platforms.

- Observe player reviews for signs of tampered experiences.

Appendix B

This appendix provides a consolidated set of notes that summarize the principles behind runtime variable protection. These notes offer quick reminders for teams who have already read Chapter 4 and wish to confirm that their implementation follows best practices.

Design Notes for Secure Variables

- A secure variable should never directly store its true value.

- A secure variable should use a reversible transformation that is not immediately obvious.

- A secure variable should maintain redundancy to detect edits.

- A secure variable should use multiple independent representations.

Reliability Notes

- All security operations should occur within predictable and controlled code paths.

- The decryption logic should remain private and centralized.

- Internal transformations should not break under rapid updates.

- Edge cases should be tested thoroughly, especially under heavy gameplay load.

Behavior Notes

- Variable updates should appear natural over time.

- Abrupt changes should trigger internal warnings.

- Freeze detection should operate independently of rendering or frame rate conditions.

Integration Notes

- Secure variables should be used only where needed due to performance considerations.

- They must remain invisible to Blueprints when possible.

- They must not be logged in development builds unless intentionally recorded.

Appendix C

This appendix provides a curated selection of tools, plugins, and utilities that support security minded development. The tools listed here are not mandatory, but they can greatly improve detection, validation, profiling, and structural consistency.

Unreal Engine Tools

- Unreal Insights for performance and anomaly monitoring

- Memory profiling tools for identifying unusual allocation patterns

- Data Validation Editor for automated checking of DataTables and assets

- Config Editor for reviewing configuration exposure

External Analysis Tools

- Static analysis tools for reviewing code quality

- Binary inspection tools for verifying packaged executable integrity

- Log aggregation tools for collecting behavioral anomalies

- File integrity tools for verifying PAK and asset stability

Development Plugins

- Plugins that centralize gameplay logs or telemetry

- Blueprint exposure auditing plugins

- Tools that assist with automated regression testing

Appendix D

This appendix gathers extra notes that help developers maintain a stable and predictable environment, especially when investigating potential tampering or verifying protections.

Debugging Notes

- Use controlled test environments to avoid false positives.

- Verify debugger detection behavior across multiple machines.

- Ensure detection does not activate during legitimate development workflows.

Monitoring Notes

- Maintain consistent timestamps for in-game event validation.

- Track execution delays to identify potential stealth debugging.

- Use internal counters to detect unusual loops or function calls.

Engine Notes

- Monitor key engine subsystems that often become hook targets.

- Validate that subsystem behavior remains consistent across patches.

- Confirm that no exposed interfaces provide unintended access.

Glossary of Terms

Glossary of Terms (Expanded Edition)

This glossary defines important vocabulary used throughout the book. It consolidates terminology from every chapter so readers can reference all core security, Unreal Engine, and cheat-related concepts in one place.

A

A/B State Verification

A validation technique that checks two different internal representations of a value for consistency

A/B Testing Trap

A decoy mechanic where the game intentionally returns slightly different values to detect if an attacker is comparing them

Action Frequency Analysis

Detecting macros by measuring actions per second

Activation Gate

A gameplay requirement that must be satisfied before a reward or event triggers

Active Memory Region

A portion of RAM currently allocated by the game for runtime values

Address Space

All memory addresses that the process can access during execution

AES-256

A strong encryption algorithm used for protecting save data

AI Manipulation

The act of controlling enemy behavior by modifying internal AI parameters

AOB (Array-of-Bytes) Scanning

Searching for unique byte patterns to locate functions or variables in memory

API Surface

All callable functions or interfaces exposed to tools or users

Application Layer Hook

A hook inserted into high-level logic, often more visible than a low-level hook

Artifact Drift

A mismatch between packaged files and their expected signatures due to tampering

Asset Extraction

Pulling data from packaged game files using third-party tools

Asset Integrity Manager

A runtime validator ensuring assets have not been modified

Attack Surface

All points where an attacker may interact with or compromise the system

Attack Vector

A specific method used to compromise a game, such as memory editing or DLL injection

Atomic Operation

An operation that completes without risk of interference from another thread

Authentication Token

A unique identifier used for validation or decryption tasks

B

Baseline Value

The expected or default value before any transformations are applied

Behavioral Signal

Any measurable action that indicates tampering or automation

Binary Patch

A modification to machine code inside the executable

Blueprint Exposure

The visibility of functions or variables through the Blueprint system

Blueprint VM Reflection

The reflection layer exposing BlueprintCallable features

Breakpoint

A controlled pause in code execution for debugging

Buffer Window

A small region of stored values used for comparison or anomaly detection

Build Pipeline

The sequence of steps used to compile, package, and deploy the project

Build-Time Security

Ensuring the build process does not ship debug features or sensitive files

C

Call Stack

The ordered list of function calls active at a given point in runtime

CBC (Cipher Block Chaining)

An encryption mode where each block depends on the previous one

CBS (Composite Behavior Score)

A score for detecting bots using weighted behavioral signals

Change Drift

A deviation between expected and actual values during gameplay

Cheat Engine

A popular tool for scanning and modifying game memory

Checkpoint Integrity

A guarantee that checkpoint data has not been altered

Ciphertext

Encrypted data unauthenticated without its key

CVar (Console Variable)

An engine level configuration value accessible through console systems

Code Injection

Overwriting or inserting new logic inside a game's process

Cold Path

A rarely executed code path that may reveal hidden debug logic

Collision of Values

A situation where two unrelated values appear identical when obfuscated

Component-Based Security

Distributing state across components to reduce predictability

Config Exposure

Sensitive data revealed in configuration files

Controlled Modding API

A restricted interface provided for safe modding

Cryptographic Save Envelope

A secure container combining encrypted data, salt, IV, and cryptographic signatures

D

Data Drift

A gradual deviation from expected values detected during monitoring

Data Entropy

The randomness level of stored data, often checked in encrypted files

Data Injection

Supplying manipulated or harmful data through save files or configs

Debug Signature

Any recognizable pattern left behind by a debugger

Debugger

A tool used to inspect or control program execution

Derived Key

A cryptographic key generated from salts or installation-specific data

Diffusion

A cryptographic property that spreads small changes across large outputs

Digital Fingerprint

A unique signature used to validate authenticity

DLL Injection

Forcing a foreign module into the game process

E

Early Hook Detection

Monitoring the startup sequence for unexpected injected modules

Encrypted Segment

A specific region of data stored in cipher form

Entropy Spike

A sudden rise in randomness, often caused by manipulated data

Event Replay

Re-running previously captured events to bypass progression rules

Event Spoofing

Triggering an event without completing its required conditions

Event-Driven Logging

Recording security signals only when triggered

Exec Function

A function callable from the console

F

Fail-Safe State

A safe fallback triggered when tampering is suspected

Fallback Key

An alternate key used when primary data is invalid

Fidelity Check

Verifying the consistency of related systems

FProperty

Reflection metadata describing class properties

Freeze Detection

Detecting memory that refuses to update

Function Hook

Redirecting execution from a function to attacker code

G

GIDS (Gameplay-Integrated Deception System)

Deceptive in-game traps that only a bot would interact with incorrectly

Global State Mutation

Altering variables that affect the entire game

H

Hard Countermeasure

A strong reaction to tampering, such as save rejection

Hardware Breakpoint

A CPU-level breakpoint invisible to simple detection

Hash Mismatch

A difference between expected and actual data hashes

HMAC

A signature used to ensure data authenticity

Honeypot Variable

A decoy value meant to trigger tamper detection

I

Implausibility Detection

Ensuring values make logical sense

INI Sanitization

Stripping forbidden settings from config files

Initialization Vector

Random bytes used to make encryption nondeterministic

Input Entropy

The randomness of player input used for macro-detection

Input Timing Analysis

Detecting macros via timing patterns

Integrity Check

A verification method ensuring data was not modified

K

Key Rotation

Periodically generating new encryption keys

L

Latency Spike

A sudden delay that may indicate debugging or breakpoints

Latent Action Abuse

Using Blueprint delays or timelines to gain unfair rewards

Layered Defense Model

Building multiple security layers instead of one perfect solution

Legacy Offset

A stale memory location used by outdated trainers

Load Order

The sequence that modules load into memory

M

Macro-Detection

Identifying automated inputs by measuring timing patterns

Man-in-the-Process Attack

An attack where injected code modifies logic at runtime

Memory Alias

Two different pointers referencing the same memory

Memory Fragmentation

Scattered memory allocation that may mislead scanners but cannot stop advanced tools

Memory Noise Pools

Fake variables designed to look meaningful

Memory Scan

Searching for values in RAM

Metadata Leak

Accidentally exposing sensitive information through metadata

Modular Hook

A hook placed inside a modular engine subsystem

Modding Interface

A controlled access point for external creators

N

N-Frame Drift Analysis

Checking value changes across several frames

Noise Entropy

Randomness used to disguise sensitive values

NOP (No Operation)

A patch that disables an instruction

O

Obfuscation Layer

A transformation applied to hide raw values

Offset Chain

A series of offsets leading to a variable

One-Way Mapping

A transformation that is easy to compute but difficult to reverse

P

PAK Encryption/Signing

Security applied to packaged assets

Patch Window

A period after release where trainers update

PDB (Program Database)

A debug symbol file that should never ship

Pointer Path

A series of pointers leading to a value

Pointer Scanning

Finding stable reference paths for cheats

Process Environment Block (PEB)

A structure containing process metadata

Protected Core

The systems shielded from modding or external access

Q

Query Entropy

Random behavior inserted into validation queries

Quick Scan Exposure

Values that can be detected using Cheat Engine's initial scan features

R

Redundant State

Multiple internal representations of a value

Reflection Exposure

Visibility of internal systems through metadata

Reputation Scoring

A long-term trust metric for save slots

Rollback Detection

Identifying when older save data is loaded intentionally

Runtime Memory Tampering

Editing values in RAM while the game runs

S

Salt

Random data added to keys or hashes

Save Envelope

The combined package of data, metadata, and cryptographic material

Save File Manipulation

Editing or replacing saves to bypass progression

Scatter Pattern

Placing values unpredictably in memory

Secure Core

Progression-critical systems protected against tampering

Secure Wrapper

A data structure storing values in transformed form

Semantic Obfuscation

Making variables abstract before exposing them to Blueprints

Shadow Variables

Secondary representations used for cross-validation

Side-Channel Detection

Detecting tampering through indirect timing or performance metrics

Signature Drift

Changes in pattern scans caused by updates

Soft Countermeasure

A subtle penalty for tampering

State Fingerprinting

Checking whether variable combinations are logically valid

Symbol Stripping

Removing debug symbols from a build

T

Tamper Artifact

A detectable change caused by tampering

Tamper Vector

The specific pathway used in an attack

Telemetry Buffer

A rolling buffer storing security events

Temporal Integrity

Ensuring timestamps progress correctly

Thread Scanning

Enumerating threads to detect suspicious activity

Token Validation

Verifying that internal values represent authorized states

Trainer

Packaged cheating software

Trampoline

A jump instruction redirecting logic to attacker code

Trap Script

A decoy script meant to detect automation

U

UGameViewportClient Override

Preventing console creation by overriding viewport behavior

Unreal Object Model

The memory and structural design of Unreal objects

Update Divergence

A mismatch between expected and actual value progression

V

Value Drift

Gradual divergence from expected values

Value Obfuscation

Transforming data so the true value never appears directly

Vaulting Behavior

A macro response where movement patterns follow unrealistic paths

W

Watchpoint

A memory location monitored for changes

Weak Entropy Range

A predictable range of values that reduces protection strength

Whitelist Enforcement

Limiting modding or editing privileges to approved actions only

X

XOR Obfuscator

A lightweight bitwise transformation used to mask data

Y

Yield Spike

A CPU stall caused by a breakpoint or hook

Z

Zero-Fill Attack

Overwriting sections of memory with zeros to erase checks or bypass systems

Index

A

Android shipping considerations
    APK modding, 214
    JNI debug entry, 213
    logcat system, 213
    mitigation strategies, 214
    sandbox model, 213
Anti-debugging techniques
    debug (*see* Debugging techniques)
    frame delays, 81
    subsystem-based approach, 81–83
    timing-based methods, 81
Application programming
       interfaces (APIs)
    debugging, 64
    modding and cheating system, 326–329
Asset protection model
    encryption and decryption
       operations, 303–304
    FAESUtility, 303
    files/binary data, 304
    flowchart, 291, 292
    game data (*see* Game data protection)
    integrity system, 294–297
    map registration process, 302
    operations, 294
    packaging configuration, 293–294
    PAK files, 293
    tampering strategies, 292–293
    UAssetIntegrityManager, 295
Attackers
    assets and data extraction, 18

    blueprint/exec functions, 17–18
    capabilities, 11
    categories, 37
    cheat engine, 14
    code injection, 15
    critical state, 27–28
    exploit layer patterns, 30–31
    mental model, 11
    methods, 19
    motivations, 10
    predictable patterns, 26
    red team analysis, 56
    runtime memory, 36
    targeted elements, 18
    text-only memory map, 29
Automation tools
    detection (*see* Detection systems)
    gameplay loops, 227
       camera-control, 227
       farming loops, 227
       frame-step, 228
       menu systems, 227
    input system, 224
    keyboard/mouse events, 225
    pulses/flooding, 226
    timing assumptions, 228
       microseconds, 228
       predictable cooldown systems, 229
       unrealistic sequences, 229
    unlimited-rates, 226
    unreal games, 224
    virtual devices, 225

B

Behavior correlation
action diversity *vs.* gameplay
context, 255
composite evaluator, 257
detectors, 256
entropy *vs.* camera control, 255
fatigue/distraction/reaction, 256
principles, 254
timing and movement, 254
Blueprints
accessibility, 145
annotation analysis, 150
BlueprintCallable, 148–149
callable console commands, 161–162
Construction Scripts (CSs), 159–161
C++ method, 151–152
Data Assets, CurveTables and
DataTables, 169–171
event dispatchers, 154–155
exploitation, 147–148
exposure vectors, 147
function, 145
graphs, 150, 164–165
honeypots/traps, 166–167
interface method, 157–159
latent actions, 167–169
metadata annotations, 149–150
reflection system, 146
semantic obfuscation, 171–173
setter functions, 163
skill unlock paths, 175
state fingerprinting, 156
state machines, 173–175
structured audit process, 150
survival game, 175
variables, 155–157, 162–164
widget, 152–154

Build-time configuration
community tool, 289
DebugGame/development, 278
debug symbols and PDB files,
280–281
development configuration, 288–289
editor dependencies, 282
flags, 284
pipeline hardening, 285, 288
plugins and modules, 277, 282–284
practical techniques, 275, 276
reverse engineers, 289–290
security concern, 276–277
security perspective, 277–278
shipping builds, 278
target rules file, 278–280
test builds, 278
validation process, 285–287

C

Cheat Engine game
workflow, 36
Cheating system, *see* Modding and
cheating system
Cheating techniques
access survival game, 6
blueprint exploits, 6
community collaboration, 13
content discovery, 13
destroying progression, 6
experience points (XP), 2
influencer amplification, 13
long-term consequences, 7
modern tools, 5
primary attack surfaces, 11
results, 5
reviews, 2

taxonomy, 11–12

technical strategies, 9

trainer request hubs, 13

Unreal Engine (*see* Unreal
Engine games)

XP inflation, 6

Composite Behavior Score (CBS)

behavior correlation, 254–257

evaluation, 251–254

subsystem contributes, 251

weighted correlation scoring, 253

Console/developer access

configuration files

attacks/protection, 195

restrictions, 195

rule file, 195–196

validation system, 197–202

Cvar system, 178–179, 183–189

exec functions, 190–195

game security, 177

hidden debugging toggles, 215–216

input protections, 182–183

modules, 182

pipeline hardening, 202

Android, 213–214

blacklist, 203

editor-only modules, 202–206

FModuleStripper, 204

Linux, 211–212

pak files, 206–207

platform rules, 208

strip modules, 203

target settings, 207

unsafe flags, 207–208

Windows, 209–211

runtime exploitation, 214–215

shipping build, 180–181

trainer/modding tool, 177

Console variables (CVars)

categories, 178, 188

cheat frameworks, 178

debugging/internal testing, 179

FCVarSecurityManager, 184

modifications, 189

non-whitelisted read-only, 183–188

rendering categories, 188

security layer, 188

security model, 183

security restrictions, 185

security system, 189

UConsole class, 178

UFUNCTION(Exec), 179

variables, 179

Construction Scripts (CSs), 159–161

Correlation analysis, *see* Behavior
correlation

C++ programming, 151–152

Cryptographic system

components, 102–104

key derivation, 94–96

mechanisms, 92–94

save envelope, 91

scenario, 91

serializes and deserializes data, 103

structure of, 91, 92

D

Debugging techniques

capabilities, 61

dead-code guards, 84

delayed responses, 84

detection (*see* Detection techniques)

driven analysis techniques, 62

external tools, 59, 60

gameplay dynamics, 65

Debugging techniques (*cont.*)
  hook functions, 66
  injection detection (*see* Injection
    detection)
  integrity checks, 84
  internal aspect, 60
  kernel-level assistance, 65
  memory/code integrity checks, 84
  memory patching strategies, 62
  monitor module, 65
  pipes/stealth attachment, 64
  runtime intrusion pathways, 60
  stealth game, 85
  structural consistency, 63
  Windows APIs, 64
Deception system
  bait-trap system, 263
  branching scenarios, 261
  design principles, 261–262
  deterministic instructions, 258
  GIDS, 258–265
  human responses, 258
  macro-detection architecture,
    264–265
  meaningless distraction events, 260
  pseudo-interactive targets, 259
  soft-penalty systems, 265–269
  strategies, 259
  timing opportunities, 259
  trap component, 262–264
  variations, 260
Decryption, *see* Encryption/
    validation systems
Detection systems
  action frequencies, 242
  behavioral patterns
    looping paths, 238
    macro patterns, 238
      movement recognition, 238–239
      Window, 239–241
  CBS (*see* Composite Behavior
      Score (CBS))
  deception system, 258
  frequency evaluation, 243
  input patterns, 229
  input timing analysis, 230
    burst frequency, 230
    intervals, 230
    statistical variance, 232
    UInputTimingAnalyzer, 231–234
    variations, 231
  safe/subtle countermeasures
    delayed strategies, 245
    principle, 245
    response manager, 246–248
    safe soft penalties, 248–249
    UMacroDelayResponseS
      ubsystem, 247
    USoftPenaltyComponent, 249–251
  state validation, 234–237
    component, 234, 236
    UStateLockedInput
      Component, 235–237
  tracking rates, 242
  UActionFrequencyTracker, 242
Detection techniques
  CheckRemoteDebuggerPresent, 68–70
  external debugger monitoring, 68
  fundamentals, 66
  hardware breakpoints
    side-channel approaches, 74
    timing analysis, 70–73
    traditional integrity, 71
    working process, 70
  IsDebuggerPresent, 66–68
Dynamic link library (DLL), 61

E, F

Encryption/validation data
    AES decryption, 97–99
    logic/IV generation, 98
Encryption/validation systems
    construction sandbox game, 114–115
    key design principle, 112, 113
    loading data, 108
        SecureSaveLoader.cpp, 110–112
        SecureSaveLoader.h, 109–110
        threat model, 108
        verification sequence, 108
    rollback technique, 114
    secure envelope, 105
    skill tree corruption, 113
    threat modeling, 90
    writer workflow, 106–107

G, H

Game data protection
    defensive technique, 297
    formats, 297
    obfuscation system, 298
    runtime verification, 299–301
    sensitive configuration, 298
    table-driven configuration, 300
    XOR operation, 298, 299
Gameplay-Integrated Deception System
    (GIDS), 258–265

I, J, K

Injection detection
    artificial input events, 85–86
    capabilities, 61
    DLL injection, 61, 78
    entry points, 65
    enumerate modules, 78
    module enumeration, 78
    optional memory regions, 79–81
    scanning, 81
    suspicious substrings, 78
    thread scanning, 74–77

L

Linux
    object injection risks, 212
    ptrace, 211
    shipping considerations, 211
    stdout/stderr suppression, 212

M, N

Macro automation
    modification, 219
    single-player environments,
        220–221
Map registration process, 302
Micro-friction systems, 268
Modding and cheating system, 323
    API builds, 326–329
    architectural practices, 325
    categories, 325
    cheats, 330
    engine systems/gameplay
        components, 326
    experimental modding, 329
    internal gameplay systems, 326
    modifications, 328
    motivations, 323–324
    protected portion, 324
    safe boundaries, 325
    UI layouts and mini-maps, 329

Monitoring system, 307
    behavioral suspicion, 318
    characteristics, 308
    correlation subsystem, 321
    crash logs/reports, 320–321
    event-driven logging, 311–313
    integrity-related events, 314
    logging system, 310, 311
    map integrity failures, 322
    post-launch system, 307–309
    routing events, 313
    scoring mechanism, 320
    security-relevant events, 309–311
    security signals, 308
    signal sources, 313–315
    suspicious activity, 318–320
    telemetry buffer, 316–318

O

Obfuscation system, 298

P, Q

Process Environment Block (PEB), 66
Progression curve modeling
    types, 131
    UProgressionCurveSave, 131–132
    XP, gold/difficulty, 131
Protection system
    cross-field validation, 129–130
    device fingerprints, 124–125
    duplication loop, 141
    hard countermeasures, 140
    honeypots/decoy, 119
    identical save states, 126–127
    implausibility detection, 121–122
    layered tampering detection, 118–119

manipulation techniques, 117
memory-based stat manipulation, 142
metadata tracking, 122–124
open-world RPG, 141–142
progression, 131–132
reputation scoring
    save slot, 134
    USaveReputationModel,
        135–136
reverse-diff analysis, 133–134
rollback detection, 122–124
save duplication, 124–125
session correlation, 127–129
snapshots, 126
soft countermeasures, 139
tampering detection, 140
temporal integrity, 122–124
trap variable pattern, 119–120
unified detection pipeline,
    136–139
validation layers, 136

R

Reflection system, 146
Reverse-diff tamper
    reconstruction, 133–134
Reward degradation systems, 267
Runtime memory
    attackers, 36
    categories, 37
    characteristics, 36
    defensive capabilities, 39
    defensive systems, 37
    editing tools, 35
    encrypted/redundant
        representations, 39
    float wrapper philosophy, 38–39

layered approach, 35

reflection system, 38

secure float (*see* Secure float
implementation)

structural characteristics, 38

Runtime variable protection

behavior, 336

debugging, 337

design notes, 335

engine subsystems, 338

integration, 336

monitoring system, 337

reliability notes, 335

S

Save data system, 89

authenticity, 91

casual editors, 90

categories, 90

confidentiality, 90

cryptographics (*see*
Cryptographic system)

encryption (*see* Encryption/validation
systems)

hex editor, 89

HMAC SHA256 helper, 99–101

integrity, 90

objectives, 90

operations, 105

protections (*see* Protection system)

reverse-engineer, 90

SecureSaveWriter.h, 105

tools-assisted modifiers, 90

version compatibility, 91

Secure float implementation, 40–42

components, 41

decryption paths, 42

external modification, 43

freeze detection, 48–50

FSecureFloat.cpp, 41

FSecureFloat.h, 40

historical values, 51

history-based analysis, 50–52

integration decisions, 55

key rotation, 46–48

layered protection, 43

noise pools, 53–55

primary and shadow storage, 44

RotateKey method, 46

security layers, 40

shadow variables, 43–46

Security checklist, 331

architecture, 331

behavioral monitoring, 333

blueprint graphs, 334

blueprint/reflection, 332

console/config, 334

detection techniques, 333

memory layout/predictability, 332

noise values, 333

PAK files, 334

post-release, 334

runtime variables, 332

save system, 333

Semantic obfuscation, 171–173

Shipping builds

Android, 213–214

benefits, 180

build configuration, 276, 278

INI files, 195

modules, 182

overrides, 181

target rules file, 278

UNoConsoleViewportClient, 180

viewport client, 180–181

Single-player security, 1
    assumptions, 3
    attackers, 18–19
    categories, 3
    cheating (*see* Cheating techniques)
    defensive techniques, 19
    designing game, 4
    layered model, 7
    motivations, 10
    narrative conflict, 4–5
Soft-penalty systems, 265
    categories, 266
    cooldown inflation, 268
    detection pipeline, 270–272
    escalation, 271
    gameplay systems, 273
    hard blocks, 266
    long-term achievement, 269
    micro-friction systems, 268
    progression gates, 267
    progression tracking, 269
    reward degradation systems, 267
    soft locks, 267
    suspicion-to-penalty, 269–270
    timing detection, 273–274
Soft *vs.* hard countermeasures, 139

T

Tamper resistance
    attackers patterns, 30–31
    checklist, 33
    component-based architecture, 31
    components and validation layers, 22
    conceptual patterns, 21
    derived values, 31
    developer mistakes, 30
    distribution, 32
        gameplay architecture, 21
        health system, 32–33, 56
        indie action game, 33
        key aspects, 23
        predictable patterns
            attack surface, 27
            critical state, 27–28
            cross-validation, 28
            harm security, 26
            redundancy, 28
            unpredictability, 28
        realistic security design, 56, 57
        runtime defenses, 33
        runtime memory (*see*
            Runtime memory)
        secure design, 29
        security benefits, 31
        security foundation, 22–23
        text-only memory map, 29
        Unreal Engine, 23–26
Thread scanning
    differences, 75
    DLL injectors, 74
    enumeration, 77
    identifiable patterns, 75
    injection/hooking tools, 74
    ToolHelp API, 75–77
    Tools, plugins, and utilities
    development plugins, 337
    external analysis tools, 337
    unreal engine tools, 336
Trainer and macro automation, 219
    automation (*see* Automation tools)
    ecosystems
        behavioral macro, 224
        gameplay systems, 223
        input events, 222
        input system, 222

overview, 221

timing-based attack, 223–224

traditional anti-cheat
systems, 222

macro (*see* Macro automation)

U, V

UFUNCTION(Exec) functions

attackers benefit, 190

FExecScanner, 190–194

internal testing, 179

reflection system, 190

restriction, 194–195

scanning process, 191

two-layer approach, 190

Unreal Engine games

assets and data extraction, 18

blueprint/exec functions, 17–18

code injection, 15

debugging, 60 (*see also* Debugging
techniques)

Lua automation, 15

reshape progression, 16

runtime memory model, 23–26

garbage collection/object
allocation, 25

memory exploration, 24

memory fragmentation, 25

predictable layout, 24

reflection system, 24

save file, 16

security checklist, 331

scanning process, 14

array-of-bytes (AOB), 15

pointer targets, 14

tools, 336

trainer platforms, 16

XP progression system, 17

Unreal Engine projects

build-time security, 275–290

User interface (UI), 4

W, X, Y, Z

WeMod (Wand), 11

Widget Blueprints

bypassing progression, 152

interactive element, 152

SecureUIActionGateway.cpp, 153

UI event graphs, 152–154

Windows

absolute paths, 210

console, 209

debug pipes, 210

feedback loop, 209

malicious DLLs, 210

remote thread, 211

search paths, 210

threads, 209

GPSR Compliance
The European Union's (EU) General Product Safety Regulation (GPSR) is a set
of rules that requires consumer products to be safe and our obligations to
ensure this.

If you have any concerns about our products, you can contact us on

ProductSafety@springernature.com

In case Publisher is established outside the EU, the EU authorized
representative is:

Springer Nature Customer Service Center GmbH
Europaplatz 3
69115 Heidelberg, Germany